Catholic Roots and Democratic Flowers

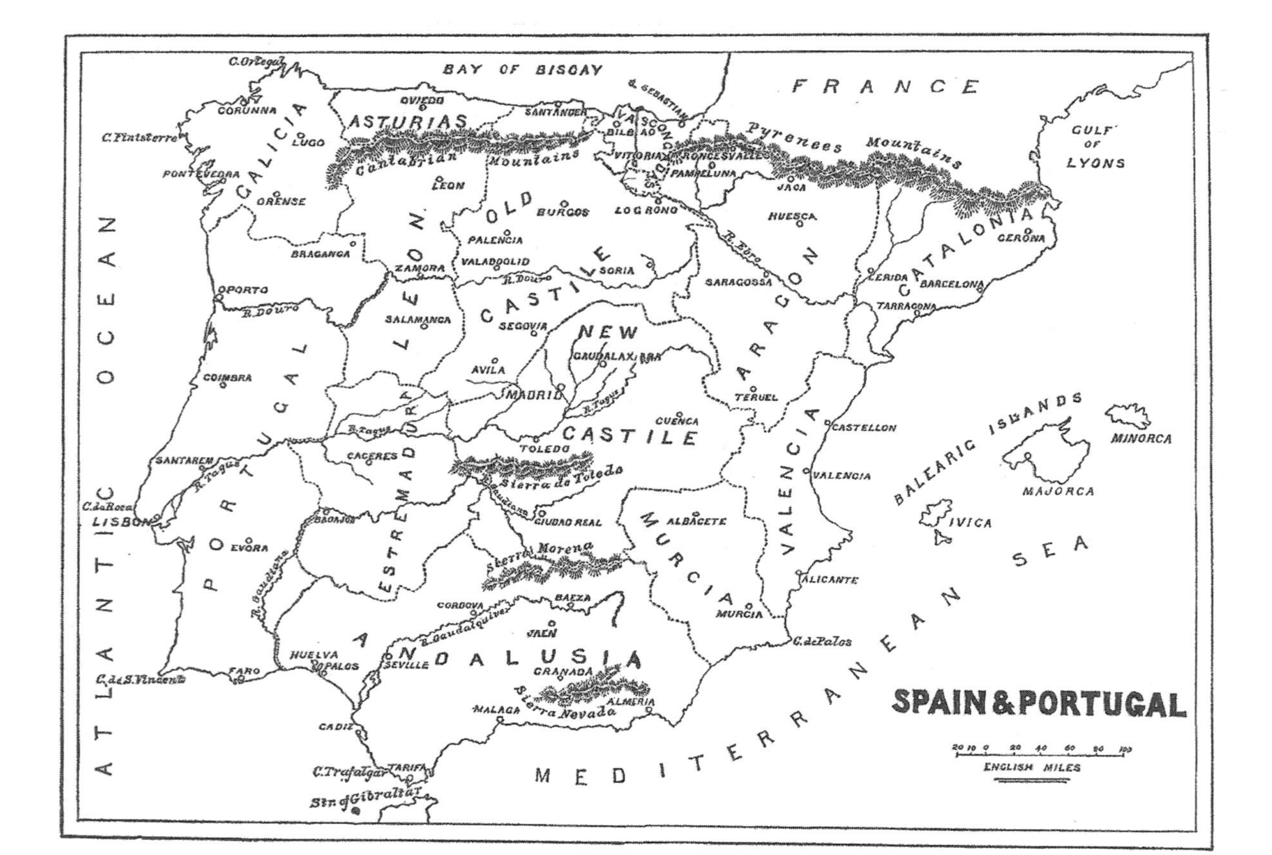
SPAIN & PORTUGAL
ENGLISH MILES
20 10 0 20 40 60 80 100
BAY OF BISCAY
FRANCE
GULF OF LYONS
ATLANTIC OCEAN
MEDITERRANEAN SEA
BALEARIC ISLANDS
MINORCA
MAJORCA
IVICA
GALICIA
ASTURIAS
VASCONGADAS
CATALONIA
ARAGON
LEON
OLD CASTILE
NEW CASTILE
VALENCIA
MURCIA
ESTREMADURA
ANDALUSIA
PORTUGAL
Pyrenees Mountains
Cantabrian Mountains
Sierra de Toledo
Sierra Morena
Sierra Nevada
C. Ortegal
C. Finisterre
C. da Roca
C. de S. Vincente
C. Trafalgar
C. de Palos
Str. of Gibraltar
CORUNNA
LUGO
PONTEVEDRA
ORENSE
OVIEDO
SANTANDER
S. SEBASTIAN
BILBAO
VITORIA
RONCESVALLES
PAMPELUNA
JACA
HUESCA
GERONA
LERIDA
BARCELONA
TARRAGONA
LEON
BURGOS
LOGRONO
PALENCIA
VALADOLID
SORIA
ZAMORA
BRAGANCA
OPORTO
R. Douro
R. Ebro
SARAGOSSA
SALAMANCA
SEGOVIA
GAUDALAXARA
AVILA
MADRID
R. Tagus
TERUEL
CUENCA
TOLEDO
CACERES
COIMBRA
SANTAREM
LISBON
EVORA
BADAJOS
R. Guadiana
CIUDAD REAL
ALBACETE
CASTELLON
VALENCIA
ALICANTE
MURCIA
CORDOVA
R. Guadalquivir
BAEZA
JAEN
GRANADA
MALAGA
ALMERIA
SEVILLE
HUELVA
PALOS
FARO
CADIZ
TARIFA

Catholic Roots and Democratic Flowers

Political Systems in Spain and Portugal

Howard J. Wiarda and
Margaret MacLeish Mott

Westport, Connecticut
London

Library of Congress Cataloging-in-Publication Data

Wiarda, Howard J., 1939–
Catholic roots and democratic flowers : political systems in Spain and Portugal / Howard J. Wiarda and Margaret MacLeish Mott.
p. cm.
Includes bibliographical references and index.
ISBN 0–275–97018–3 (alk. paper)—ISBN 0–275–97022–1 (pbk. : alk. paper)
1. Democracy—Spain. 2. Spain—Politics and government. 3. Democracy—Portugal. 4. Portugal—Politics and government. I. Mott, Margaret MacLeish, 1956– II. Title.
JN8221.W52 2001
946′.0009′04—dc21 00–061168

British Library Cataloguing in Publication Data is available.

Library of Congress Catalog Card Number: 00–061168
ISBN: 0–275–97018–3
0–275–97022–1 (pbk.)

First published in 2001

Praeger Publishers, 88 Post Road West, Westport, CT 06881
An imprint of Greenwood Publishing Group, Inc.
www.praeger.com

Printed in the United States of America

The paper used in this book complies with the Permanent Paper Standard issued by the National Information Standards Organization (Z39.48–1984).

10 9 8 7 6 5 4 3 2 1

To a remarkable group of teachers,
who first taught us about Iberia, Latin America,
and the interrelation between them.

Irving A. Leonard, Lyle N. McAlister,
Donald C. Worcester, Harry Kantor,
and Alva Curtis Wilgus

CONTENTS

Preface ix

1. Introduction 1
2. The Long Sweep of Iberian History 9
3. The Franco and Salazar Regimes 39
4. The Transitions to Democracy 61
5. Political Culture: The Iberian Melody 81
6. Interest Groups and the Political Process 105
7. Political Parties and Elections 125
8. Government and the Role of the State 145
9. Public Policy: Domestic and Foreign 163
10. Conclusion: Roots and Flowers 191

Selected Bibliography 203

Index 209

PREFACE

Spain and Portugal have emerged as very important countries, both in their own right and as key nations in American foreign policy. And yet we lack a good, solid, readable book about them that can be used as a textbook by college and university students or to which an interested general reader can turn for understanding. For a long time during the authoritarian dictatorships of Francisco Franco in Spain and Antonio Salazar in Portugal, it was difficult to do serious research and writing about either country, and the few good books published then have long been out of print. Since the overthrow of the Salazar/Caetano (Marcelo Caetano was Salazar's successor) regime in 1974 and the death of Franco in 1975, a wealth of detailed information has been published about specific features of each country. But we lack (1) a broad overview that examines Spanish and Portuguese history and culture and seeks to understand contemporary social, economic, and political development in historical context, and (2) a balanced, serious, provocative, comparative treatment of both Iberian countries in a single volume.

One can think of many reasons for having a new book on Spain and Portugal: the endlessly fascinating history, culture, and sociology of Iberia; the longevity, character, and shaping influences of the Franco and Salazar regimes; the exciting transitions in both countries (revolution in Portugal, evolution in Spain) from authoritarianism to democracy; the use of Spain and Portugal as models for democratic transitions in Latin America and now Central/Eastern Europe and globally the entry of both countries into NATO, the European Economic Community, and now the European Monetary Union; the economic booms in both countries that have made them models of growth and of foreign aid success; the dynamism and energy of these two societies as they undergo perhaps the world's most rapid modernization; and the continuing tensions in them as they look back on a turbulent history and toward an uncertain future. Above all, we are interested in Spain and Portugal because they continue to exhibit so many continuities with the past even while rushing pell-mell toward modernity. We think there is a unique distinctive, special Iberian history, culture, and political process at work here that is fascinating in its own right and may offer lessons from which other newly democratic and developing nations can learn.

Solid reasons obviously exist for doing separate books on Spain and Portugal. But here both countries are treated comparatively and in parallel fashion within a single volume, utilizing an intellectual framework common to both of them. The reasons for this parallel treatment are as follows: (1) the striking similarities between these two countries on a variety of historical, social, cultural, and political dimensions; (2) their parallel development patterns and trajectories; (3) the fascinating shades of differences as well as similarities between them; (4) their geographic location isolated from the rest of Europe and facing the Mediterranean and the Atlantic in that westernmost promontory of continental Europe called the Iberian peninsula; (5) their close identification together in both the popular mind and the tourist brochures; and (6) their exciting transformation to democracy and modernity that offers inspiration to other countries. Let's face it: Spain and Portugal are "different" from other countries, yet they are very close, not just geographically but historically, culturally, sociologically, and politically, to each other.

Related to this last theme is the suggestion—and the underlying thesis of the book—that Spain and Portugal, even with their recent democratization, economic and social development, and integration into Europe, are still often distinctive. To us, it is both their similarities with other modern European societies as well as their differences that make them interesting. Iberia's uniqueness over the decades has ameliorated as both countries have democratized, modernized, and joined the European community of nations, but in many respects both countries retain important elements from their past. They have energetically embraced the New Europe even while wrestling with the issue of what is valuable and worth retaining from history. For a time, because they long lagged behind the rest of Europe, Spain and Portugal sought to be more "European" than the Europeans themselves; more recently they have sought again to rediscover their own background and culture and to reassess what is valuable and worth saving in that tradition.

Anyone who has ever visited or traveled in Iberia knows immediately and often vividly that she/he is not in Germany, Scandinavia, or what Spaniards and Portuguese call the "Anglo-Saxon world." But then the question becomes, even while avoiding simplistic national stereotypes: What is it precisely that makes Spain and Portugal different, unique? And how has that changed under the onslaught of new democracy, societal modernization, consumerism, the EU (European Union), and the rapidly encroaching global culture of rock music, blue jeans, and Coca-Cola? It is toward the analysis and dissection of how Iberia is different and where and how it corresponds to broader, European and global processes of change that this book is dedicated. Hence, although the book provides comprehensive treatment of the history, religion, culture (especially political culture), economics, sociology, and politics of Iberia, it also examines the larger issues of development and democratization and where Spain and Portugal fit—or fail to fit—in these larger social and political processes.

A few words should be said about the sociology of this book and the authors' approach to it. Both authors spent many of their early, formative years living, working in, and studying Latin America; both of us feel extremely comfortable in the language, culture, and society of Latin/Hispanic civilization. But wherever we lived and studied in Latin America, we were both struck by many of the same features: a patrimonialist political culture, a top-down social and political system, a persistently organicist and corporatist society and polity even in the face of democratization, a set of values and beliefs undergirded by Catholic religious assumptions even in an age of secularism and pluralism. So, by quite independent paths, we both determined that, to understand Latin America, we had to go back to the roots of these systems in Spain and Portugal. And that, in turn, led to an ongoing fascination with those two countries in their own right, as well as to the question of their conformity, or not, to the broader, post–World War II European polity model of democracy, social welfare, and a modern mixed economy.

One of the authors began going to Iberia in the early 1970s, lived in Portugal for a time, served as an adviser to the U.S. State Department during the Portuguese Revolution of 1974, later lived and traveled extensively in Spain, and returns to Iberia on a yearly basis; his published work includes seven books and monographs on Iberia and a host of articles and book chapters. The other author became familiar with Iberia in the 1990s, when she lived, traveled, and walked through Spain along the famous *Camino real* (royal road); her published work includes several articles and papers on Spain as well as an as-yet-unpublished doctoral dissertation on the intellectual, cultural, and religious roots of Hispanic civilization.

At one level, this is a factual book about Spain and Portugal that can readily be used as a text in courses on European, Iberian, and Hispanic culture, politics, and civilization. But at another level, it is a book that tries to understand and interpret Iberia: What makes it tick? Where and how is it different from/similar to other countries? What are its underlying values and political culture? And how much have underlying realities changed in Spain and Portugal in recent decades to go along with the undoubted economic, social, and institutional changes? Hence, the book contains challenging ideas as well as facts, interpretation as well as chronology, ways of understanding as well as history. The book is a synthesis that brings together in coherent, integrated, and readable form a large body of research and writing that has been done on Spain and Portugal in recent decades, but it also contains some original research and ideas that may make it challenging and of interest to senior as well as junior students of Iberia and Hispanic civilization.

The writing of this book would not have been possible without the assistance of thousands of persons, some known, some nameless, who have helped us understand Spain and Portugal over the years. These include students, fellow scholars, government officials, and many persons in all walks of Spanish and Portuguese life. Howard J. Wiarda wishes especially to thank his family: Dr. Iêda Síqueira Wiarda, Kristy Lynn Williams, Dr. Howard E. Wiarda, and Jonathan S. Wiarda (born in Portugal), who shared so many of these travels and experiences of living abroad. Margaret MacLeish Mott wishes to thank her parents, William H. MacLeish and Margaret M. MacLeish, for introducing her to Iberian-Latin culture, and Alison Mott for her invaluable comments.

Numerous organizations have also supported this long-term work, including the Center for International Affairs at Harvard University, the Center for Strategic and International Studies (CSIS) in Washington, D.C., the Department of Political Science at the University of Massachusetts/Amherst, and the community of Marlboro College in Marlboro, Vermont. Financial support was provided by the Social Science Research Council, American Philosophical Society, Rockefeller Foundation, Mellon Foundation, National Endowment for the Humanities, Tinker Foundation, Luso-American Development Foundation, the Twentieth Century Fund, and the Graduate Program at the University of Massachusetts. Lawrence Graham, Michael Kryzanek, William Salisbury, and Larman Wilson have read and commented on earlier versions of this manuscript. We are grateful to all these institutions and individuals who have been wonderfully supportive of our work but, for good or ill, the analyses and interpretations that follow are our responsibility alone.

Chapter 1

INTRODUCTION

A DIFFERENT PATH TO DEVELOPMENT

On the night of February 23, 1981, gun-wielding Civil Guard officers, claiming the backing of the king, stormed into the Spanish Parliament and took the government hostage. The coup itself was not particularly surprising; Spain has a history of military interventions. Nor was the insinuation of regal support out of line: Spanish monarchs have historically aligned themselves with the army against democratic activities. There was no reason to think that this king would act differently. Not only was Juan Carlos of noble descent, he was a member of the Bourbon dynasty, he had also been hand-picked for the throne by the authoritarian dictator General Francisco Franco. Neither the earlier Spanish monarchs nor the subsequent dictator favored parliamentary rule. What made this moment unique in Spanish history was Juan Carlos's response. Instead of supporting the coup, Juan Carlos, dressed in full military regalia, immediately appeared on Spanish TV and ordered an end to the insurrection. Speaking in defense of democracy, the new constitution, and the rule of law, the king, who seeks to speak for the entire nation, effectively ended the practice of military intervention in Spanish politics. The symbol of Spain's absolutist past was now in favor of rule by democratic means.

A year before Juan Carlos rose to the throne in the mid-1970s, junior army officers in Portugal in 1974 toppled their equivalent of the Franco regime.

Using Marxist rhetoric to voice their discontent, these young army officers demanded an end to the authoritarian methods that had governed Portugal for nearly half a century. Although leading banks and businesses were nationalized, and many nervous investors fled the country, matters never got completely out of hand. There was neither civil war nor communist takeover. Instead, a parliamentary democracy was established and, by the early nineties, many of the nationalization programs were reversed.

Portugal, like Spain, now enjoys a healthy economy, a functioning democracy, and social pluralism. These two countries, both saddled with authoritarian regimes for much of the century, now find themselves in tandem once again. This time, however, the common ground is not repressive politics but democracy, social modernization, and a dynamic mixed economy. Spain accomplished this impressive task under a monarchy that dated back to the early seventeenth century, and Portugal achieved the same results despite a radical insurrection. These unusual events make us question some basic assumptions about democratic development. When did monarchs ever lead their people towards democratic rule? How often do military insurrections transition into a pluralist democracy?

It is questions like these that make Spain and Portugal worthy of study. The models of democracy and development fashioned in the United States and Western Europe often fall short when applied to the Iberian peninsula, the southwestern extension of Europe that comprises modern-day Spain and Portugal. The political development of Spain and Portugal challenges many universal assumptions; that is, monarchies aren't necessarily regressive and Marxist uprisings do not inevitably lead to totalitarian states. Obviously there is something else going on under the superficial truths of some of these development models.

The political development of the Iberian peninsula has a long history of being out of step with the rest of Europe. What historians refer to as the Dark Ages was far less unenlightened in Spain and Portugal. Under the control of the caliph of Cordova, Al Andalus, as Islamic Iberia was known, was home to schools and libraries that advanced scientific studies, particularly mathematics and engineering. Muslim regimes on the Iberian peninsula modeled a tolerant religious pluralism that allowed for Christians and Jews to follow their respective faiths. These enlightened practices continued into the era of Christian rule. The royal court of Alfonso X, for instance, promoted philosophy, music, and the arts. The *Siete Partidas,* the great legal compilation completed in 1284, had provisions for representative government and a limited monarchy.

Alongside this tradition of pluralism, codified law, and cultural productivity, Iberia has also been the site of intense repression. Throughout the rise of European liberalism, Iberia has often responded with authoritarianism, torture, and forced conversions. When Martin Luther's reforms were implemented in northern and central Europe, Spain launched the Counter-Reformation. As Henry VIII was reducing the authority of the Church in England, the Spanish monarchy was encouraging the expansion of the Inquisition. This polarity between Protestant and Catholic nation-states continued into the twentieth century. When Allied forces in World War II vanquished the fascist regimes of Adolf Hitler and Benito Mussolini, Spain and Portugal continued to hold on to their right-wing dictatorships. While much of Western Europe moved toward political pluralism and democratic governments, the repressive regimes of Spain and Portugal maintained absolute power.

The study of politics in Iberia offers an alternative model of political development. Some of the defining factors which are relevant to Protestant northern Europe and the United States (separation of church and state, separation of powers) may not be as central to democratic rule in Spain and Portugal as earlier conceived. Political systems may become more democratic without an American-style limited government. Authoritarian systems, on the other hand, may not be as "fascistic" as commonly thought. Rather than necessarily repressing the rule of the people, a centralized, top-down political system may, paradoxically, further democratic development by providing a solid economic and institutional foundation. What has been essential in Protestant northern Europe and North America might be less necessary in the Catholic countries to the south. Democracy itself may look different depending on the distinct cultural and sociopolitical tradition.

We can see this difference in the way democracy is defined in Iberia. Though Spaniards tend overwhelmingly to favor representative democracy, when pressed for a definition, some illiberal answers emerge. Some say democracy means "patronage," a favor for a favor, implying a system of mutual obligation rather than a neutral forum of autonomous actors operating in their own self-interest. A majority assumes that the state will play a large role in shaping policy as opposed to the market forces of a laissez-faire solution. Democracy, in this regard, does not imply a "black box" model of government whereby the state merely responds to "inputs" from the public by generating policy "outputs." Far from being a neutral tool of varying conglomerates of interests, the state is the body that decides what is best for its people.

A second component of democracy, representation, is often understood in Iberia as group or corporatist representation, not as individual representation. That elite actors within functional groups act under the guidance of the government is not inconsistent with Iberian understandings of democracy. Interest groups' independence from the state, so dear to American's understanding of pluralism, is not as essential in this orchestrated, top-down system. Having interest groups coopted by the state, which is the practice in much of continental Europe, indicates political efficiency, not, as in liberal terms, political corruption.

What this means is that Iberians may, at times, view order as more important than liberty. This preference for order is consistent with their long history of political instability and intermittent civil wars. In unstable times or under emergency conditions, democracy has been forced to give way to strong governments—for the good of the people. Rather than see absolute rule always as an abuse of power, which follows the reasoning of John Locke and the American founders, Iberians tend to understand absolutism within a Thomistic natural law framework. Within this Catholic structure, stability and universal harmony is privileged over individual rights. The ruler, as the natural head of the body politic, guides his people toward their better selves. The personification of what Rousseau called "the general will," the ruler understands the needs of the people better than they do themselves. Far from being a limited officeholder, the Iberian leader traditionally embodies the spirit of the land.

Because the politics of Iberia followed a different road to modernity, the existing models of liberalism and Marxism don't always apply. Unlike the recipes followed by the United States and other Western European countries, Spain and Portugal achieved democratic status without having to completely dismiss the Catholic Church or overthrow an absolute monarch. Democracy came into being without a popular revolution (the revolution in Portugal was initially a military insurrection; popular involvement followed the army revolt), as was the case in the American and French revolutions. Without a complete revolution, the religious and historical roots of governance were never torn out of the political soil. Instead, new theories, such as democracy and liberalism, were grafted onto the deep-rooted plant, creating a hybrid of old customs and new ideas.

These concepts are troubling in a world which often sees power divided neatly and rigidly between liberals and Marxists, authoritarians and democrats, socialists and capitalists. Countries that took a secular, free market, limited-governmental-powers approach to development, like the United States, are easily categorized as democratic. Countries that took an absolute, statist, totalitarian approach are equally easy to label; those are the ingredients of an antidemocratic regime, such as Hitler's Germany and Mao's China. The history of Iberian political development, however, confuses these neat polarities. The governments of Spain and Portugal have been both religious and limited, authoritarian and representational. Spain and Portugal hosted both the Inquisition and some of the more enlightened monarchs in Western history. Although both Spain and Portugal were isolated and underdeveloped for much of the first half of the twentieth century, they are currently experiencing growth rates of miraculous proportions. Far from conforming to traditional political models, Spain and Portugal tend to explode them.

Instead of forcing Iberian patterns into models that cannot account for them, this book considers the history and political development of the Iberian peninsula on its own terms. We seek to consider Iberian politics outside of the usual liberal/Marxist polemic. This perspective offers a third alternative to a highly polarized and much too simple perspective of the world. The corporatist, organicist, statist framework, which we develop here, continues to explain much of Iberian political behavior, and it is with the benefit of that explanatory model that we proceed.

WHY STUDY THE POLITICS OF SPAIN AND PORTUGAL?

Besides the theoretical benefit of challenging existing universal models, there are several other rewards that are specific to the study of Spain and Portugal. First, for students interested in the philosophical development of Western thought, Spain and Portugal offer an often overlooked alternative. The classic Iberian political thinkers were all theologians: Francis of Vitoria and Dominic Soto were Dominicans; Luis Molina and Francisco Suaréz were Jesuits. Political ends, therefore, were understood as Christian virtues. Although some of the conceptual tools included supernatural actors, such as angels and saints, this did not diminish the use of careful reasoning. Reason cemented a person's faith; it upheld the existing religious hierarchies. Unlike the Enlightenment tradition, espoused most forcefully by British philosopher John Locke, reason did not support individual inalienable rights but rather made clear a person's place in the great chain of being.

Second, many of the features of Iberian politics—Catholicism, authoritarianism, corporatism, patrimonialism—are apparent in Latin American politics as well. The regime of Juan Perón in Argentina, for instance, introduced a populist understanding of democracy, efficient through a strong authority, in which the means used to bring about modernization were not highly questioned given the social ends. Numerous regimes in Latin America , left, right, and now democratic, have similarly been cast in the Iberian mold. By studying Spain and Portugal, therefore, we are studying the social and political blueprints for much of the Western hemisphere.

Third, Iberia presents an alternative to the polarization of modern secular states and religious fundamentalism. Modern capitalist countries are increasingly being attacked for their secular values and loss of moral purpose. Fundamentalist movements in the Christian, Islamic, and Jewish communities define themselves against the moral bankruptcy of their secular governments. Spain and Portugal, by including religion as part of their civic equation, suggest a method of being both modern and devout, ceremonial and constitutional.

Fourth, Iberia provides an example of a nation built on Christian and Islamic principles. From 711 through 1492, Islamic rulers provided a strong political presence on the Iberian peninsula. Along with the occasional battles between Christians and Moors, there was also the practice of *convivencia*, the peaceful cohabitation of Christians, Muslims, and Jews. Whether on the battlefield or as partners in a negotiated peace, Iberian political development was greatly influenced by Islamic as well as Catholic understandings of government. As is the case in the Marxist/liberal polemic, and the secular/religious divide, Spain and Portugal offer a point on a continuum between the highly charged polarities of Islam and the West.

Finally, there is the unique relationship between Spain and Portugal and the rest of Europe. Perhaps because it is a peninsula, isolated from the European landmass by the mountainous terrain of the Pyrenees, or for many of the cultural and political reasons outlined above, Spain and Portugal have generally been considered different from the rest of Europe. Comments such as "Africa begins at the Pyrenees" or "Europe ends at the Pyrenees" speak to a long history during which Spaniards and Portuguese were not considered European. With democratization, the integration of Europe, and the prominent roles played by Spanish and Portuguese officials in both the North Atlantic Treaty Organization (NATO) and the European Union (EU), Spain and, to a somewhat lesser extent, Portugal are rapidly moving from a place on the periphery to the core of European integration. How successfully that center holds will depend on Europe's capacity to recognize Iberia's unique contribution to modern political development as well as its similarities.

POLITICS WITHIN CULTURE

What follows is a look at the political development of Spain and Portugal, particularly the transition to democracy, as a Catholic, corporatist phenomenon. We begin with the history of both countries, paying particular attention to repeating patterns and recurring conflicts. Not only are we interested in historical events but we are also interested in how those events advanced or retarded national identity and political institutions. We look at techniques used by the central government to maintain their legitimacy as well as regional and corporate efforts to reduce their absolute rule.

Chapter 3 focuses on the Franco and Salazar regimes. Both Spain and Portugal experienced dictatorships for a large part of the twentieth century. Whereas the history chapter traces the processes of nation building, the Franco and Salazar chapter introduces some of the political machinery established during the twentieth century. In political science terms, this chapter describes the process of state formation. Although much has changed since the transition to democracy, the bureaucratic apparatus of the central government is still very much in place.

The fourth chapter describes the remarkable occurrences highlighted at the beginning of this introduction: the transitions to democracy in both Spain and Portugal. This is the final chapter that follows a historical narrative, bringing the chronology up to the current time.

The second half of the book breaks with the earlier chronological ordering and takes up the central themes of the book. Chapter 5 focuses on the political culture of Spain and Portugal: its Catholic, Thomistic roots and the naturalness of a vertical hierarchy even within a democratic context. Chapters 6 through 9 take up key components of democracy and analyze them through the prism of Spanish and Portuguese political culture. Each component is given its own chapter: interest groups (chapter 6), political parties (chapter 7), the role of the state (chapter 8), and public policy (chapter 9).

Since the fall of the Soviet Union, democracy has been touted as "the only show in town." Yet that too-simple, post–Cold War mentality is losing credibility as the many faces of democracy emerge. Without the Eastern bloc nations to provide a stark contrast, the Western nations are looking less cohesive and more distinct from one another even as they all claim to be democratic. The "only show" turns out to have some surprising variations depending on where it is being shown. This book endeavors to enrich our understanding of two recent democracies that have arrived on the scene. Our hope is that readers will not only come to appreciate the rich traditions and political dangers represented in Spain and Portugal but will develop a broader understanding of what it means to be democratic.

Chapter 2

THE LONG SWEEP OF IBERIAN HISTORY

A country is shaped not only by the events of the past but by how the nation makes sense of those events. Military battles and heroic legends help a nation understand its collective self. Soldiers, kings, and democrats model the cultural norms for a nation's citizens. Battles, in retrospect, tell us what causes citizens were willing to die for. For instance, the American national identity was forged in the battle against the troops of the British monarchy. The values we were willing to die for—representation, liberty, and self-government—became the defining characteristics of our country. We understood ourselves and our collective purpose to be distinct from the British crown. The Civil War, on the other hand, threatened our national identity. The values that Southern Americans were willing to die for—states' rights and an American form of feudalism—were no longer viable components of the national identity.

Imagine the complications of crafting a national history stretching over a millennium of civil wars and internal battles. Battles against foreign aggressors, such as the Moors and the French, reinforced a sense of national identity. But battles between the inhabitants of the peninsula confused what it meant to be Spanish, what it meant to be Portuguese. Some people were willing to die for the monarchy; some were willing to die for republican rule. Some people were willing to die for Islam, some for Catholicism. Some people were willing to die for their region; few were willing to die for the central government. The formation of Portugal's national identity is less complicated than that of Spain; many of the battles fought there were against Castile, the politically dominant region in Spain.

What follows is a brief history of Spain and Portugal that highlights the tensions between central authority and local control, between national identity and regional customs. We will look at the heroes of Spain and Portugal and consider their legends in terms of formulating cultural norms. We will look at how external battles fortified cultural values and how internal battles reinforced ideological differences. Those ideological differences can be categorized in terms of polarities which, in different forms, are woven throughout Iberian history:

authoritarianism vs. democracy
corporate rights vs. individual rights
central government vs. regional government
religious values vs. secular values
mercantilism vs. free market economy

The history of political development in Spain and Portugal is largely expressed in terms of these five disputes and the alliances formed within the terms of those debates.

THE EARLY PEOPLES

Iberia has been inhabited since the Paleolithic era. About thirty-five thousand years ago, cave dwellers hunted reindeer, escaped lions and tigers, and painted scenes of their lives on the walls of their homes. These vivid, lifelike pictures suggest a trained aesthetic not normally associated with "cavemen." Deep in the recesses of a cave, bison, deer, horses, and cattle race across the walls and ceilings in dramatic depictions of the hunt. Whether these cave paintings invoked magical powers or chronicled tribal heroes is unclear. What is clear is that the earliest known inhabitants of the Iberian peninsula, like their distant relatives, knew how to glorify the kill.

Around 7000 B.C., perhaps because the herds could no longer support the cave dwellers, fishing and hunting tribes gathered along the rivers of the peninsula. Their eating habits have been revealed through the archeological digs that have uncovered huge kitchen middens containing the remains of shellfish and crustaceans as well as the bones of oxen, deer, sheep, horses, pigs, wild dogs, badgers, and cats. Around 3000 B.C., Neolithic people began constructing dwellings and practicing agriculture. Polished stone tools and ceramics were now included in the legacies left by these ancient peoples along with remnants of their elaborate funerary monuments, called dolmens. By the advent of the Stone Age, about 2000 B.C., regional differences begin to appear, due to the chopped up geography of the peninsula.

It is worth spending a moment on the effect of geography on regional differences. Just as Iberia is cut off from Europe by the Pyrenees Mountains, so the various regions within the peninsula are separated by natural borders. Many of the regions of Spain are closed in by mountain ranges, each with its own climate, necessitating a distinct agriculture and land use. Olives grow well in southern Andalusia but can't survive the moisture of northern Galicia. Oranges flourish on the Valencian coast but suffer terribly in the extreme climate of the central plateau, known as the *meseta.* Northern Portugal is mountainous and cold, but the south is blessed with sunshine and beaches. Although the entire landmass of Iberia is smaller than Texas, it has the geographical variations of a continent.

The physical realities of the peninsula have prohibited much agricultural development. Unlike nearby French farmers, Iberian farmers have had to contend with poor soil, an intricate web of mountain ranges, and rivers that are largely unnavigable. Because of this fractured environment, the Iberian peninsula was incapable of developing the kind of agricultural economy common to central Europe. Instead, economic development occurred in the ports and cities along the coast of the peninsula, and through the extraction of silver, copper, and tin from the interior mountains.

In the twelfth century B.C., Phoenician traders arrived on the Atlantic and Mediterranean coasts of the peninsula in search of some of these metals. They founded trading posts at Cádiz, Valencia, Málaga, and Sevilla. The Greeks arrived in the seventh century, founding their own colonies on the Mediterranean and Atlantic coasts. When the Carthaginians replaced the Phoenicians and closed off the Straits of Gibraltar to the Greeks, a battle ensued as the various trading groups attempted to take control of the southern half of the peninsula. The Carthaginians eventually gained the upper hand and lost power only when Carthage was defeated by the Romans during the Punic Wars in the third century B.C.

Celts began arriving from north of the Pyrenees during the eighth, seventh, and sixth centuries B.C. Perhaps because of the familiarity of the climate, many of these Celtic tribes remained, bringing with them their sheep and pastoral lifestyle. They mingled with the Iberos, the native people, giving rise to a new identity, Celtiberians. This ethnic identity is still prominent in Galicia, the northwest province of Spain. Gallegos are proud of a tradition that includes over one thousand years of fierce fighters and even bagpipes (*gaitas*).

THE ROMAN IMPACT

Roman military legions began to enter Iberia around 200 B.C. as part of their campaign against Hannibal. It took Rome nearly two hundred years, until 19 B.C. to subdue the fierce Iberians. Resistance was strongest in Asturias, in the northern Cantabrian Mountains, and among the Lusitanians living in the western part of the peninsula. The first great national hero of Portugal was the Lusitanian warrior chieftain Viriato, who kept the Romans out of his jurisdiction for several decades until he was finally murdered in his sleep. Legend has it that he was murdered by his own people, who had betrayed him for Roman bribes.

Despite a deep-seated resistance to Roman rule, the Iberians eventually accepted the infrastructure of a centralized government. Lusitanians and Asturians might maintain regional loyalties but they certainly benefited from the infrastructure of the Roman Empire. The Romans built roads, bridges, and aqueducts, many of which are still in existence. They increased trade, agriculture, and production of mineral resources. Along with this economic development, the Romans instituted a centralized, bureaucratic government and a universal legal code.

Iberia was divided into a number of jurisdictions, each with a Roman center of justice and administration, and subject to Roman law. Senates were established, schools of Greek and Latin were opened, and eventually the fortress mentality of Lusitanians, Celtiberians, and other indigenous groups, was replaced, to some extent, with civilized life in a town. Latin became the lingua franca of the peninsula. When Rome converted to Christianity, the inhabitants of the peninsula converted as well.

Roman rule imposed a class structure on the peninsula. Former warrior chieftains were given a rung on the social ladder. Social and political identity was drawn from one's social class, not from one's region. The emperor, off in Rome, sat at the top of this social hierarchy with the various classes of people laid out beneath him, the slave class providing the foundation. The hierarchy itself was considered a matter of natural law. Just as fathers ruled over their children, and husbands ruled over their wives, so the emperor ruled over his people. Following Aristotle's model of an inclusive hierarchy, in which everything in the world is lined up in an ascending order of being, various corporate groups (i.e., the army, the intellectuals, the pagan priests, the artisans) found their place in a naturally determined vertical landscape. One understood oneself as a member of a group with carefully delineated privileges and obligations. Hierarchy provided order, which was pleasing to the gods. Individual rights and social equality, on the other hand, were disruptive to the natural order of being.

It is important to recognize that, in the ancient world, slavery operated within an economic sphere, not a racial one, as was the case with slavery in the Americas. Slaves were regarded as things *(instrumentum vocale)* while they were the property of masters. Once freed, the slave became a Roman citizen. Slavery, in other words, was not a condition of being, as was the case with racial slavery, but a condition of property, from which one could be released. One was not necessarily born into slavery, although that did occur. Citizens became slaves both involuntarily—as a result of war, piracy, or kidnapping—and voluntarily—as a means of paying off a debt. Freemen who wished to pursue political careers often sold themselves to the authorities in an ancient form of bonding insurance. Children were sold off to slavery in order to pay off their parents' debts. The condition of women most closely approximated race-based slavery. Unlike a male child who might grow out of his servitude, females were never granted the rights of citizenship and so spent their lives as the property of their husbands or fathers.

Through absolute control and a highly unified political apparatus, the Roman Empire was able to maintain control as it expanded horizontally. The unifying attributes of the expanding empire—language, government bureaucracy, religion, infrastructure, and a codified law—reinforced a visceral allegiance to Rome. Once it was finally subjugated, "Hispania," the Roman term for the peninsula, responded sympathetically to the absolute, intolerant conditions employed by the Romans. In some ways, Hispania became more Roman than Rome.

Besides creating a healthy respect for the power of empires, the Romans also introduced the practice of ceremonial crowd control. The political institutions of Rome included not just a centralized, bureaucratic system, but popular ceremonies of brutality. The events in the coliseum served several purposes at once. They established the superior strength of the ruling elite who could command such an enormous spectacle. They educated the masses about the unfortunate consequences of seditious activities. And they offered sacrifice to the Roman gods, which was always a good idea. The masses learned that it was better to be in the stands shouting than to be on the coliseum floor getting bludgeoned to death. These blood baths were not just popular entertainment, but a ritualized way of returning a chaotic state to order.

The bullfight, interestingly enough, represents a uniquely Iberian response to this instrument of imperial domination. A subjugated people took an activity that had generally led to martyrdom and reconditioned it as an heroic ballet. The Roman coliseums brought Christians to their knees before the lions, but the Iberian coliseums reminded the crowds of the power of the lone fighter. The hero is one who can resist the powers of the state, whether the agents be fierce animals or well-trained soldiers. The first national hero of Portugal, remember, was not a Roman jurist but a rebellious Lusitanian. The Iberian tradition, in other words, reveres honorable rebels as much as the rule of law.

In the early fifth century, when the Roman Empire began to crumble under the onslaught of barbarian attacks, three Germanic tribes—the Suevi, the Alani, and the Vandals (whose brutality gave rise to the term *vandalism*)—entered the peninsula and destroyed many of the Roman accomplishments. On their heels came the Visigoths, who remained on the peninsula establishing small kingdoms. Unlike the Romans, the Visigoths did not operate under imperial motives. There was no absolute or centralized ruler to resolve conflicts between the kingdoms, nor a bureaucratic system to coordinate their competing needs. Destruction of the Roman infrastructure, however, did not return the peninsula to pre-Roman conditions. For one thing, Latin maintained its usefulness as the common language. The second important unifying element was Christianity. The process of Christianizing the peninsula, begun under the Romans, was solidified under the Visigoths. The fourth Council of Toledo, under the guidance of St. Isidore, directed that all Iberian churches use the same hymns and liturgy. The various kingdoms may not have conformed to universal legal practices but they did conform to universal religious practices, all of which were conducted in Latin. The Roman Catholic Church replaced the Roman bureaucracy as the glue which held the separate political entities together.

In as much as it constrained political behavior, the Church acted as a sort of constitution. Any petty rivalries or terrible abuses of power were subject to the spiritual censure of the Church. A Visigothic king bent on personal power and private ends would be at odds with a powerful Church which, following St. Augustine, understood political legitimacy in terms of its conformity to the basic Christian principles of charity and justice. A cruel and tyrannical king was, by definition, not a Christian king and therefore not worthy of being served.

This ethical constraint, however, was somewhat weakened by the *Patronato Real*, or royal patronage. This legal contract between the king and the local parish provided military protection for the Church and its property in exchange for a portion of the tribute the church received from local landowners. Under the terms of the contract, the Church had a military defense always on hand and the king was guaranteed a spiritual mediator to argue against any of his temporal sins. Placating the Christian God was now as important as placating the Roman authorities had earlier been. A powerful ruler guilty of an occasional usurpation of power might need a number of masses said on his behalf once he was laid to rest. The grace offered by the priest and the official prayers offered after death must have freed the conscience of the warring king faced with the ethical dilemmas of the battlefield, particularly when most of the victims were Christians. That dilemma was eased in 711, when the Moors crossed the Strait of Gibraltar from North Africa and entered Spain. Now the Visigothic kings had a new enemy, whose slaughter would not pose a moral problem for their souls.

ISLAMIC SPAIN: AL-ANDALUS

Many explanations may be offered for why the Moorish warrior tribes, the Berbers, attacked the peninsula, many more explanations than there are historical sources. One theory is that the Visigoths, with their internecine squabbling, made for an easy target. Some even suggest that one of the Visigothic kings invited the Moors over to destroy a Christian rival. Another factor might be the warrior ethos of the Berbers, who understood political legitimacy in terms of military might. The great Islamic social scientist Ibn Khaldun (d. 1406) wrote that "fortitude has become a character quality of theirs, and courage their nature" (95). Their methods provided the term *barbarian,* that is, someone from the Barbary coast. Political fortitude was not about developing a civilization, as was the case with the Romans, but about maintaining one's willingness to die in battle for the cause of Islam. In order to be a good citizen, a Berber had to demonstrate that he was ready to fight.

An additional factor was political. The segmentary system employed by the Umayyad Dynasty, based in Damascus, did not hinge on feudal loyalties but tribal allegiance. The Islamic fighters were not, in the strict sense of the term, a warrior class, but a tribe of people unafraid of battle. Unlike the Roman Empire, with its strict hierarchy of functional groups of people, the ruling Arabian dynasties, first the Umayyad and then the Abbasid, were as vulnerable to attack from other desert tribes as they were from their political enemies. For this reason, it was often in the dynasty's best interests to send the Berbers elsewhere to prove themselves. Otherwise, they might attack the ruling Arabian dynasty only to show they could.

Besides the cultural norms of the Berbers, Islam itself cultivated a warrior mentality. In the fourth Sura of the Quran, believers are urged to "exchange the life of this world for the hereafter, fight for the cause of God; whoever fights for the cause of God, whether he dies or triumphs, We shall richly reward him" (4:74). Being a good Muslim, in other words, involved being a good fighter, and those fighters needed battles to prove their faith. The fighting prowess of the Moors was certainly proved in Spain and Portugal. Within a few decades of landing, most of the Iberian peninsula was held by the Moors. Once again, pockets of resistance lingered in the northern caves and hideouts of the Cantabrian Mountains, but, all in all, the Visigothic kings lost their autonomy and became the reluctant subjects of the caliph, the Arabic leader who ruled from a luxurious palace in Cordova.

In terms of Spain's and Portugal's national identity, Moorish influences, unlike those of the Romans and the Visigoths, posed a political problem. The Moors, and the Arabs who followed them, were theologically unable to be absorbed into the existing Roman Catholic social and political structure. The North Africans might improve the aqueducts and bridges, they might introduce lovely geometrical mosaics in their architecture, they might offer advancements in science and math, but their offerings would always be scorned by the creators of national identity, the Christian historians. No matter how useful or sophisticated the offering, it was always understood as the gift of the infidel, the unbeliever, and therefore had to be denigrated and downplayed. There might be some confusion as to whether the obedient town-dweller or the rebellious fortress-dweller was a better citizen, but there was no disagreement when it came to religion. The good Spaniard, the good Portuguese was always a good Christian.

This is not to say that the Moors did not influence Christian behavior although, until recently, few Spanish or Portuguese scholars wished to admit it. In the words of historian Desmond Seward, "even today Arab traits are found in the Spanish character: dignity and courtesy, the sacred duty of hospitality, fantastic generosity, intolerance, an inability to compromise, and a ferocity which is not so much cruelty as indifference to physical suffering."[1] A respect for absolute authority was coupled with a fascination with transcending one's fear of death. As with all foreign ideas, these concepts were given a particularly Iberian, now Catholic, gloss, in the form of the religious military orders.

The Spanish and Portuguese religious military orders, that is, the Orders of Alcántara, Santiago, Avís, Montesa, Calatrava, and the Knights of Christ were fashioned after the Templars and Hospitalers, military religious orders developed during the Crusades. Prior to the formal incorporation of these orders, the peninsula was home to *hermangildas,* small bands of local Christian farmers. Once these *hermangildas* were exposed to the techniques of the Almohad *rabitos* (the Islamic holy warriors), they acquired a quasi-religious character. These "monks of war" often took vows of chastity, poverty, and obedience. They loved God so much they no longer feared death or bodily injury. Without wives to provide for or children to feed, these devout fighters were able to give all they had in this world for the eternal blessings of the next.

The highly religious nature of the military orders may have improved the fighters' discipline, but it did create some problems of loyalty. While the *Santaguistas'* ferocious battle-cry, "*Rubet ensis sanguine Arabum*" (May the sword be red with Arab blood) may have served the needs of a developing Catholic nation, the chain of command did not always end at the throne. It was the Pope, Alexander III, not a Visigothic king, who formally recognized the Order of St. James. When various factions of Christians took to fighting amongst themselves, the orders were often represented on both sides. When the fight was against the Moors, the Christian nation was able to forge a formidable alliance. When the battle line was drawn on other than religious grounds, the results were disastrous. As with the earlier Arabian dynasties, it became essential for the ruling Catholic monarchy to keep its military might employed at external boundaries. Better to send the young fighters on military conquests, than risk political instability at home.

Along with the cult of the holy warrior, Islamic rule also brought a new type of slavery to the peninsula, domestic slavery. The Quran allows for polygamy and the keeping of concubines. The heaven depicted in the Quran offers beautiful women as the reward for living a devoted life. Christian leaders termed that sinful and on that basis sought to induce gallant young Galicians to go to war against the Muslims. Legend has it that the *Reconquista* (the Christian reconquest of the peninsula from the Moors) formally began when the Christian king Ramiro I refused to surrender one hundred virgins as part of the annual tribute to the Islamic caliph of Cordova. Reality indicates that many Iberians found pleasurable reasons to convert to Islam. Although some historians argue that the role of the wife was one of many crucial differences between Islam and Christianity that made assimilation and cohabitation impossible, there was often less confrontation than one might imagine.

As the *Reconquista* progressed, generally proceding from the north of the pennisula to the south, many Muslims remained in the reconquered Christian territory (they were known as the Mudéjars). Likewise, Christians remained in Islamic-controlled terrain (the Mozarabs, from the Arabic *must'rib,* "Arabized"). These groups had certain legal privileges and tax consequences, known as *fueros,* or corporate rights. The state recognized the group by allowing it to live in a certain neighborhood and engage in certain businesses. Participation in the political process, limited as it was, was not accorded to individuals but to groups. Along with protected legal status (which often was costly in terms of increased taxation), these subcultures exchanged customs with the dominant society. Much evidence also exists of intermarriage between Christians and Muslims. In places like Toledo, where both Mudéjars and Mozarabs resided, some Christian women adopted the custom of wearing veils.

Another indicator of tolerance between Christians and Muslims can be found in the early Inquisition records. Initially, Muslims and Jews were treated very differently. The Muslims who converted to Christianity under pressure from the throne, called Moriscos, were not subject to the extensive persecution of the newly Christianized Jews. In the tribunal of Toledo, for instance, the number of Muslims prosecuted in the first years of the Inquisition was less than one hundred, while at the same time, over two thousand five hundred people suspected of judaizing (practicing Jewish rituals while passing as Christian) were brought before the Holy Office. Despite the theological posturing, Spanish Catholics and Muslims did share more common ground than Spanish Catholics and Jews.

The shared values of Muslims and Christians are embodied in the Spanish hero El Cid. A Christianized version of a Berber-style hero, El Cid not only engaged Muslim volunteers in his own army, he also served, for a brief period, the Muslim emir of Zaragoza. When Christian forces from Aragon attacked Zaragoza, the warrior El Cid, the ultimate "man-on-horseback," came to the emir's defense, following a medieval code that privileged feudal loyalties over religious beliefs. Zaragoza, an Islamic emirate, was subject to Christian Castile. The Aragonese attack, therefore, was not a religious battle but an encroachment on Castilian sovereignty. When, in 1092, El Cid seized the Muslim city of Valencia, he did not enslave the vanquished Muslims, as was the custom. Instead, he permitted "the honorable men among you, who have always been loyal to me" to stay in their homes with their wives, to retain one servant and one mule but no weapons. The rest of the Muslims were permitted to leave Valencia and set up a neighborhood, with corporate rights, in nearby Alcudia, where they might have their own laws, their own judges, and their own ruling council. El Cid is also credited with being the first to inflict defeat on the advancing Almoravids, a particularly fierce Berber tribe. He represents a Christian who was not made soft by civilization, a warrior who respected feudal obligations as well as the honor of his opponent.[2]

The *Reconquista* afforded opportunities for Christians and Muslims to exchange customs, create business relations, and to develop a religious pluralism in the form of corporate rights. That Christians finally took back the peninsula says as much about the decay of the ruling Arabian dynasty and the resultant petty squabbles between the various Arabic *taifas* (small city-states) as it does about the military strength and cunning of the Christian forces. The struggle against the Moors, however, did for the Iberians what the Romans had done several centuries prior. It unified the peninsula under a common banner; yet this time the banner read not *pax romana* but militant Catholicism.

THE *RECONQUISTA* AND CORPORATE RIGHTS

Were the legends completely accurate, the *Reconquista* would have finished with a completely unified Iberia. By all accounts, the fight against the infidels should have created a cohesive community of Christians fighting for their country and their patron saint, St. James. In fact, regionalism was reinforced through the system of *fueros*. Warriors who fought to defend the Catholic faith were rewarded on a material level through ownership of the conquered land as well as the labor of the people living there. Towns that were able to incorporate and hold off the Moorish invaders were granted municipal *fueros,* allowing them a good deal of autonomy from the emerging regional governments. Regional *fueros* allowed for patronage of the local church, the creation of a municipal government, and a reduced tribute to the king. They also allowed for local solutions to local problems, thus creating an interesting patchwork of legal practices. In sharp contrast to the unified law of Roman rule, in medieval Iberia the punishment for various crimes differed greatly from town to town.

Not only communities were granted *fueros*. Functional groups, such as guilds and religious brotherhoods, were also awarded their own *fueros*. Membership in a corporate group determined the amount of one's tribute, the length of one's military obligation, as well as many other aspects of political life. Citizenship, in other words, was understood, not on an individual basis but in terms of one's membership in a corporate group. Notions of one man, one vote, or individual rights had no place in this corporate, organic conception of government.

Although this tradition does not conform to Anglo-American understandings of representative government, which are based more on individualism, we can see how this organic system would limit the absolute powers of a central ruler as indeed they did. Representatives of the various corporate groups occasionally met, along with the nobles, in an assembly or *cortes*. The first *cortes* assembled in Aragon in 1163, followed by one in Leon in 1188. Castile's *cortes* first met in 1250. The *cortes* and the *fueros* imposed some limits on the central authority, providing Iberia with its own particular tradition of a limited government.

The creation of Portugal as an independent nation occurred amidst the struggles for the throne of the kingdom of Leon, the then ruling court in Spain. A former province of Leon, the territory known as Portucalense was separated from central government by a range of rugged mountains. In 1096 Alfonso VI, king of Leon, granted sovereignty of Portucalense to Henry, the husband of his favorite, albeit illegitimate, daughter, Teresa. Henry's autonomy, however, was tempered by the customs of vassalage; having been given a region to govern, Henry was obligated to maintain loyalty to the Leonese court. Henry dutifully observed his feudal obligations up until Alfonso's death in 1109, when a civil war broke out between Aragonese, Galician, and Castilian barons, all of whom claimed title to the Leonese crown. Henry maintained his region's autonomy by pursuing a policy of nonalignment in the Spanish struggles of ascendancy. Both this policy and the territory were inherited by his wife, Teresa, after Henry's death in 1112.

Eventually Teresa's sovereignty was compromised. After a six-week war in 1127, Portucalense once again submitted to the feudal obligations of Leon. Teresa's son, Afonso Henriques, however, refused to submit to the Leonese demands and rebelled against his mother. With the support of barons and lower nobility, Afonso overthrew Teresa and invaded Galicia. After hearing Afonso Henriques's claims that parts of southern Galicia were within Portuguese dominion, the new Leonese king, Alfonso VII, marched on Portugal (the vernacular name for Portucalense). By the end of the battle, Afonso Henriques was recognized as a king in his own right, and Portugal had its autonomy. What had been a province of Leon, became a nation in its own right, unified under the rule of Afonso Henriques.

In Spain the situation was complicated by the vast negotiations between the central government and the regional barons. All of these groups were governed by organic laws spelling out their rights and obligations in relation to royal authority. When the central authority was in question, as when Alfonso VI died, the societal corporate groups were dominant and often at war. Once the supreme commander was installed, generally through military right, the corporate groups were subordinated.

Military efforts, however, were not the only mechanism for creating a centrally recognized leader; legal instruments were also effective at establishing unity and order. Compacts between kings and vassals established a system of hierarchy and obligation. The *Siete Partidas,* a compilation of laws and customs commissioned by Alfonso X and completed in 1284, set forth the privileges and obligations assigned to each corporate group. Rather than risk having these corporate rights wielded against the central authority, the *Siete Partidas* incorporated them within the body of law of the central state. *Fueros* were legitimate not just because they were accepted locally but because the central authority recognized their legitimacy.

The third factor, besides military might and legal instruments, that brought subordinate groups under the control of the central government was religious orthodoxy. The Inquisition, the first national institution on Spanish soil, became a most effective instrument in bringing the various regions and corporate groups in line with the wishes of the central government, even while it drove the most dynamic elements in Spanish society out of the country.

THE INQUISITION AND THE JEWS

The Inquisition has long been held over Spain's head as an example of its cruelty. The dealings of the Holy Office form a large portion of the Black Legend, the anti-Catholic, anti-Hispanic propaganda generated by England during the time of Henry VIII's divorce from Catherine of Aragon and maintained over centuries of Anglo-Iberic disputes. British and American historians and novelists of the nineteenth and early twentieth centuries played on existing prejudices as they denounced Spain for its supposed cruelties. Not only was the Spanish character cruel but so were its religious institutions, especially the Catholic Church and the Inquisition. Washington Irving and William Prescott raised the specter of a juggernaut of death, of "an eye that never slumbered, an unseen arm ever raised to strike." These authors contributed to an already accepted legend: the Spanish Inquisition was nothing more than justice run amuck.

Justice, throughout history, has not necessarily been known for its mercy. While unrepentant Judaizers were burnt at the stake in Toledo, poachers in the king's forest outside London were also being drawn and quartered for treason. All over Europe, justice came down with a heavy hand. What is central to this discussion of Iberian political development is that the glue which held the peninsula together was not allegiance to the state but devotion to the "One, True Faith," that is, Catholicism. The crime most dangerous to the health of the body politic was heresy, not treason. The Inquisition was the first institution since the Romans to unify the peninsula under a uniform legal code.

Given the propaganda generated around the Inquisition, it is worth while to spend some time exploring the conditions under which the Inquisition in Spain came to power. For much of the fourteenth century, Jews, living in Jewish neighborhoods, prospered as merchants and international traders. They were allowed to practice their religion as long as they didn't attempt to convert Christians. The kings benefited not only from their business acumen but from the higher taxes imposed on all non-Christians. Most kings recognized not only the economic benefits but the intellectual rewards of having a thriving Jewish community within their realm. Jewish intellectuals, such as Maimonides, unscrambled ethical and metaphysical problems for the Christian courts. The separate all-Jewish neighborhoods, or ghettos, also served the needs of a people whose religion necessitated strict dietary and domestic practices, a kosher market, and an accessible synagogue.

Although the political arrangements may have served the needs of the merchant class and the royal elite, a large portion of the population resented what they saw as the rising affluence of infidels. Spurred on by demagogic priests, lower-class Christians, beginning in 1391, rose up en masse and destroyed the Jewish ghettos of Castile. The anti-Semitic fury quickly spread to Valencia and Catalonia. Jews were forced to convert under threats of death or slavery to the Muslims. The royal authorities watched helplessly as the lower classes vented their economic frustrations on the Jews.[3]

As a result of these uprisings, many Jews converted to Catholicism. As New Christians, they now had all the benefits of citizenship, including lower taxation, without the stigma of being Jewish. The financial and intellectual talents which had served them as Jews were given greater leverage as New Christians. Far from destroying their adversaries, the zealous mobs had only given them more political power. Again the frustrations arose, only this time there were two adversaries: Jews and *conversos,* the name for Jews who had converted to Catholicism. The lower classes, often inflamed by the disgruntled priests, claimed that the *conversos* had not truly converted but were still following the laws of Moses. The Jews and the *conversos* were blamed for natural disasters and diseases such as the plague. If Christians were suffering, it was because of the Jews and, by association, the false Christians.

Given the uncertainty of medieval life, it is not surprising that many Iberians, wishing to hedge their afterlife bets, followed both religions. Ample evidence indicates that families switched back and forth between Judaism and Christianity in an attempt to appeal to both the Old Testament and New Testament gods. At the same time, we can believe that many of the *conversos* truly changed their faith. Given the resentment of the Old Christians, however, their conversions remained suspect.

It fell to the Inquisition to determine the validity of a Christian's faith, not just what a person did but what he or she truly believed inside. Only Christians were subject to the jurisdiction of this ecclesiastical tribunal. Jews, Muslims, and, after the Conquest, Indians in the New World, were outside the jurisdiction of the Holy Office. Protestants, on the other hand, having been baptized, were at great risk of being denounced, as were blasphemers and visionaries. The Inquisitors, trained in the nuances of theology and philosophy, tested the faith of the members of the body politic to see whether they were as Christian as they claimed. Rather than allowing for mob justice, the Inquisition created an institutional valve for letting off the lower classes' steam of resentment. Disgruntled demagogues might appeal to the Holy Office instead of inciting their parishioners to riot. The continued presence of Jews, however, was considered too dangerous to a polity now considered to be in a state of spiritual crisis. Twelve years after the Holy Office was instituted in Spain, the Jews were expelled.

Many of the Jews went to the New World. The expulsion order was issued just a few days before Columbus set sail for the New World, and it is believed that many Jews and *conversos* helped finance the expedition in their desperation to find a safe haven. King Ferdinand's treasurer, Luis de Santangel, who was instrumental in convincing Queen Isabella to support Columbus's project, was a kinsman of another Luis de Santangel, burned at the stake for continuing to practice Jewish rituals after converting to Christianity. The treasurer Santangel personally raised half the money needed for the enterprise, suggesting a very strong connection between the plight of the Jews and the discovery of the Indies.

Most of the Jews remained in the Old World. Some went to Amsterdam or Venice or other European or Mediterranean cities that permitted a Jewish neighborhood. King Manuel of Portugal allowed many Jews to reside in Portugal as long as they were willing to pay for the favor. Not only did the royal coffers gain in this bargain but the ports of Lisbon and other Portuguese cities were blessed with the influx of a merchant class. In 1497 Manuel, in order to find favor with the Spanish Monarchs, Isabella and Ferdinand, ordered all Jews to be brought forward for baptism. Rather than risk an exodus which would have damaged the Portuguese economy, Manuel insisted on conversion without enforcement. In other words, as long as the merchant pretended to be Catholic, by attending mass and celebrating the Holy Days, the king and his agents would look the other way. When Portugal instituted its own Inquisition in 1547, a wave of crypto-Jews returned to Spain, which by then had relaxed its inquisitorial efforts and was ready to take advantage of the returning merchant class.

Not only did the Inquisition manipulate the merchant class, it also weakened the authority of the various regions. Several regions claimed that their *fueros* exempted them from the Inquisitor's gaze. Galicia and Aragon were somewhat successful in keeping out the Holy Office and its spies. However, since much of the social discontent operated across the regions on a class basis, being resistant to the "curative" powers of the Holy Office brought suspicion upon oneself. The Holy Office was not beyond prosecuting the political elite or even prominent church officials. Those who criticized its harsh methods, and there were many Old Christians who felt this way, were subject to denouncement.

THE HAPSBURGIAN MODEL

The rule of Queen Isabella and King Ferdinand form a central part of Spanish national identity. Their marriage, in 1469, joined the important kingdoms of Castile and Aragon. Ferdinand, trained as a federalist in Aragon, respected the various regions' councils of state and parliaments. He brought new respect for *fueros* to Castile and was known as one of the more skillful diplomats of his time. He used his political finesse to include Catalonia and Valencia in his project to unify Spain. Ever cognizant of the constitutionally distinct regions, Ferdinand and Isabella worked to bring the political institutions of the various regions in line with the Christian notions of government. Each member would have its own honor and all members would be guided by Christ, as personified by the most Catholic kings, Ferdinand and Isabella.

Under their leadership, a royal militia was organized, the Inquisition was established, Navarre was annexed, and Columbus was licensed to set sail for the Indies. After visiting the tomb of St. James in Compostela, they vowed to rid the peninsula of all non-Catholics. After two hundred years of dormancy, they reanimated the battle against the Muslims and overthrew the emirate in Granada. In the same year, 1492, the Jews were expelled from Spain. Ferdinand and Isabella were absolute in their authority and intolerant of anything that smelled even faintly of heresy. The methods and institutions of the Catholic Monarchs, as they were named by the Pope, became the blueprint for subsequent governments.

We might look at this repressive system with a certain amount of horror. Freedom of religion, one of the founding elements of American independence, was completely absent from the government set up by the Catholic Monarchs. For a government to tell its citizens what they should believe is overstepping the bounds of good government as we understand it. But for a nation which understood itself in terms of a Christian mission, good government was obligated to turn sinners into people who might be saved. One of the great political philosophers of the Spanish Golden Age, Juan de Mariana, described Ferdinand and Isabella as "they who restored justice, previously corrupted and fallen into decay, to its proper place." What Protestant rulers in England and Holland referred to as repressive and cruel, the Catholic Iberians understood as harmonious with God's divine plan. Given the terrors of eternal damnation, using coercive techniques to ensure salvation was far more important for the common good than protecting individual liberty.

The authoritarian rule established by the Catholic Monarchs survived the illnesses and premature deaths of the next generations. Of Ferdinand and Isabella's five children, only one, Juana, survived and, according to legend, her sanity took a severe downturn with the death of her husband, the archduke of Austria, a member of the reigning Hapsburg dynasty. When the husband, Philip "*el Hermoso*" (the handsome one), died, Juana became "*la Loca*" (the crazy one), leaving her young son, Charles I to take the throne under a regency. Because Charles had been reared in Belgium, knew no Spanish, took the Spanish throne while still a teenager, and brought strange Flemish customs into the sober Spanish court, he never gained the respect of his Spanish subjects. The early part of his reign was marred with populist uprisings protesting the large number of foreigners in the Spanish court. These seditious revolts were suppressed only with enormous bloodshed.

When the emperor of the Holy Roman Empire, Maximilian I, died, Charles inherited his title in 1519. Spain, an emerging colonial empire in its own right, became the coresponsibility of Charles I, who now also held the title of Charles V of the Holy Roman Empire, which stretched as far east as coastal China.

With the expansion west to the Americas, Charles V was able to claim that the sun never set on his dominion. Castilian hearts, however, never shone for him.

Although the immediate heirs of the Catholic Monarchs were far less skilled at governing the Spanish people, the legitimacy of the system endured. Juana may have been crazy and Charles may have been foppish, but the system itself was sacred. Even imperial expansion was understood in terms of a religious mission, not economic largess. In his chronicles of the Conquest of the Americas, Bernal Díaz del Castillo, cites as one of the major accomplishments, "the conversion of so many souls which have been saved and each day are being saved which before would have perished in Hell."

Not only did the Conquest increase the number of souls going to heaven, but the New World's precious minerals funded religious wars on the European continent. American gold and silver financed the costly battles against Protestant sects in the Low Countries. Very little of the Aztec and Incan bullion was used to revitalize the Spanish national economy or improve the state infrastructure. The prime concern of Iberian national politics was to maintain the hegemony of the One, True Faith throughout the expanding world.

Charles was succeeded in 1556 by his son, Philip II, who continued his father's battle against the heresies of Protestantism, channeling more Incan and Aztec fortunes through Spain and into the Dutch and Flemish economies, so much so that Spain developed the reputation of being a sieve, "which whatever it receives is never the fuller," wrote an eighteenth-century British historian. Philip also consolidated powers by abolishing the *fueros* of Aragon and reducing the importance of the *cortes* of Castile, Aragón, Valencia, and Catalonia. Laws that had needed the concurrence of the *cortes* were now proclaimed by councils that had no ties to the various regions but operated under Philip II.

The reign of the Hapsburgs, which began with Philip, "*el Hermoso*," included an enormous flowering of Spanish culture and ideas. Spain became the center of philosophical resistance against the new European and Renaissance ideas of secular humanism. The Counter-Reformation provided a rich climate for the plays of Félix Lope de Vega y Carpio, the novels of Miguel Cervantes, the paintings of Diego Rodríguez de Silva y Velázquez and Domenikos Theotokopoulos, "El Greco," and the political philosophy of Juan de Mariana and Francisco Suárez. Despite, or perhaps because of, the extreme positions taken by the ruling monarchs, Spain, which from 1580 to 1640 now included Portugal, found itself vaulted to the forefront of European culture. The *Siglo de Oro,* "the century of gold," did not just refer to a precious metal from the New World. It indicated a time when Spanish thought, language, imagery, and artistic productions were gathering a worldwide audience.

At the same time as Lutheranism, Calvinism, and the Anglican church were causing many Christians to abandon Roman Catholicism for Protestantism,

Spain found itself as the prime Defender of the Faith. In terms of national identity, this self-conception was extremely convincing and politically useful. In terms of economic development, however, this statist, feudal, mercantilist economy effectively drained the resources of Iberia and Latin America. Counter-Reformation Iberia, by insisting that the troubles of this world were naturally subordinate to the glories of the next, did not cultivate the Protestant work ethic. Instead, the Hapsburgian model, locked in a rigid, hierarchical, authoritarian system, fostered an ethic with little concern for domestic productivity and with an obsession for piety and order. In England and the Netherlands, philosophers and intellectuals were rediscovering the vast potential of reason and free enterprise; but in Spain and Portugal, philosophers used reason to legitimize the existing hierarchy.

This is not to argue that England and the Low Countries were necessarily more "evolved" or "developed" than the Iberian peninsula. In fact, John Locke, one of the key Enlightenment thinkers, whose political theories shaped the American founding, pointed to Spain's exemplary custom of land use. In his famous *Second Treatise of Government,* Locke holds up the Spanish practice of permitting "a Man . . . to plough, sow, and reap, without being disturbed, upon Land he has no other Title to, but only is making use of it" (II§36). In John Locke's day, fallow Spanish pastures might be worked by landless farmers, who, upon cultivation, could and did claim ownership. Far from being a backward corner of Europe, Spain exemplified, in some regards, a more generous society.

Nor can it be said that early Protestant regimes were more tolerant than the Counter-Reformation Catholics. According to ecclesiastical historian Patrick Collinson, "[b]oth backed up instruction with corrective, even coercive pastoral discipline, a force for order and deference so useful to secular governments that it is doubtful whether the emergence of the centralized authoritarian state would have been possible without it" (266). Whereas Calvinism may have cultivated the accumulation of capital, it would be a distortion of history to see it as a pluralistic society. As Collinson reminds us, "[b]oth Catholic and Protestant regimes gave, as they thought, honor to God by burning [heretics] on an unprecedented scale" (266).

IBERIA IN DECLINE

Following the Golden Age of the sixteenth century, the Hapsburg dynasty went into a tailspin. Familial inbreeding is one explanation for this decline. Without strong leadership at the top, the Hapsburgian model could not function effectively. Besides the increasing imbecility of the rulers, the costs involved in staging global religious battles were exorbitant. Despite the huge amount of gold and silver coming in from the New World, the battles against the heretics decimated the resources of the peninsula both in terms of bodies and bullion. Not only did Spain lose much of its able-bodied citizenry to foreign wars, but many of the brightest emigrated to take advantage of opportunities in the New World. We have already mentioned the exile of the Jews, which resulted in the loss of an economically and intellectually vibrant community. Besides the factors of war, conquest, and forced exile, the plague also contributed to a severely depleted census. Added to this politically unstable mixture was a burdensome and unequal tax policy. Eventually, those who were left revolted. In 1640 massive uprisings took place in Catalonia and Portugal; thereafter Portugal was once again recognized as an independent nation.

Had there been a strong ruler at the top, things might have gone differently. As it happened, the Hapsburg heir destined to rule at the end of the seventeenth century was sickly and apathetic. The rule of Charles II (1661–1700) is recognized as a veritable disaster for Spain. Unable to resist outside influences, he was constantly manipulated by his advisers. Without the strength of leadership at the top, the entire system almost gave way. What had begun as a effective, zealous, albeit intolerant, dynasty, ended up as a universal symbol for political decadence.

The Hapsburgs were replaced in the eighteenth century by the Bourbons, a royal family from France. The Bourbons embodied all that was modern, progressive, and European about France, but they were not particularly concerned with the traditions of the peninsula. A succession of able, effective Bourbon monarchs introduced many of the advances of the continent: street lighting, improved roads, a mail service, public buildings, reforestation, a canal system, and the draining of wetlands. Along with these technological and bureaucratic efficiencies, the Bourbons also brought in European styles of dress and behavior. These foreign customs were not always well received by the Spanish masses. As the Bourbon dynasty continued to introduce "modern" European notions to the peninsula, the Spanish people, who were often more conservative than their leaders, became increasingly resistant and resentful. It was one thing to stimulate intellectual life, another thing entirely to impose European dress. Further, while a change in the system of taxation might have been welcomed, new restrictions on the Church were not.

The anticlerical policies of the Bourbons were directed against a Church that had become disenchanted with absolutism. The Jesuits, in particular, were outspoken critics of regalism. Suárez and Mariana, prominent Jesuit political theorists, had argued for a natural law compact between the people and the king. In an Iberian version of constitutionalism, Suárez had used Thomistic reasoning to replace the absolute position of the "divine rights of kings" with the "divine rights of the people." Political legitimacy required social justice, argued the Jesuits, not absolute power. This democratic position was not particularly popular with the ruling establishment. The Bourbons were against public charities financed by the Church; charity was antisocial because it destroyed the poor's initiative. Eventually, the Jesuits were expelled and the political theories of Suárez and Mariana were banned. Once again, a vibrant portion of the population was expelled.

In Portugal, the Marquês de Pombal, an eighteenth-century nobleman who ascended the rigid class system through personal charisma and a politically astute marriage, also imposed modern European programs through an absolute rule. Taking advantage of an earthquake in 1755 in Lisbon, Pombal rebuilt the city according to more modern methods, giving Lisbon the distinction of being Europe's first planned city. For this engineering success, Pombal was promoted to chief minister in the court of José I , a ruler known for his indolence. Following an assassination attempt on the king, Pombal manipulated the situation to his advantage by having any political enemies systematically destroyed. Pombal also expelled the Jesuits, confiscating their possessions and closing their schools. He created mathematics and philosophy departments that stressed scientific methods in the universities. Portugal, like Spain, would become a modern, enlightened nation whether the people liked it or not.

As Pombal and the Bourbons demonstrate, enlightened goals are not always achieved through enlightened methods. There was no room for democratic participation. Reforms were enforced from above, not generated from below. Catholic absolutism was replaced by Enlightenment absolutism without the necessary social support. At least the Catholics had the support of the Spanish people. The progressive reforms, generated by a powerful elite, depended on an emerging middle class for their social support. In order to carry out modernization, these reformists needed an obedient population who valued intellectual matters over religious superstitions and commercial acumen over political control.

Two Spains and two Portugals developed as a result of this deep ideological split. On the one side were traditional Catholics, both of the landed elite and rural peasant classes, who venerated the old ways. On the other side were modern, middle-class, and largely urban Catholics who were interested in moving Spain and Portugal closer to the commercial practices developing elsewhere in Europe. The two Spains and the Portugals shared little common ground, except for an inability to compromise. Eventually the tensions between the two sides erupted into a protracted period of civil war.

CIVIL CONFLICT IN THE NINETEENTH CENTURY

We have discussed at some length the conflict between national identity and regional differences. We have also discussed the struggle between Catholic intolerance and the need for a cosmopolitan merchant class. As Spain and Portugal entered the nineteenth century, these tensions were further exacerbated by the introduction of "foreign" republican and secular ideas to modernize and become more like the rest of Europe. In the past, ideological differences had been erased through religious intolerance; people who thought differently, that is, Jews, Muslims, and Protestants, were forced to conform to the One, True Faith or they were eliminated through death or expulsion. The conflicts of the nineteenth century were complicated in that Catholics disagreed amongst themselves as to how best to proceed.

Traditional Catholics were conservative, authoritarian, and believed in a highly centralized government. The social bases of traditional Catholics were the monarchy, the nobility, and the landowners and peasants of the countryside. Progressive Catholics, in contrast, no longer believed in the absolute ways of the past. They were intrigued with the possibilities of commerce and science, of humanism and the Enlightenment. The social bases of the progressive Catholics were located in the cities and comprised mainly the emerging middle class, merchants, and intellectuals. Not only were these progressive Catholics interested in natural science, they were equally interested in the science of governments. Instead of the divine rights of kings, an absolutist position, progressives were interested in constitutions and other political institutions. These ideological differences gave rise to what scholars have called a "split in the Iberian soul," with its origins in the eighteenth century but reaching full scale conflict in the nineteenth.

With the outbreak of the French Revolution in 1789, monarchs across Europe began to fear for their lives. Countries that had been at war with one another, now put aside their differences in favor of royal solidarity. Mutual assistance treaties were signed by Portugal with Spain and England in 1793. That same year the Bourbons attempted to help their doomed French cousins by sending the Spanish army, reinforced by six thousand Portuguese troops, across the Basque frontier. A year later, the French launched a major counterattack, sending the Spanish-Portuguese army back over the border.

On the elite level, across Europe, all sorts of political bargains were being negotiated. Manuel de Godoy, chief minister and virtual dictator of Spain, after attacking the newly established French Republic and observing the rise of Napoleon's empire, decided that it was in his favor to join forces with France against Britain. When Napoleon decreed that all nations of Europe should break relations with Britain, Portugal, a longtime ally of the English court, refused to obey. Having been offered one-third of Portugal as his personal reward, Godoy ordered Spanish troops to join French forces in a successful invasion of Portugal. When economic misery and a series of military losses caused a popular uprising in March of 1808, Godoy was dismissed and

Ferdinand ascended to the throne. The French immediately forced Ferdinand to abdicate, and Joseph Bonaparte, Napoleon's brother, was named king of Spain. A large French army was brought in to defend the new regime.

It should come as no surprise that members of the Spanish elite would welcome Napoleonic rule. The *afrancesados* welcomed a return of Bourbon social planning and economic engineering. Like the Bourbons before him, Joseph Bonaparte proclaimed the dissolution of religious houses. While that may have ingratiated him with the *afrancesados*, the Spanish citizenry reacted quite differently. Loyalty to the Catholic Church became once again the identifying characteristic of a good Spaniard. The move against the religious houses provoked nationalist fervor and armed resistance. The citizens of Zaragoza kept the French out for more than a year. In Asturias, the French were routed by local forces. An army of Valencians temporarily forced the French out of Madrid. The War of Independence, which lasted from 1808 to 1814, unified regions and classes against the infidel French.

Yet unity depended entirely on fighting a common enemy. Once the French were defeated, those who favored a constitutional government fought with those who wanted to reestablish absolute monarchy. In the absence of royal authority, a majority decision was eventually reached to invoke a *cortes* at Cádiz. This medieval institution was traditionally understood as a council to the king. Although representative in practice, membership was restricted to elite members of the various corporate groups. Many of the representatives who gathered in Cádiz were operating under medieval assumptions: once the deposed king Ferdinand VII ("the desired one") returned, the *cortes* would disband. Other representatives saw this as a traditional Spanish instrument that might be reworked into a more liberal form of government. The latter were clearly in the majority and were able to pass a constitution in 1812 that set forth the guidelines of a limited government. Favoring property qualifications over social status, the constitution effectively subverted the traditional hierarchy by privileging the rights of the commercial class and making no special provisions for the Church or the nobility. Traditional property restrictions were repealed, giving the liberals a freer economy in which to operate.

When Ferdinand VII returned to the throne in 1814, he refused to recognize the constitution. Six years later, an army insurrection reestablished the supremacy of the constitution through rule by *pronunciamiento*. This "referendum in blood" expressed the army's willingness to shed blood without having actually to engage in battle. For three years, the *pronunciamiento* held until the French army intervened. In the midst of this political chaos, most of the Spanish-American colonies revolted and declared their independence. Many of these revolts were provoked by what the colonists saw as dangerously liberal tendencies in the mother countries, the constitution of 1812 being a prime example. The arrival of the infidel French only confirmed the colonists' suspicions that the Motherland had lost her spiritual bearings and was on her way to perdition. Given the wars that followed, they may have had a point.

The Carlist Wars centered around questions of royal succession. When Ferdinand died, he left no male heirs. Instead he left his wife, Maria Cristina, as regent for their daughter, Isabella. Ferdinand's brother, Don Carlos, a popular traditionalist, was heir presumptive. On the one side were the Carlists, the supporters of Don Carlos, who insisted that legitimacy depended on a male line. This position attracted agrarians (landowners and peasants), regionalists, and traditional Catholics. The other side coalesced around the regency, the same groups who had been attracted to the constitutional government—centralists, anticlerical liberals, urban-dwellers—who benefited from an international economy rather than a fixed social hierarchy. These groups battled and regrouped off and on between 1833 until 1876. Throughout that period, the regency and its liberal supporters barely maintained the upper hand.

Liberals could agree only on a few points, Maria Cristina not being one of them. By 1840 the army forced her to resign. Liberals agreed they were against the Church and for economic progress but they disagreed on the best way to achieve an anticlerical, laissez-faire future. Moderate liberals were not against absolute measures to achieve their ends. Progressives, who drew support from the urban masses, wanted a more democratic method. Although both moderates and progressives believed in the development of individual rights, they were unclear whether they followed a Lockean or Rousseauian tradition. Did government take a passive role, as in Locke's theory of government by consent, or did it actively and authoritatively express the general will, the ideal system put forth by Rousseau?

The liberal position was not supported by many of the traditional corporate groups: the nobility, the Church, and the regionalists. What is surprising is that one traditional corporate group, the army, was for a time a key component in Spain's liberal rule. Since the Enlightened absolutism of the Bourbons, the army had come around to a more progressive vision for Spain. This is not to say that the military was in favor of a broad-based democracy. It clearly wasn't. The army, as a national force, operated most efficiently from a strong center, bringing law and order to the unruly masses. The result of this alliance between the army and liberalism meant that progress could never involve decentralization. Each time the government attempted to enact programs that involved a devolution of power, as in land reform, the army stepped in and took over, either by coup or *pronunciamiento*. Liberalism, in Spain, was not at odds with a military dictatorship.

The situation in Portugal in the nineteenth century paralleled much of that in Spain. A problem of royal succession was initially resolved by a constitutional charter. Eventually war broke out between absolutist and liberal factions. However, Portugal, unlike Spain, developed a method for handling these two opposing forces. *Rotativismo*, the practice of alternating the two parties, the Regenerators and the Historicals, at regular intervals, and sharing in the patronage that accrued with control of the government, produced a relatively stable government until the end of the nineteenth century.

THE REPUBLICAN INTERLUDE

In 1878 a group of Portuguese republicans organized itself into a formal party. Membership was drawn from the intellectuals, teachers, and journalists, as well as from the commercial class. Portuguese republicanism stressed nationalism, universal suffrage, separation of church and state, and the abolition of the monarchy and the noble families that were firmly established in Portugal. Republicanism appealed to those who felt that the old ways were keeping Portugal out of step with the rest of the world.

When the back room negotiations that constituted *rotativismo* were brought before the public eye, the masses were not sure how to respond. Instead of applauding a system which produced stability through secret pacts, the masses refused to play along. Neither of the two traditional factions were able to gain a majority. Instead, a small number of republicans managed to be elected to the parliament, enough to create a political stalemate. Parliament was dissolved, a dictator was appointed by the king and, after an unsuccessful coup attempt, a military crackdown was imposed, creating more social unrest. Eventually, the dictator stepped down and a new round of elections began; however, neither of the traditional parties was able to forge a majority. When the Portuguese army failed to back the monarchy, the royal family fled to Britain. On October 5, 1910, a provisional republican government was organized.

From 1910 to 1926, the Portuguese First Republic attempted to hold control. Inexperienced in republican, democratic rule, the ministers and governments came and went on an average of every few months. Chaos reigned and one historian counted more bombs thrown in Lisbon during that period than in any other European country.[4] By violating Catholic assumptions of order and discipline, the republic was unable to garner much popular support. The tradition that did remain was the family-oriented patronage politics that had characterized the earlier monarchy. Rival clans continued to "rotate" in and out of office, giving all the factions a turn at the great public watering trough: the national treasury. By the 1920s, the economy was in deep trouble, and a fraudulent bank note scheme devalued both the government as well as the currency. In 1926, fed up with the political and economic mess, the army stepped into power, paving the way for the dictatorship of Salazar.

Unlike Portugal, when Spain moved to a republican government, the change was fueled by a sense of being terribly out of sync with the rest of the world. When Spain lost Cuba, Puerto Rico, and the Philippines to the United States in the Spanish-American War of 1898, the country suffered a major loss of confidence. Not only was a substantial portion of its remaining colonies taken by a young upstart nation but only one of the old nations, Germany, had sided with Spain. The response to this international loss of face, was a flowering of new, often short-lived political parties, most centered around the founder's personality. Regionalists used the national disaster as an excuse to disassociate themselves from "the corpse of Castile." Anarchists seized the opportunity to critique archaic, absolute government; often their critiques involved terrorism. In this unstable climate, Alejandro Lerroux organized a number of antimonarchist and liberal splinter groups into the Radical Republicans, a national party that appealed to the middle class and the industrial Catalans.

As is often the case in Iberian politics, the army was central in deciding the future of politics. A long-standing battle in Morocco, which none of the various parties was willing to finance enough to win, had reduced the army's morale. Officers who had served in Morocco returned to wartime inflation and low, fixed wages for military personnel. Increased terrorism and social unrest, brought on by ideological wars and economic instability, reached a level where another *pronunciamiento* was issued, bringing General Miguel Primo de Rivera into power.

Primo de Rivera ruled through military dictatorship from 1923 to 1930. His partially corporatist regime foreshadowed the system established by Franco. He dissolved parliament and sponsored public works to curb unemployment. Through his protectionist policies and mercantilist practices, the economy recovered temporarily. A fully funded and better supplied army won the war in Morocco in 1926. These successes convinced many in next-door Portugal, who were dissatisfied with their own attempts at republican rule, to return to the stability of an authoritarian ruler. A coup in 1926 in Portugal ushered in a military dictatorship which eventually came to be led by General Óscar Fragoso Carmona. Unlike Primo de Rivera, Carmona was a master at balancing the various factions. Both Catholic and republican, he negotiated a center position between pro- and antimonarchists and pro- and anticlerical officers.

Had the international economy not collapsed in 1930, Spain's Primo de Rivera might have held power for longer. His regime was further weakened by the absence of a positive program. His coalition, such as it was, was founded on negatives: they were against parliamentary government and extreme political parties. When the economy went sour, he lost the support of the banking community and, more importantly, the good will of the army and the king. Forced to resign, Primo de Rivera went into exile and died shortly thereafter.

It is at this point in history where the political stories of Spain and Portugal take divergent paths. In 1928 General Carmona, in a shrewd political move, named António de Oliveira Salazar as his minister of finance. This professor of political economy from the University of Coimbra took complete control of all government expenditures. Within his first year, he not only balanced the budget but created a governmental surplus, the first in over a decade. It was quickly apparent that the minister of finance was doing a better job of running the country than the succession of military prime ministers. Through strict measures, Salazar reduced government inefficiency and improved revenues. For these improvements, he won the respect of the young intellectuals and military officers. For his economic successes, he won the respect of the banking and commercial community. A practicing Catholic, Salazar also had the backing of the Church, which had suffered from the anticlerical positions of the First Republic. The political system that Salazar established, the New State (*Estado Novo*) is treated in greater detail in the following chapter.

In Spain, Primo de Rivera did not achieve the political success of his Portuguese counterpart. The elections following his exile voted in a substantial number of antimonarchist parties. The king, Alfonso XIII, sensing a civil war, appealed to the army for support. Hearing that the army would not support the king against the will of the people, Alfonso abdicated and, in 1931, the Second Republic was ushered in. A coalition was formed whose goals included reform of the army, a return to regional autonomy, economic redistribution, social reform, and separation of the Church from governmental and educational programs. Niceto Alcalá Zamora became president and called for immediate elections in which the Republican Left (Izquierda Republicana—IR) came out ahead.

The events that follow represent a tragedy of differences. The coalition that Manuel Azaña, the leader of the Republican Left headed, promised a gradual transition to socialism. The pace of change angered the radical left and the goal disenfranchised the right. Efforts to reform the army provoked a *pronunciamiento* and Azaña was forced to back down. Problems with the army, however, were secondary to the ideological differences within his coalition. The Marxist-leaning socialist party, the Spanish Socialist Workers' Party (Partido Socialista Obrero Español—PSOE) was unwilling to cooperate with the middle-class bourgeois IR . Meanwhile the world economic depression had deepened. While Marxists were arguing with republicans over ideological issues, unemployment and inflation were on the rise. Society began to fragment and polarize. The Carlist civil wars of the nineteenth century were about to be reenacted in their final, bloodiest, and most violent form, compounded now by real class and ideological conflict.

Liberals and socialists were the dominant elements in the republic during its first two years, facing strong opposition from the right. During the next two years, power passed back to the conservative elements but, given the intensely polarized climate, they could not govern effectively either. The economy remained in the depths of depression, and the political parties remained severely factionalized. Violence began to spread as each of the major parties established its own militia—private armies that were well-armed and wreaked havoc on the opposition. Civil society gave way to mob justice. One day conservative leaders were gunned down, the next day socialists were assassinated. The army, watching the spreading chaos, alarmed by the strength of the left as well as all the guns in the hands of irregular civilian groups, grew restless.

The political pendulum began to swing wildly. In 1935–36, it swung way back to the left. The left at this time consisted no longer of moderate liberals and republicans but was dominated by socialists, communists, and anarchists. In many respects the socialists were even more extreme than the communists, calling for the overthrow of capitalism and the establishment of a dictatorship of the proletariat. Chaos and violence spread. The left-wing parties now formed a radical, Popular Front government. Fearing the establishment of a Bolshevik regime, the Spanish army, important parts of which were located in the Spanish enclaves in North Africa, issued a *pronunciamiento* against the republic and invaded the peninsula. The republican government responded by opening the arsenals in the major cities and giving guns to the workers and to the Popular Front political parties. With these acts, full-scale civil war began.

The Spanish civil war raged from 1936 to 1939. It was one of the bloodiest and most vicious civil wars of all times. On both sides there were scenes of mind-numbing violence and brutality. Republican forces raped and murdered nuns, the army forced suspected republican sympathizers—old men, women, and children—to walk off cliffs. The stakes were high and the ideological passions were fervent. The war epitomized the history of the time: the left saw it as the battle between liberty and repression, the right as the war between order and chaos. It attracted worldwide attention, with intellectuals, writers, and activists of all kinds flocking to Spain to write about the conflict and/or join it. American authors, such as Ernest Hemingway and John Dos Passos, saw the conflict as the epitome of republican virtues fighting against absolute tyranny. British author and former communist George Orwell discovered in Spain that the Soviet Union was interested only in power, not the masses' liberation from servitude.

The Spanish civil war also attracted the attention of the major world powers. An outbreak of violence, easily understood as the battle between fascism and communism, created political alliances along ideological lines. The Soviet Union offered support to the republican forces. Fascist Italy and Nazi Germany gave military assistance to the Spanish army, using Spain to test techniques they would employ during World War II. When a junta of generals formed a government in Burgos, Germany and Italy immediately recognized it. Yet these external players only contributed a piece of the picture. The left was never able to galvanize around a shared Spanish value. The fascist right, on the other hand, was able to seize the banner of nationalism. When the young founder of the Falange, a quasi-fascist party, was executed by republican forces, the right had its Catholic martyr. José Antonio Primo de Rivera, the former dictator's son, became the symbol of all that made Spain Spanish. He was devout and willing to die, committed to order and the blessed hierarchy of the Church.

With rising nationalist sentiments, superior organization and firepower, the Spanish army, under the leadership of General Francisco Franco, slowly turned the tide of the battle. This Catholic, disciplined, ascetic leader rode into victory with the support of monarchists, centralists, and the Church. In a decisive battle outside of Madrid, Franco invoked once again the powers of St. James (Santiago). When the battle was won, Franco reinstituted the *Votos de Santiago*, a medieval tribute paid to the cathedral in Campostella that housed the saint's bones, and restored Santiago as the patron saint of Spain.

National identity in Franco's Spain reached back to a medieval Catholicism. Those who were good Spaniards were those who fought for God, Spain, and St. James. Liberals and socialists, those vanquished during the war, became the new breed of heretics. On churches across the regions, the names of those who died for God and Spain were inscribed. Those who died for godless reasons, the members of republican Spain, were dumped in common, unmarked graves; the poet Federico Garcia Lorca lies among them. Religious intolerance became political intolerance. Spain moved into the twentieth century, still in one piece, but with her creative, intellectual, and economic powers exiled or carelessly buried underground. Portugal had experienced the same conflicts and polarization between republicanism and authoritarianism, anarchy and order, individualism and corporatism, secularism and religion, but as usual in less severe form than Spain.

NOTES

1. Desmond Seward, *The Monks of War: The Military Religious Orders* (New York: Penguin, 1995), 144.

2. Cited in Benjamin Keen, *Latin American Civilization: History Society, 1492 to the Present* (Boulder, Colo.: Westview, 2000), 30.

3. For recent revisions on the Spanish Inquisition, see B. Netanyahu, *The Origins of the Inquisition in Fifteenth-Century Spain* (New York: Random House, 1995); and Henry Kamen, *The Spanish Inquisition: A Historical Revision* (New Haven: Yale University Press, 1997).

4. Douglas Wheeler, *Republican Portugal: A Political History, 1910–1926* (Madison: University of Wisconsin Press, 1978).

Chapter 3

THE FRANCO AND SALAZAR REGIMES

Francisco Franco ruled Spain from 1939 until his death of natural causes in 1975, a period of thirty-six years. Antonio de Oliveira Salazar ruled Portugal from 1928 (when as finance minister he became czar of the nation's economy; he was appointed prime minister in 1932) until his incapacitation in a fall in 1968, a longer reign (forty years) even than Franco. In addition, Salazar's regime continued for six more years under the leadership of his protegé, Marcello Caetano, until it was overthrown in the Portuguese "Revolution of Carnations" in 1974.

The regimes of Franco and Salazar were two of the longest-lived regimes in the world in the twentieth—or any other—century.[1] In longevity they matched or surpassed the earlier rule of Ferdinand and Isabella, Charles I, and Philip II. In their authoritarian, organic, corporatist, and top-down structures, they were also very much in the tradition of these earlier monarchs. The difference is, by the mid-twentieth century, Spain and Portugal had changed greatly since these earlier times, so it is worth questioning if the type of regimes erected by Franco and Salazar was still appropriate in this modern context or if they would only be reconstituted by repression and violence.

Franco and Salazar were not just long-lived authoritarians, however; nor will we understand them if we simply dismiss them as "dictators" or "fascists." In fact, the Franco and Salazar regimes were much more complex than such simple labels imply—and more important. First, the echoes of Franco and Salazar still resound in Spain and Portugal; the influence of their regimes are still evident in political discourse, and in some quarters there is nostalgia for the order, stability, and discipline that characterized their rule. Second, Franco and Salazar presided over an unprecedented period of economic and social change; without that growth and modernization it is doubtful if the later democratization of their two countries would have been possible. Third, Franco and Salazar were adherents of corporatism as an ideology and system of national sociopolitical organization and sought to elevate corporatism into a position as a "third way" alternative to either American- or British-style liberalism or to Soviet-style communism. They also suggested corporatism was more closely attuned to Iberian history and realities (Catholic, organic, structured, legalistic, top-down, ordered) than was either the liberal or Marxist alternative, and that this same corporatist third way was also appropriate for Latin America.

In one sense, the Franco and Salazar regimes were the culmination of the long Catholic and authoritarian tradition presented in the previous chapter; in another sense, they ushered in the modern period in Iberian history and paved the way for society-transforming change and democracy; in still a third sense, their impact—both positive and negative—continues to reverberate in Spanish and Portuguese politics today.

EARLY ORIGINS AND COMING TO POWER

Antonio Salazar was the son of small-town shopkeepers in the north of Portugal. He and his family were austere, hard-working, and strongly Catholic. A brilliant student, he attracted the attention of local priests, who provided his early education and sent him to Portugal's historic Coimbra University. He at first studied for the priesthood but switched to law and economics. Economics in Portugal in those days was pre-Keynesian and a branch of law.

As a young professor in the 'teens and early 1920s, Salazar was witness to the chaos and instability of Portugal's First Republic, 1910–26. His values were order, stability, and hierarchy; Salazar did not share the British, American, or Portuguese-republican values of democracy or egalitarianism. Instead, he was caught up in a number of Catholic political movements that stressed the organic, integral, and corporatist structure of society. He was also influenced by Mussolini's coming to power in Italy in 1922, not by totalitarianism or genocide but again by the ideas of an organic and corporatist society. The question was: Which of these influences would dominate in the young Salazar: the "softer," more pluralist corporatism of free association of the Catholic social movement or the "harder" state corporatism of Mussolini? The answer for Salazar: both.

During the early 1920s Salazar remained active on behalf of conservative and Catholic causes, denounced the republic for its instability and godlessness, and applauded the military coup that overthrew the Republic in 1926. But the military lacked an ideology or program; when they asked Salazar to serve as finance minister in 1928, they got not only an economic czar but an entire Catholic-corporatist "third-way" ideology as well. He spent the next four years reforming the economy and consolidating his power, and moved up to prime minister in 1932. In the same year he completely restructured Portuguese labor relations, interest group activities, and state-society relations along corporatist lines, based on the principles of functional or group representation and class harmony rather than geographic or individual representation (liberalism) and class conflict (Marxism). He also employed censorship, authoritarianism, and police state controls against his enemies. The pattern of Salazar's rule, with only slight variations, was thus set for the next thirty-six years.

Francisco Franco's early career in Spain was very different from Salazar's, but the two ran parallel at various points, and their styles and systems of rule were remarkably similar. The Franco family came from Galicia, in the far northwest of Spain, which is much like the area in northern Portugal from which Salazar came. It was similarly poor, austere, and very Catholic; like Salazar, the young Franco was brought up in a Catholic family and a social milieu that emphasized stability and order and had little use for the liberalism, egalitarianism, and "advanced" ideologies of the large urban centers.

Whereas Salazar had grown up training for the priesthood, young Franco had grown up as a product of military academies. But both institutions were similar in many respects, stressing order, discipline, hierarchy, authority, and self-control. Moreover, these two, the Church and the army, were among the few institutions in Spain and Portugal of those days providing avenues of upward mobility for the able, ambitious children of the lower middle class. And whereas Salazar excelled in the disciplined, hierarchical, cloistered halls of Coimbra University, Franco was recognized by his military superiors for his organizational and leadership skills. He graduated first in his class at the military academy, earned numerous awards and commendations as a young officer, and was famously the youngest general in Europe since Napoleon. Much like Salazar, his accomplishments at an early age attracted the attention of higher-ranking admirers and mentors who helped guide and advance his career.

As a young military officer, Franco watched with apprehension as the First Spanish Republic came to power in 1931. Then, again like Salazar in Portugal, his worst fears were realized as the republic degenerated into instability, bitter factionalism, widespread violence, and virtual societal breakdown. His suspicions of civilian politicians and party politics deepened as he witnessed their rhetorical excesses, demagoguery, and vote-trading. The wild swinging of the Spanish political pendulum from left to right and back again, the coming to power in 1936 of the radical (socialist and communist) Popular Front, the dispensing of guns to workers and peasants and the formation by all the parties of armed party militias, the accelerating violence and assassinations, and the fear that a Bolshevik-like Marxist-Leninist revolution might occur in Spain seemed to confirm Franco's, and the army's, worst fears.

Along with most of the army, Franco was stationed in Spanish North Africa when the 1936 civil war began. He was not yet the highest-ranking general in the army, but his skills and talents were known by his fellow officers. He and his forces soon were called back across the Strait of Gibraltar and joined the conservative nationalists in their uprising against the republic. Meanwhile, some of the senior generals died, were killed, were elbowed aside, or retired. By the end of the war in 1939, Franco not only was the highest-ranking general but the republic had been crushed, the Nationalists had emerged victorious, and he was de facto the effective ruler of Spain.

THE CHANGE TO CORPORATISM

In the 1920s and 1930s—the period between the two world wars of the twentieth century and including the Great Depression as well as political breakdown in a number of European countries—corporatism was a very popular idea.[2] Corporatism was presented as a "third way" between liberalism and Marxian socialism; its popularity, as an alternative, was enhanced as liberalism and capitalism seemed to be breaking down in the 1930s depression and since, to most of the Spanish and Portuguese people, Soviet communism was completely unacceptable. A major branch of corporatism grew out of Catholic social teachings of the late nineteenth and early twentieth centuries, as the Church sought to formulate a positive ideology to compete with other challenging ideologies and to secure the Catholic flock in an increasingly secularized world. But corporatism also had bureaucratic, organizational, and nonreligious forms as well. So while Catholic corporatism flourished for a time in Iberia and Latin America, Protestant and secular forms also emerged in northern and central Europe.

There are two main definitions of corporatism; both of them are important for understanding Spain and Portugal. The first definition suggests that corporatism is an ideology, like Marxism or liberalism, a way of life, a set of beliefs, a general pattern of political understanding. Corporatism in this sense means a political world view derived from Aristotle and St. Thomas Aquinas:

that government is good and natural; that it need not, therefore, be checked and balanced; that the well-ordered political system is integrated, disciplined, hierarchical; that all groups and individuals are secure and fixed in their station in life. Corporatism thus pictures society as an organic whole with all its parts interrelated. A corporatist political system is made up of corporately organized groups recognized in law as having juridical personality and having duly recognized rights and responsibilities.

In Spain and Portugal the main historic "corporations" or corporative units of society, traced back to feudal or even earlier times, were the family seen as the building block of society, the local community or town, the parish or neighborhood association, the Catholic Church, the military orders, the guilds of sheepherders, silversmiths, and other trades, and the university or religious orders. Typically, supreme authority in a corporatist regime is centered in a governing body based not on individual or geographic representation (one person, one vote) but on functional representation from the groups indicated above. Because historically they derive their ideas so strongly from medieval Catholic political philosophy, corporative regimes of this kind have been particularly prevalent in the Catholic countries of Europe (Spain, Portugal, Austria, Italy, Belgium, even France) and Latin America. Often viewed as a conservative ideology because of its foundation in medieval Catholicism and its emphasis on order and authority, corporatism also adapts to change by incorporating newer social groups (such as business and labor) into its vision and structure of a coordinated, interdependent, structured political system. Depending on one's perspective, one can consider corporatism as either a rediscovery by Spain and Portugal of their historic and nationalistic roots as described in the previous chapter, or a regressive, reactionary throwback to an earlier authoritarian era. In Spain and Portugal, both of these interpretations were strongly held, which helps explain why the Franco and Salazar regimes were—and remain—so controversial.

The second definition of corporatism sees it as a general model of the political system with no particular cultural, religious, or regional base. Corporatism in this sense is not an ideology or belief system but a particular way of structuring state-society relations that is hierarchical, disciplined, monopolistic, and state-centered. Corporatism is thus a political-organizational model like pluralism or totalitarianism. Defined this way, corporatism may exist in Protestant and secular nations as well as Catholic ones, in advanced industrial nations as well as developing ones. This type of corporatism seeks mainly to regulate and control business and labor organizations under an authoritarian-bureaucratic system.

The confusion—and the controversy—comes from the fact that, under Franco and Salazar, Spain and Portugal embodied both of these definitions of corporatism. Their regimes represented combinations and often uneasy overlaps of the Catholic ideological tradition of corporatism and the bureaucratic-authoritarian one, with the balance between these two conceptions shifting over time. Let us look at each of these regimes concretely, beginning with Portugal.[3]

At least initially, Portugal was closest to the ideological or Catholic-corporatist conception. Salazar had been a seminarian, trained for the priesthood, and active in Catholic social movements; he was thoroughly imbued with the Catholic-corporatist conception. He disliked both Marxism and liberalism, seeing the former as instigating bloody class conflict and the latter, with its strong individualism, as undermining the organic unity of society. He believed corporatism would be the ideology of the future, a way of bringing conflicting groups and classes together through a system of Catholic harmony. He sought to restructure Portugal according to its "natural" corporatist units: the family, the parish, the neighborhood, and so on. He distrusted political parties, parliaments, and interest group pluralism—that is, Western liberalism—as divisive and leading to conflict. He tried to restructure Portugal not on the basis of "imported" liberal institutions but on its own historic, indigenous, and nationalistic—that is, Catholic and corporatist—bases.

Salazar, therefore, set out to reorganize Portugal's political institutions on a corporatist basis. Recall that the military regime that had seized power in 1926 and called Salazar to be finance minister two years later lacked an ideology other than knowing that it disliked the chaos and disorder of liberalism and republicanism; they were, therefore, willing to give Salazar a free hand to implement his own ideology. So in 1932–33, upon consolidating his power as prime minister, Salazar began the corporatist restructuring. In a virtual avalanche of legislation in some ways reminiscent of Franklin D. Roosevelt's first one hundred days, Salazar promulgated a new constitution, a new set of laws governing labor relations, and a series of measures governing interest group activities.

The 1933 constitution, for example, proclaimed Portugal both a republican and a corporative state. One house of parliament was to be based on geographic representation, the other on functional or corporatist representation. The Catholic Church, the armed forces, the Portuguese wine industry, and other major entities, all were guaranteed a set number of seats in the second or Corporative Chamber. A high-level Council of State, similarly with representation from all major corporate groups in society, was to serve as an advisory body. A new cabinet-level ministry of corporations was created to preside over all the new corporatist bodies.

A new labor statute also issued in 1933 forced business and labor to join in a system of obligatory adjudication; in keeping with the class harmony theme, both worker strikes and employer lockouts were forbidden. Next came a series of decrees reorganizing all interest groups and their interrelations; labor unions were restructured as *sindicatos,* business groups as guilds, fishermen (a major industry in Portugal) in "houses of fishermen," common people in "houses of the people." University personnel, doctors, engineers, all professional associations were obliged to follow suit. In all these reforms the principles followed were class harmony rather than conflict or pluralism and organic unity over diversity and pluralism.

Along with the corporatist political agencies, the government created a large number of new regulatory agencies to preside over the economy and, Mussolini-style, to introduce economic as well as political corporatism. These included a vast number of new agencies, directorates, and offices designed to replace a free-market economy with a statist or mercantilist one. These agencies vastly increased the power of the state to intervene in all areas of economic life and to set prices, wages, and production quotas through state directives rather than market mechanisms. During the 1930s, thus, Portugal instigated a corporatist or state-directed economic system to go along with its reorganized corporatist political institutions.

The capstone of this entire system was supposed to be the "corporations," not joint-stock companies as we know them but agencies to supervise each sector of the economy (such as wine, fish, wheat) and, once again, to guarantee worker-employer harmony. But the organization of the corporations was repeatedly postponed by crises—first by the depression of the 1930s, then by the Spanish civil war (1936–39), then by World War II. By that time corporatism as an ideology and sociopolitical program had been discredited by its perverted practice under Nazism and fascism, which had been defeated in the war. Salazar remained a corporatist intellectually and politically and strongly antiliberal, but as a pragmatist he recognized the futility of trying to put into practice an ideology that had been repudiated. So after World War II, Portugal drifted, without an ideological compass; by the time Salazar finally created the corporations in the 1950s and 1960s, they performed such tasks as regulating labor relations and administering social welfare—roles not very much different from those performed by labor ministries or social security agencies in other Western countries.

In the meantime, objective observers learned a great deal about the actual functioning of such corporatist regimes, as compared with their idealistic ideology. First, the Salazar regime, rather than treating labor and capital as harmonious equals as the ideology said, instead was much harsher on worker groups than it was on employers. Second and related, the regime came to accept the arguments of elite big business that corporatism in the economy was too risky an undertaking for such a fragile country; hence, while workers were forced to join government-run *sindicatos*, business continued to enjoy considerable freedom of action. Third, although many of the young Catholic intellectuals that designed and wrote the early corporatist laws and constitution favored a softer, pluralist "corporatism of association"; the regime's actual practices were those of "corporatism of the state"—harsher and more authoritarian. Finally, although with its emphasis on such constituent units as neighborhood, family, and parish, as the building blocks of society corporatism sounded like a philosophy of decentralization, grass roots participation, and local control, in fact the corporatist system served as an agency of centralization and top-down state control.

By contrast, Franco was never so committed to the corporatist ideology as Salazar had been.[4] He was a military man, more practical, less doctrinaire. He supported many of the same values as did Salazar: discipline, order, hierarchy, Catholicism (pre–Vatican II), social control. Many of his civilian advisers and government officials were committed corporatists. But Franco had not been brought up in the Catholic-corporatist ideological movement as Salazar had and was not as wedded to it. For Franco, corporatism was a useful organizational tool, a way of defining his regime but not locking it in, a way of filling organizational space, a means of organizing national society when all other means (liberalism, Marxism) were seen as bankrupt and exhausted.

Salazar had been invited by the Portuguese military to come to power and put his ideas into practice, but Franco was the triumphant general in a bloody civil war following the unraveling of the First Republic. In 1939 Franco found himself rather like the Portuguese generals in 1926: triumphant in a military uprising against the republic but, other than the usual military preference for order and discipline, lacking a formula for governing. Hence, he turned to the Spanish Falange movement, a right-wing, quasi-fascist group, to provide the ideology, model, and political program that Franco lacked. The Falange advocated a corporatist restructuring of society, but it was much closer to the Italian form of fascism than to the Catholic-corporatist ideals of Portugal's young leaders.

The Falange, thus, provided Spain with the corporatist political model and ideology that Franco and his fellow officers lacked. In the early years of the Franco regime, the Falange was undoubtedly influential, leading many to label the government "fascist," a label that stuck as an indication of disapproval even after its accuracy as an adjective had faded. For Franco never allowed the Falange—or any other group—to acquire too much power. Instead, he kept most of the power concentrated in his own hands. He used the Falange to help organize his regime politically, but real decision-making power remained concentrated in Franco himself. After World War II, when the Falange's usefulness to him declined, he shunted it aside and, with it, a good part of the corporatist system and ideology.

Under Franco, Spain had an authoritarian government that was at least partly corporatist. Unlike Portugal, it had no formal constitution but instead a series of charters, laws, and statements of national principle laid down over the years and considered the fundamental laws of the nation, constitutionally binding. Spain had a chief-of-state (Franco), a council of ministers (cabinet), and a *cortes* (parliament). The *cortes* was a consultative body as it had been in early Spanish history, not an independent legislative one. Representation was, as in Portugal, by corporative bodies or functions: armed forces, religious bodies, economic groups, labor unions (*sindicatos*), municipalities, professional associations, and the Falange itself. Spain also had a high-level advisory body, the Council of State, similarly based on corporatist representation, but it performed few important functions and, like the *cortes*, never developed as an independent body.

Spain had a Ministry of Syndicates, comparable to Portugal's Ministry of Corporations. It oversaw the country's national Syndical Organization, which was the only officially recognized bargaining agent between labor and management. In keeping with the corporatist principle of class harmony, all employees and employers were obliged to belong to the syndicate or corporative body appropriate to their field of economic activity. Thirty such syndicates were eventually created, covering all of Spain's major economic sectors. Labor and management were supposedly coequally represented in each syndicate. It should also be noted that the syndicates were vertically organized rather than horizontally. Instead of all the workers being gathered together in one big labor movement like the AFL-CIO (horizontal organization), in Spain the syndicates were organized by industry. For example, the wine-makers' syndicate would include not only workers and employers together but also all those involved, vertically, in the growing, harvesting, bottling, sales, and distribution of wine products. Each syndicate, in turn, was divided into subgroups including neighborhood associations, community organizations, and guilds and brotherhoods of various kinds. By forcing workers into the same associations as employers and by preventing workers from organizing horizontally across all economic sectors, the regime prevented a strong, unified, disciplined labor movement from emerging.

With less ideological commitment to Catholic social corporatism than Salazar, the authoritarian or state-corporatism features were more prevalent in Spain right from the beginning. Recall also that Spain had just emerged from a vicious civil war and feelings of hatred and revenge were strong. Thousands of Spaniards from the republican opposition were killed, jailed, or sent into exile by the Franco regime. And because the threat of radical (socialist, communist, anarchist) trade unionism was considered great, the regime came down hard on the unions, using corporatism not to achieve class harmony but to control and suppress organized labor. Corporatism in Iberia could have been a constructive, socially just, nation-building formula; instead, it became an instrument of dictatorship. Rather than serving as a uniquely Spanish and Portuguese expression of modernization and reconciliation, the corporative system instead became an agency of authoritarian control, subordinate to the state and to one-man rule.

Eventually, the Spanish corporative system changed functions, as had the Portuguese. Its importance was downgraded, and the Ministry of Syndicates became a combined labor-social welfare ministry. It still kept close tabs on labor unions, but it also administered new programs in health, unemployment, and pensions. The corporatist ideology of the 1930s was increasingly ignored, even by the Franco regime. Meanwhile, the system opened up somewhat, not to still-despised liberalism, but to somewhat greater interest group activity and even a measure of pluralism, including a pragmatic willingness to deal with previously suppressed labor groups.

AUTHORITARIANISM AND REPRESSION

Many adjectives have been used to describe the Franco and Salazar regimes, not all of them useful. They have been described as "military dictatorships"; but Salazar was a civilian and both he and Franco, while relying on the military, never allowed the armed forces to rule, dominate, or interfere with their own decisions. Another term used is "clerical" or "theocratic dictatorships"; but while these were strongly Catholic regimes in terms of the religious basis of the political culture, they were also pragmatic and did not allow the Church any more than the military to govern. A third designation is "fascist" but that is not quite accurate either: while there were some fascist sympathies and tendencies in both regimes, particularly in the pre–World War II period, in fact both Franco and Salazar took strong action against the real fascists in their countries, and neither regime pursued genocidal policies, dreamed of world conquest, propagated a totalitarian ideology, or developed a full-fledged fascist party. A police state? It is true that both regimes employed sometimes brutal and repressive methods, particularly in the 1930s, but over time they became less repressive and eventually opened up their regimes somewhat not to liberalism but to greater pluralism and less strict controls.

If these descriptions are not entirely accurate, then how do we describe the Franco and Salazar regimes? Not by employing bumper sticker labels but by analyzing them carefully. A good starting point is Juan Linz's distinction between authoritarian and totalitarian regimes,[5] a distinction that was not always apparent to the victims of these regimes but is helpful in understanding them. Linz argues that both the Spanish and Portuguese regimes should be understood as occupying an intermediary position, clearly not liberal, not totalitarian either, but in between these two major types, an authoritarian regime that has its own distinctive politics and dynamics.

First, with regard to interest groups: Spain and Portugal did not allow completely unfettered interest group pluralism (liberalism), but they did not completely snuff them out (totalitarianism) either; rather, Spain and Portugal allowed limited pluralism, which they then gradually expanded over time. Second, ideology: Franco and Salazar did not allow all ideas to compete (liberalism), but they did not have a totalitarian ideology like fascism either; instead, they had a "mentality" (discipline, order, conservatism, Catholicism) which they believed but did not seek to spread by forced indoctrination as totalitarianism did. Third, mass mobilization: both liberal and totalitarian regimes try to mobilize their populations (the latter by force) to participate in politics, but the Franco and Salazar regimes relied more on apathy, indifference, and the depoliticization of their populations from earlier frenetic activity. Fourth, political parties: while democratic politics are competitive and totalitarianism means total dominance by a single party (fascist or communist), Spain and Portugal had neither of these; rather, they had large political patronage machines that served some but still limited (not "total") purposes. A fifth difference is that Spain and Portugal had no messianic totalitarian leaders like Hitler or Mussolini; instead, Franco and Salazar were poor public speakers, shunned large mass rallies, and were uncharismatic. Sixth and again distinguishing them from totalitarian regimes, Franco and Salazar followed no genocidal policies and never carried out the wholesale slaughter (genocide) of huge masses of people.

In terms of typologies, therefore, the Franco and Salazar regimes were authoritarian, conservative, Catholic, and corporatist; they were obviously not liberal but not totalitarian or fully fascist either. Moreover, they were in keeping with a long tradition of Spanish and Portuguese regimes that called for strong, unified, organic government tempered by religious, cultural, and societal norms and held in check by strong corporate groups such as the Church or the army. These were not democratic regimes by our standards, but they were not entirely outside the Spanish and Portuguese mainstreams either—although at various times their repressive policies went beyond the pale and at the end both regimes became old, tired, and out-of-date. Moreover, they represented one (the authoritarian) historic tradition in Iberian politics but not the other, more liberal tradition that had developed since the eighteenth century; and in Spain and Portugal of the twentieth century some accommodation between these two traditions was required rather than the one dictatorially seeking to rule completely without—and repressing—the other.

Let us now turn from characterizing these two Iberian regimes to analyzing their dynamics. First, both Franco and Salazar were strong, forceful, dominating personalities and skillful political operators; they did not rule by repression alone. It is sometimes said that Salazar was a front for the army or the Church and that Franco fronted also for the military or Opus Dei (a secretive Catholic organization), but recent scholarship indicates it was really Franco and Salazar who personally ran these regimes.[6] They made all the important decisions and were not fronts for anyone. The Church and the military bolstered these regimes to be sure, but ultimate authority rested with Franco and Salazar.

A second institution meriting further mention was the official party. In Spain it was the Falange, later rebaptized as the National Movement; in Portugal it was the *União Nacional* (National Union), later renamed the National Popular Action. These two "parties" were mainly national patronage agencies, screening candidates for government jobs and dispensing favors, access, and government contracts in return for loyalty and service. It was the classic feudal system of mutual obligation now dressed up in modern garb and called a political party. In fact, both Franco and Salazar (like George Washington and Charles de Gaulle) hated political parties, thought them divisive, and believed they detracted from the unity and integrity of the state. The official parties of each regime served as forces to keep the faithful in line, as brokerage agencies between the state and the citizenry, and as guardians of the regime's traditional belief systems. Only incidentally did these parties write platforms or run candidates in elections since all opposition parties were proscribed, no other candidates were allowed, and the official party always won. These were political machines that served the Franco and Salazar regimes in various ways but were never at the real center of power or decision-making.

Third, Franco's and Salazar's control was supported by the armed forces and secret police. Behind the constitutional structure, the armed forces were the ultimate arbiters of political authority. Although Franco and Salazar governed, they both depended on the good will of the military. As the highest ranking general (the *generalissimo*), Franco generally had good relations with the military; so did Salazar, though in Portugal there were some tense periods and several failed coup attempts. Meanwhile, these regimes pampered and privileged the armed forces and gave them an elevated place in society—like the military orders of old. Rather than fighting external enemies, the military primarily maintained internal peace, operating more like a police force. Though the armed forces were important, it was Franco and Salazar who dominated.

Both Spain and Portugal had secret police organizations and networks of informers. The police were especially active during the early years when these two regimes were consolidating their hold on power. In Portugal the police were used to harass and repress opposition trade unions and political parties, and to jail and exile opposition politicians. In Spain in the aftermath of the 1936–39 civil war, the police or *guardia* were especially brutal, and thousands of Republican loyalists were exiled or killed (from which the "fascist" label often stems). But after the 1940s, the secret police were less active and less brutal. They kept tabs on the population but the controls were often relaxed and inefficient. Most people, unless they became political activists, went about their lives having no contact with the police. By this time both the Franco and Salazar regimes were firmly established and they had neither the need nor the desire—unlike Hitler—to use widespread brainwashing, terror, or torture techniques. On the other hand, if one was politically active, one could expect to be watched, harassed, jailed, or exiled. The result was that few people talked politics except to close friends and family in private. By the early 1970s, however, both regimes were freer than before and, within limits, it became possible to express oppositionist views.

For a long time the Catholic Church provided these regimes with another instrument of control. Both regimes were strongly grounded in Catholic principles, and they worked out close, mutually supporting arrangements with the Church. But by the end of the long Franco and Salazar regimes, two things had happened: (1) the Church itself was changing, becoming more liberal, and (2) these two countries became less religious. As a result, the Church slipped from being one of the three or four most important props of these regimes to being only ninth or tenth in influence.

It may be recalled that in the Spanish-Portuguese tradition of Catholic political and religious thought outlined in chapter 2, a considerable degree of authority and discipline is viewed as necessary to counter mankind's sinful, anarchic nature. But both Salazar and Franco (especially the latter) went considerably beyond these permissible limits; indeed, they sought to use the very Catholic basis of their culture and society to justify both the authoritarianism of their regimes and the repressive measures used. But over time these justifications began to wear thin.

Another instrument of control was the huge state and administrative structure in Spain and Portugal. Under Franco and Salazar, the size of the state increased dramatically until it accounted for 25–30 percent of the gross national product and employed an even higher percentage. The power of the state, of bureaucratic regulation and controls, was everywhere. Franco and Salazar used state power to reward their friends and harass their enemies, and one could not get a government job or contract without joining the official party. One does not rebel or express opposition against a government that is paying one's salary.

Although the Franco and Salazar regimes did not begin as class-based regimes, over time they became that way. Recall that they used the corporative system to clamp down harder on labor than they did on business. In addition, both regimes came to depend on the business/banking/industrial class because, without a successful business class, the economy—and with it their regimes—would suffer. More than that, both regimes came to favor certain business groups, showered them with government contracts, borrowed money from them, and became dependent on them. These banks and businesses became critical centers of power, provided personnel for cabinets and other government positions, and dominated much of government decision-making. Under corporatism, labor and capital were supposed to be equal but in fact the business groups dominated much of the economic and political life, and in Portugal these large conglomerates with their vast overseas holdings help explain why Portugal held onto its African colonies long after the time when it should have granted them independence.

If we put together all these instruments of control—army, party, secret police, religion and the Church, one-man rule, censorship, state controls, class favoritism—the whole structure of authoritarianism in Spain and Portugal was considerably greater than the sum of its parts. For some four decades the regimes of Salazar and Franco dominated most—but not all, since that would have made them fully totalitarian—areas of national life. However, there were many cracks and gray areas in these regimes in which some limited politics could and did take place and which opened wider over time.

OPPOSITION POLITICS

The Franco and Salazar regimes had dealt harshly with the opposition, particularly at first and especially with socialists and communists.[7] Opposition parties, unions, and publications were broken up, destroyed, or forced to reorganize under the corporative system; many opposition leaders were killed, jailed, or exiled. Sizable colonies of republican exiles from the Spanish civil war spent long decades away from their country—in Latin America, France, England, and other locales. Often the regimes in Spain and Portugal were not very discriminating, persecuting liberals, democrats, social Christians, and social-democrats as well as those on the far left.

While the bulk of the repression was directed against the left, the right did not escape either. That may be surprising if we think purely ideologically, but in fact, as politicians concerned with power, Franco and Salazar were hostile to all challengers to their rule, left or right. For example, in Portugal, Salazar took strong action against the fascist Integralist movement headed by Rolão Preto because it challenged his authority; in Spain Franco used the Falange movement and incorporated some aspects of its ideology, but he never let it dominate his administration and over time made it marginal to his regime. Under

Franco and Salazar, all groups and parties outside of the regime felt the dictatorship's heavy hand.

While repression was characteristic of the early Franco and Salazar regimes, eventually the opposition tired of the battle, became reconciled to the fact of these regimes' longevity, or were cowered and beaten into submission. But by the late 1960s and 1970s, as some of the dictatorial controls were relaxed, the opposition was again emboldened. Some oppositionists returned from their long exiles, the oppositionist underground was revived, and new opposition groups emerged.

At this stage we can distinguish between five different opposition orientations. In practice, there were many other small or minigroups, few of which were willing to work together. Both Spain and Portugal have adages that go: "When two Spaniards [or Portuguese] come together, there is a political party; when they part, there are two more." This analysis of the emerging opposition factions in the last years of Franco and Salazar is important because a number of these groups formed the nuclei of the political parties that formed after the dictatorships.

The exiles may be divided into two major groups. The communists were mainly in exile in the Soviet Union and Eastern Europe with small groups in other countries as well; they later formed the main communist parties of Spain and Portugal once the Franco and Salazar regimes were gone. The non-communist opposition (socialist, social-democratic) was concentrated in Paris and London, with some exile communities located elsewhere in Europe, the United States, and Latin America. Some of the non-communist oppositionists eventually tired of exile, reconciled themselves to the longevity of the Franco and Salazar regimes, and moved back to Madrid and Lisbon, largely abandoning politics. But others stayed in exile until the end, only returning after Franco died and the Salazar-Caetano regime was overthrown and then organizing the movements that would quickly become major political parties. Most of those who left Spain and Portugal during this period did so for economic reasons—to escape the poverty of their own countries and find jobs elsewhere—not for political reasons.

Within Spain and Portugal three other broad groupings are worthy of note. First, there were individuals within both regimes who were known as dissenters and had their own agendas and followings. Despite the authoritarianism of the two dictatorships, they were sufficiently pluralistic to allow (within limits) distinct points of view and some degree of factionalism. Of course, hard-line right wingers were present, but at different points there were also liberals, Christian-democrats, and reformers pushing for policy change. With the demise of authoritarianism in the mid-1970s, a number of these leaders came forward to form the nuclei of democratic political parties.

A second category of oppositionists formed secretive "study groups." These were often young professionals, university professors, and journalists of a usually liberal or social-democratic orientation who did not want to go into exile. Since opposition political parties were not allowed, they were called study groups instead. They held semisecret meetings, wrote study papers on policy issues, and tried to get their points of view across in clandestine newspapers and even the mainline press during periods of relaxed censorship. A number of these study groups emerged as political parties once the dictatorships ended.

A third category was the underground. Usually dominated by communists and socialists, they formed clandestine "workers' commissions" in factories and workplaces. Sometimes they challenged and rivaled the official government-run unions and were often the subject of police harassment. But at other times the government, wishing to keep the economy humming, dealt with these groups realistically and worked out collective bargaining arrangements with them. This process was sporadic and irregular, but it did reflect the more open climate in Spain and Portugal in the late 1960s and early 1970s. Once Franco died and the Salazar-Caetano regime was overthrown, these groups too emerged from the underground and formed the base of the new parties and labor unions.

ECONOMIC AND SOCIAL MODERNIZATION UNDER AUTHORITARIANISM

During the years of World War II and its aftermath in the late 1940s and early 1950s, Spain and Portugal remained very poor countries, among the poorest nations in Europe. Portugal had a per capita income of less than two-hundred dollars per year; Spain's was about three-hundred dollars. These figures are close to Third World levels. The German U-boat blockade of the continent during the war had led to shortages of everything and produced widespread malnutrition, starvation, and disease. The two Iberian countries escaped a German occupation by remaining neutral or nonbelligerent in the war, and they also were spared bombing and widespread physical destruction, but social and economic conditions were abysmal. Nor, because of their "fascist" regimes, were they able to qualify for U.S. Marshall Plan aid immediately after the war.

Portugal entered the 1950s as still a predominantly traditional, rural (80 percent), illiterate (80 percent) nonindustrial country. The south of the country was dominated by large estates and a still-feudal social system; the north consisted mainly of small, inefficient farms; the only industry was in and around Lisbon. Spain was bigger and somewhat more advanced with heavy industry in the north and around the major cities of Madrid, Barcelona, and Valencia; but Spain was also predominantly rural (70 percent). During the 1950s, however, two major trends occurred which began to lift both countries out of their poverty: (1) Spain and Portugal began to benefit from the general European recovery and prosperity of the time, and (2) both countries took steps to reform and modernize their outmoded economies.[8]

In 1953 Salazar enacted the first of several five-year plans to modernize the economy. The plan lowered some tariff barriers, opened the country to foreign investment, and stimulated trade and commerce. It did away with the worst features of the old autarkic or closed economic system and provided a stimulus to manufacturing and industry. Coupled with the booming European economy of the time, these steps helped stimulate Portuguese economic growth. Per capita income doubled by the early 1960s and then doubled again by 1974. Most Portuguese had never had it so good economically, which is why many later looked back to this era, the last decade of authoritarianism, as the best period of their lives.

The Spanish economic takeoff was even more dramatic. Spain started from a larger, richer base with greater resources and a market four times that of Portugal; nevertheless, the government's action was a major turning point. In 1957–58 Franco restructured his cabinet, bringing in a group of growth-oriented technocrats (many of whom were associated with the mysterious Catholic lay organization Opus Dei), a move which, similar to what had occurred in Portugal, opened up the economy, encouraged trade and investment, and replaced autarky with a freer market. In both countries the state continued to play a strong directing role in the economy even while giving freer run to market forces.

The results were spectacular. Foreign capital began to pour in; new factories sprang up around the country; manufacturing and industry increased dramatically. Prosperity began to increase; a more skilled labor force was created; women flocked to work in the new factories; and the social transformation of Spain began. People ate better, looked healthier, and grew taller; Spain began to move from the Third to the First World. During the 1960s and on into the early 1970s, economic growth was a spectacular 7, 8, and 9 percent per year. Dubbed the "Spanish miracle," the growth rates were second in the world only to Japan.

The economic growth of the sixties and early seventies enabled Spain and Portugal to finance new social programs which previously had been woefully inadequate. Education, health care, literacy, social welfare, life expectancy—all improved, although not dramatically. Of course, Spain and Portugal still lagged behind the wealthier and more progressive countries of Europe, but now these outdated states of the past began to evolve into modernized social states.

Economic stimulus also produced vast social changes. Spain went from 70 percent rural to 70 percent urban, Portugal to 60 percent urban. Literacy increased in the same dramatic fashion. As women joined the industrial labor force, upper- and middle-class families in Madrid reported a shortage of maids! The old class structure in both countries began to change as well: a new business/banking/commercial/manufacturing elite replaced the old landed elite—or intermarried with it; the middle class grew to 30–35 percent of the population; new and larger labor organizations were formed; the peasantry was uprooted and migrated to the cities. Whereas in the earlier conditions of extreme poverty, the end point of many Spaniards' and Portuguese' migration was out of the country, leaving behind many impoverished and depopulated rural villages, now with the economy booming more stayed at home—or returned from years of labor abroad. The cumulative effect of all these changes was broad social transformation; Spain and Portugal were becoming more modern.

Eventually these broad social and cultural changes would produce political changes as well. But during the 1960s and early 1970s, while the economy and society were being transformed, the political system remained locked in place. Franco still ruled in Spain; in Portugal, Salazar had been replaced by his heir Caetano, but the system of authoritarianism continued. That is what made these two regimes attractive as an object lesson to other authoritarians: Spain and Portugal had achieved remarkable economic and social modernization—without that leading to hated democracy and liberalism. Spain and Portugal seemed calm on the surface and authoritarianism appeared to be firmly in control; however, beneath the surface, pressure and tensions were building that by the mid-1970s would produce dramatic transformations.

TENSIONS WITHIN THE SYSTEM

We often think of authoritarian or totalitarian regimes as rigid, monolithic, and incapable of change; but even though the changes are less visible than in an open and democratic regime, dictatorships have internal tensions and change dynamics too. It's just that they're harder to spot: witness our inability to predict the collapse of the Soviet Union or, for our purposes, the demise of the Franco and Salazar-Caetano regimes.

First, in both countries there was a sharp generational gap—actually two generational splits. By the early 1970s most of the leaders of Spain and Portugal were in their seventies or even eighties: old, tired, and out of touch. Waiting in the wings was a new generation of persons in their forties and fifties, trained in the Franco-Salazar system but too young to remember the civil strife of the 1920s and 1930s. This middle generation was impatient with or had forgotten the old, ideological battles between liberalism, socialism, and corporatism and, most importantly, wanted to inherit the government, party, and private sector jobs that the older generation had monopolized for so long.

But the Franco and Salazar-Caetano regimes had been in power for so long (forty years each) that by this time there was a second and even more impatient generation of young people in their twenties and teens. They didn't remember at all the civil war, the ideological disputes, or the earlier political conflicts; instead, they wanted rock music, blue jeans, and Coca-Cola, and a new, free lifestyle. They were attuned to the freer American and European lifestyles and wanted to live like young people in democratic societies. Often nonpolitical, this generation wanted little to do with the partisan squabbles of their elders. They wanted to do "their thing," which often was contrary to traditional Iberian mores.

A second major transformation was occurring in Spanish and Portuguese culture. Through movies, television, and travel, the outside world of freer, "looser" social norms and behavior was having a profound impact. Long isolated from the cultural, social, and political mainstreams of Europe, now Spain and Portugal (especially the former) began to be more influenced by newer, secular forces. Fewer Spaniards and Portuguese attended mass, for example, and the hold that the Church and Catholic belief systems had long had on them began to decline. In addition, the freedom that Europeans enjoyed, their lifestyles, the more autonomous role of women, greater independence for young people—all these had a growing impact on Iberia. Though censorship remained in place, travel agencies in Madrid did a booming business, for instance, in bus tours to the French border town of Perpignon, where Spaniards could watch prohibited movies. In addition, tourism in Spain was attracting millions of visitors per year, and the sight of all those northern Europeans cavorting freely (and often nudely) on Spanish beaches had a major impact on local behavior. These are just a few of the many ways in which the culture and mores of Spain and Portugal were changing.

For decades if not centuries Spain and Portugal had prided themselves on being "different" from the rest of Europe: more Catholic, more conservative, more traditional. But increasingly their people no longer wanted to be different; they wanted to be "normal" and just like people in the rest of Europe. For a time this desire to be more like Europe was largely confined to the social and cultural sphere, but eventually it became political as well. And that meant democracy, not authoritarianism.

Socially and economically, vast changes were under way that would transform Spain and Portugal even while Franco and the Salazar regimes were still in power. Economically Spanish and Portuguese banking, industry, and commerce were being integrated into European norms, so both business and government practices had to change. Socially, Spain and Portugal were becoming more literate, urban, affluent, and middle class, and these changes led to impatience for a more open, free, and democratic society.

Political change lagged behind social, economic, and cultural change, but it was occurring even while the old regimes were still in power. The censorship was considerably relaxed, and clever journalists and editors could print opinions that would not have been permitted in earlier days. In both Spain and Portugal the corporatist system and the older trappings of fascism were increasingly shunted aside and ignored. The secret police were still present but seldom in heavy-handed ways, and people began over time to lose their fear of the police. Strikes were still illegal but sometimes "work stoppages" were carried out and the government forced to deal with the dissidents. Opposition political parties were similarly treated: they were still prohibited but opposition "study groups" and "think tanks" were permitted that functioned like political parties and even got some of their members into government. In short, most of the institutions of dictatorship remained in place but they were either not working, not enforced, or bypassed by the very groups they were meant to control. Nevertheless, in both countries there was still a "bunker mentality" that refused to allow real, meaningful change.

Increasingly, the Franco and Salazar regimes were seen as out of touch and sclerotic. Their leaders were viewed as doddering old men; often their aides and lieutenants ruled in their place as if they were no longer there—as indeed they sometimes, figuratively, were not. Franco, now in his eighties, was afflicted with numerous infirmities. He still exercised oversight, but the day-to-day affairs of the country were now run by others. He sought to perpetuate his rule (and the principle of organic unity) by bringing back the monarchy and carefully training the young monarch, but Juan Carlos belonged to the new generation that had different, more democratic ideas. Another blow to regime continuity came in 1973, when Franco's designated successor and fellow authoritarian Admiral Luís Carrero Blanco was blown sky-high by a Basque terrorist bomb in downtown Madrid. Franco's plans to perpetuate his system of authoritarian rule began to become unglued.

In Portugal parallel developments were under way. In 1968 the aging Salazar had collapsed in his deck chair, hit his head, and fell into a coma. He lingered on and, in a macabre pretense, aides continued to treat him as if he were still prime minister; but power was now passed to his former student and long-time ally Marcello Caetano. Caetano was more liberal than Salazar, but he was hemmed in by the old guard who wanted to retain strict control. In addition, Caetano was a cautious and indecisive leader who waffled on major policy decisions. First, he allowed freedom for trade unions, then he clamped down again. He brought some reformers into his cabinet but quickly removed them. He sought to extract Portugal from its ruinous efforts to hang onto now-rebelling colonies in Africa (Angola, Mozambique, Guinnea-Bissau, São Tomé) but was unwilling to confront the Salazar old guard on the issue for fear of being overthrown. Caetano's waffling and indecisiveness were the subject of many jokes (itself a sign that the climate was loosening up in Portugal): for example, you can always tell Caetano's car in traffic because it signals left but turns right.

By the early 1970s such vast economic, social, cultural, even political changes had occurred in Spain and Portugal that the two countries were hardly recognizable from what they had been earlier. What had once been "hard" dictatorships were now "soft" dictatorships led by enfeebled old men. These once fierce authoritarian regimes were now tired, out of date, old-fashioned, and hanging on mainly by inertia. It would not take much to topple them, as we see in the next chapter.

NOTES

1. The better biographies include J. Fusi, *Franco: A Biography* (New York: Harper & Row, 1988); Stanley Payne, *The Franco Regime, 1936–1975* (Madison: University of Wisconsin Press, 1987); Paul Preston, *Franco: A Biography* (New York: Basic Books, 1994); Hugh Kay, *Salazar and Modern Portugal* (London: Eyre and Spottiswoode, 1970).

2. Howard J. Wiarda, *Corporatism and Comparative Politics: The Other Great "Ism"* (New York: M. E. Sharpe, 1996).

3. For a detailed treatment, see Howard J. Wiarda, *Corporatism and Development: The Portuguese Experience* (Amherst: University of Massachusetts Press, 1977).

4. Jon Amsden, *Collective Bargaining and Class Conflict in Spain* (London: Weidenfeld and Nicolson, 1972).

5. Juan Linz, "An Authoritarian Regime: Spain," in *Mass Politics* ed. E. Allardt and Stein Rokkan (New York: The Free Press, 1970).

6. See especially the works of Payne and Preston cited above.

7. David L. Raby, *Fascism and Resistance in Portugal: Communists, Liberals, and Dissidents in the Opposition to Salazar, 1941–1974* (New York: St. Martin's Press, 1983).

8. The best studies are Charles W. Anderson, *The Political Economy of Modern Spain: Policy-Making in an Authoritarian System* (Madison: University of Wisconsin Press, 1970); Richard Gunther, *Public Policy in a No-Party State: Spanish Planning and Budgeting in the Twilight of the Franquist Era* (Berkeley: University of California Press, 1980); Eric Baklanoff, *The Economic Transformation of Spain and Portugal* (New York: Praeger, 1978).

Chapter 4

THE TRANSITIONS TO DEMOCRACY

The Franco and Salazar-Caetano regimes were so long-lived that many analysts had come to think of them as permanent. Indeed, a whole body of literature had sprung up focused on the presumed permanence of the authoritarianism and corporatism of the two Iberian nations.[1] Not only theorists but also political elites and practitioners from all over the world had journeyed to Iberia to see how Franco and Salazar had done it—that is, how they had achieved socioeconomic modernization for their nations without, seemingly, giving rise to the "dreaded" liberalism and pluralism.

But in the mid-1970s, both of these long-time regimes collapsed. It was not just that Franco and Salazar died after a period in office averaging nearly forty years for each, but that their whole systems and regimes collapsed as well. Actually, as we saw in the previous chapter, socially and culturally the postauthoritarian transition in these two countries had really begun while Franco and Salazar were still alive. But in the mid-1970s, with the death of Franco and the overthrow of the Portuguese regime, that process was greatly accelerated.

Thereafter, both countries—not without considerable uncertainty and trauma—embarked on a quite remarkable transition to democracy. This transition fundamentally altered the political landscape of Iberia, and we shall, naturally, be concerned with assessing and analyzing just how deep and permanent these changes will be. But the importance of the Spanish and Portuguese transitions to democracy went beyond these two countries. Along with the transition to democracy in Greece, which was occurring during the same time period, the transitions in Spain and Portugal served as models and inspirations for a whole wave of democratic openings that began in the late 1970s in Latin America, then continued in East Asia, in Eastern Europe, and even in the Soviet Union (now Russia). Although viewed earlier as models of authoritarianism, Spain and Portugal are now seen as models of democratization. Hence, whether Spain and Portugal succeed in their quest for democracy will be important most obviously to those two countries, but the issue also carries global implications.

THE PORTUGUESE "REVOLUTION OF CARNATIONS"

The Portuguese revolution began in April 1974, about nineteen months before the death of Franco. We, therefore, will look at the Portuguese transition to democracy first.

Portugal in the early 1970s was facing some difficult problems. Salazar had died, after earlier falling into a coma, but Salazar's authoritarian system lived on under the leadership of Marcello Caetano. Caetano had liberalized the regime somewhat, provided some greater freedoms, but the pace of change was too slow for many Portuguese, who were impatient with the old system and wanted to move forward toward Europe and toward freedom.[2] The economy had been performing quite well, but the growth was uneven and there were periods of slumps. The sharp rise in oil prices in 1973 hurt Portugal badly because it must import all of its petroleum. There were many other social, economic, and political tensions. The regime might have survived these problems, however, if it were not for the African wars.

The Portuguese colonial wars on three fronts in Africa—Angola, Mozambique, Guinea-Bissau—had now been going on for over a decade—longer than the Vietnam conflict for the United States.[3] Moreover, Portugal was a small and still a poor country. Yet, it was fighting wars in three countries at once that it could not afford; the wars were draining upwards of 50 percent of the national budget. In the early years of the rebellions, the Portuguese forces had done well, isolating the African guerrillas, keeping the conflict from spreading, and retaining control of the most important parts of their African territories. But later the guerrillas received better training, chiefly from the Soviet Union, as well as sophisticated weapons such as surface-to-air missiles (SAMS), which enabled them to shoot down Portuguese aircraft. During the early 1970s, the body bags containing slain young Portuguese soldiers began arriving back in Lisbon on an everyday basis. Portugal is an intimate and close-knit society in which seemingly everyone knows everyone else or is interrelated; those body bags coming home day after day and year after year were devastating to the Portuguese and fueled the fires of popular discontent.

Prime Minister Caetano had a plan to grant greater autonomy to the African colonies and thus to end the wars there, but his being tapped as Salazar's successor had been conditioned upon his continuing the struggle and hanging onto the African territories. In a series of interviews with one of the authors,[4] Caetano said he wanted to get out of Africa, but that if he moved too quickly the hard-line Salazar loyalists would have him ousted by the next day. The actual situation was that during certain periods Caetano did have enough power to move against the old *Salazaristas* and also to reach a resolution of the African conflicts, but he temporized and failed to use these opportunities.

The war was felt heaviest within the Portuguese military, for it did the brunt of the fighting and dying. One of the myths generated by the Portuguese revolution, perpetrated by those young officers who staged it and found in many academic analyses, is that they had learned to admire the African guerrillas, admired their socialism, and wished to establish that same socialism in continental Portugal. Actually, the young officers despised the African guerrillas, shared the then-common racial stereotypes about Africans, disliked having their lives and careers disrupted for long periods by several stints in Africa, and above all did not want to be maimed or killed in Africa and shipped back in one of those body bags. There were several occasions in 1972–73 when the troops on the docks in Lisbon, ready to sail to Africa, refused to go. Adding fuel to these fires were the resentments kindled by the fact that the government, desperate for officers, was giving commissions to young university graduates who had only a hasty training course that gave them rank equal to that of the military school graduates who had put in years of training. These are all personnel, professional, and institutional considerations; interviews conducted from 1972 to 1973 with Portuguese military officers found few of the "idealistic" and ideological motivations later emphasized by some other authors.[5]

By 1973–74 there were several plans, plots, and conspiracies within the armed forces. These military maneuverings overlapped with the activities of various civilian groups, who also wanted change. The Portuguese revolution was not just a military movement; therefore, it involved complex interrelations between various military factions and their counterpart civilian groups. Some of the plots revolved around senior military officials—such as General Antonio de Spínola, a colorful commander who saw himself as a possible successor to Prime Minister Caetano. The publication of Spínola's book in early 1974, *Portugal e o Futuro [Portugal and the Future]*,[6] in which he offered a way to pull out of Africa in direct contradiction to official government policy, set off a wave of discussions, plots, and counterplots. Other senior officers and their civilian colleagues were similarly jockeying for position. Meanwhile, the junior officers were also plotting, not only against the government but also often against their senior officers, whose positions they wished to inherit. The government learned about one small conspiracy launched in February 1974 and was able to put it down, but the larger discontents remained, and they soon blossomed full-bloom to the surface.

The movement to overthrow the Caetano regime began on the morning of April 24, 1974, with the playing of the song "Grandola" over the radio.[7] That song was a signal to all the conspirators that the coup was on. The old regime fell quickly—which was surprising given its tough and authoritarian image. Within two days the secret police, the official party, the corporative system, the censorship—all the controls—were in disarray or abolished. Caetano and other high officials were exiled. These changes occurred peacefully; the liberated and enthusiastic crowds put flowers in the barrels of the soldiers' guns, hence, the designation "Revolution of Carnations." Spínola led the revolution in its first days, but soon he was replaced as well.

Several things happened concurrently. First, the senior leadership of the revolution—such as Spínola, who came to function more as a figurehead than as a real power figure—was replaced by more junior persons within the armed forces. The main group was the Armed Forces Movement (MFA), made up chiefly of junior officers, who wanted and soon discovered that they liked power, that they also desired the high-level positions held by the senior officers, and further that they liked the attention and glory they were receiving at home and abroad for overthrowing the old "fascist" regime.

Second, the revolution spread to the streets. The Portuguese revolution had begun at the top levels of military and civilian life and involved a change among the leadership, a rotation of elites (familiar in Portuguese history); but it also unleashed a host of popular frustrations and discontents and soon spread to the lower levels of society. Employees rebelled against employers; government workers against office managers; clerical staff against directors; students against teachers; communicants against the Church; peasants against landowners; faculty against administrators; children against parents; hospital maintenance staffs against doctors; and so on. All the old ties and hierarchies of rank, place, and position kept intact in Portugal for so long were challenged and undermined. In short, what had begun as a fairly simple *coup d'état* launched by the army now became a genuinely popular revolution that spilled over into the streets—which the younger officers in the MFA now sought to guide and direct. Portugal, in other words, experienced two revolutions in 1974–75: one a not-untypical barracks revolt with limited goals, with its usual personal and political rivalries and complications, and the other a genuine grass-roots revolution at lower levels that showed signs of getting completely out of hand.

A third activity under way was the attempt by various parties and political movements to capture this revolution. A host of left-wing activists—Trotskyites, Maoists, Marxists, communists—descended on Portugal from Europe and the United States. The Portuguese socialist and communist parties, now returning from exile and allowed to function above ground, as well as numerous smaller groups, tried to infiltrate and influence the MFA, to capture the heretofore largely spontaneous street movements, and to control or seize political power.

The movements, demonstrations, and battles among competing groups raged all through the spring and summer of 1974. The MFA was trying to run the country, but it lacked the skills and experience to do so. The question was: Who controlled or would dominate the MFA? It was surely the left, but did that mean socialists, communists, or independent Marxists? No one knew for sure, but there was a great deal of political activity, maneuvering for power, and efforts at power grabs. The economy, meanwhile, was thrown into chaos; investment dried up; living standards began to decline; and the impressive economic growth of the previous years was reduced. The Portuguese now moved precipitously to grant independence to their African colonies, but that also resulted in the return of several hundred thousand Portuguese from the territories, adding immeasurably to the unemployment problems. At the same time, a fourth element was added to the simmering Portuguese brew: the involvement in these tumultuous events of a variety of foreign actors—the U.S. embassy, the CIA, the German Social Democratic and Christian Democratic parties, the British Labor Party, the Dutch, the Scandinavians, and others. The Portuguese revolution was no longer just a domestic concern; it became an international issue as well. The international actors mainly supported the socialist and social democratic parties and sought to keep the communists out of power.

Portugal continued to lurch along for at least another year. In the fall of 1974, the country seemed to be inexorably moving to the left, and there were dark rumors of communist power grabs and antidemocratic movements. Then in March 1975, General Spínola tried to rally what he called his "silent majority" and attempted to stage a countercoup to return Portugal to a centrist position; but that effort was frustrated by the MFA and the Communist Party. Then in November 1975, the Communist Party and its allies attempted their own power grab, seeking to gain full control of what to this point had been a still diverse, often confused, and chaotic revolution. But this effort was also put down by more moderate elements within the MFA.

After this last radical gasp, the Portuguese revolution began to settle down. The Communist Party had sought to grab power through a *putsch* and was humiliated and embarrassed in public. The MFA, while still playing a leading role, began a gradual retreat to the barracks. Within its ranks the moderates took power from the radicals. People went back to work after the heady street demonstrations of the past year and a half. The Socialist Party—which in those days represented the center of the Portuguese political spectrum and had won the 1975 election—formed a government under its longtime leader Mario Soares and was actually able to govern more or less effectively, even though it still had to bargain almost constantly with the MFA, the other parties, and the foreign influences in order to get things done. Gradually the country calmed down and the economy began returning to normal. Democracy was finally established in Portugal after it had been powerfully challenged by both the right and the far left.

Portugal is, after all, not that radical a country; it is, in fact, quite conservative in many respects; historically it had been even more strongly Catholic and traditional than Spain. And the history after 1976 was that of a gradual movement back to the center and away from extremes. The socialists governed from 1976 to 1978. However, the socialists gradually lost popular support, and from the summer of 1978 until January 1980, a series of three, short-lived, nonpolitical governments were in power. By this time conservative sentiment was already reasserting itself, and Portugal began to swing back toward the center and right.

The main beneficiary of this more conservative swing was the Social Democratic Party (PSD) under the flamboyant and charismatic Francisco Sá Carneíro. Sá Carneíro organized a coalition with other center and rightist groups, including Christian Democrats and monarchists, and called it the *Alianza Democrática* (Democratic Alliance—AD). In elections held in late 1979, AD garnered 45 percent of the vote; Sá Carneíro was inaugurated as prime minister in January 1980. But the AD's hopes of winning an absolute majority in the next elections were dashed when Sá Carneíro was killed in a plane crash in December 1980. He was succeeded as prime minister by newspaper editor Francisco Pinto Balsemão who ruled until his government collapsed in December 1982.

The early 1980s were again chaotic for Portugal but not as chaotic as the 1970s. Balsemão, not an effective leader or administrator, had lost popularity and the confidence of the president, Ramalho Eanes, and he was asked to step aside. For a short time, Socialist Mario Soares came back as prime minister in an unstable coalition arrangement that included the PSD, but many observers thought that Eanes now wanted the position. He backed away from the prime ministership, however, and in 1985 the PSD returned to power albeit once again in a minority, coalition government.

New elections were scheduled for 1987. The winner once more was the Social Democratic Party, now headed by Anibal Cavaco Silva. An engineer and a technocrat whose austere demeanor and policies reminded many Portuguese of Salazar, Cavaco Silva's party this time, without any alliance partners and without the necessity of a coalition, won an absolute majority—the first time any party had done so since the overthrow of the old regime. Finally, political stability seemed to be returning to the country.

The Social Democrats governed democratically and with full respect for civil liberties. But they also began to repeal some of the radical legislation of the mid-1970s, to open up the economy, and to restore some of the publicly owned enterprises to the private sector. Because of these policies, as well as help from the European Economic Community (EEC, which Portugal joined in 1986) and major investments from the United States, Portugal began to boom. The economy took off, the *retornados* (those who returned from Africa) found jobs, and unemployment was greatly reduced. New wealth was generated—some of it even trickled down—vast construction projects were under way, and the middle class began to grow. With these successes, the PSD won again in 1991 with another absolute majority.

Rule by the PSD and Cavaco Silva with majority electoral support lasted for nearly a decade, 1987–95. Silva preached efficiency and probity. This was the stablest period in recent Portuguese history. In addition, as a new (and poor) member of the EEC, Portugal qualified for enormous European foreign aid that built bridges, highways, and other mammoth construction projects. The Portuguese middle class swelled with the new prosperity and the heretofore quaint and old-fashioned capital, Lisbon, saw the growth of new affluent suburbs, shopping centers, and traffic jams. What had once been a "sleepy," morose, very Catholic, and very traditional country became dynamic, alive, energetic, on-the-move. The Middle Ages finally came to an end in Portugal in the 1980s and 1990s.

Silva and the PSD benefitted from the new prosperity, but over time the government lost support, became aloof, and was charged with corruption. New elections were held in 1995 in which the socialists, now led by António Guterres, won a plurality. By this time the Portuguese socialists, like their European counterparts, had largely shed their Marxism, talk of class warfare, and commitment to a nationalized economy in favor of a commitment to free but regulated markets coupled with advanced social welfare. In addition, Guterres was an amiable, nonthreatening leader who, unusual for a Portuguese socialist, went to mass regularly. He continued the growth policies of his predecessor, welcomed foreign investment, which had continued to flow in, and accelerated the modernization of Portuguese institutions. His economic policies called for austerity, privatization, and balanced budgets—little different from his conservative predecessor. The fact that generous EEC subsidies, designed to lift Portugal up to European living standards, continued contributed to Portugal's economic growth. In 1999 Guterres was elected to a new term.

The question we must ask is whether all these changes have been sufficient to overcome Portugal's historic divisions and underdevelopment and whether democracy has now been fully consolidated in the country. The answer is almost certainly Yes; indeed, it would be almost unthinkable (and also very costly since all the European subsidies would be cut off) for Portugal to revert at this stage to some form of authoritarianism. Portugal has its idiosyncracies, to be sure, and many parts of Portuguese social and cultural life remain infused by religious and quite traditional ways of doing things. But on the main issues Portugal has, for the first time, become a "normal" European country: democratic, with a modern mixed economy, committed to free market practices as well as the social safety net of a welfare state.

THE SPANISH TRANSITION

The Spanish transition to democracy was far calmer, less frenetic, and more institutionalized than the Portuguese in its early stages.[8] It was evolutionary rather than revolutionary. It ushered in a *reforma* (reform) as contrasted with the Portuguese *ruptura* (rupture) or sharp break with the past. But the Spanish transition was no less significant for taking this gradual route.

In fact, the course of the Portuguese revolution, occurring a year and a half before Franco's death, was very closely followed in next-door Spain and had a strong effect there. To the extent the Portuguese revolution was peaceful and achieved democracy, the Spanish admired it and thought of it as something their own country should do. But to the extent the Portuguese revolution initially produced disorder, chaos, and economic breakdown (frequently the case), or opened the door to a communist *putsch,* the Spanish shied away from its example. In short, depending on the circumstances, the Portuguese example could and did have both positive and negative ramifications in Spain.

Although we often treat the Spanish and Portuguese openings to democracy in tandem because they occurred around the same time, the differences between these two countries' transitions are as striking as their similarities. Here are some of the major differences:

1. Although Caetano in Portugal was effectively head of the government at the time of the revolution in Portugal and fighting to hang onto power, Franco in Spain was already by the early 1970s, quasi "in retirement" with power passing to his subordi-

nates. Hence, the Portuguese change was abrupt and precipitous while the Spanish one occurred gradually.

2. The Spanish economy, with a per capita output twice that of Portugal, provided a more solid and more comfortable base for the transition to democracy.
3. Similarly, Spanish society was more literate, more urban, more middle class, more sophisticated, already more European-minded. Sociologically, Spain had in fact begun its transition to democracy even while Franco was still alive. To a far greater extent than Portugal, Spain's values were European values (including democracy) even though the Franco era had not yet ended.
4. Spain had before it the example of the 1930s civil war; the bloody, wrenching, fratricidal nature of the conflict made Spaniards determined not to repeat that upheaval again. Portugal had no such experience.
5. Spain had a monarch who provided crucial stability and continuity in the transition; Portugal had no such institution.
6. The Portuguese revolution was initiated and led by the armed forces (principally the MFA); in Spain the transition was led by civilians, and the military remained largely nonpolitical.
7. The Portuguese revolution was a polarizing movement in which the center was ground down and almost disappeared for a time; in Spain it was the political center that guided the transition and never lost control of it to the extremes.
8. The Portuguese revolution was highly conflictual, whereas in Spain "social pacts" negotiated between labor, employers, and the state served to reduce greatly the potential for conflict and violence.

These are the major differences between the Portuguese and Spanish transitions to democracy. Now let us flesh out the story by telling it in narrative form.

Franco had ruled Spain since 1939, even earlier if one counts his rule as general of the Nationalist Forces during the civil war. But by the early 1970s, due to his age and declining health, he had progressively turned over more and more responsibilities to his subordinates and to a prime minister, who ran the country on an everyday basis. Franco still had ultimate control and it was he who made the big decisions affecting the future of the nation. But routine matters were now increasingly handled at lower levels. The old Spain, that of traditional Catholicism and reaction, had begun to fade, at least in the cities if not yet in the rural areas. The post-Franco transition, in short, had begun even while Franco was still alive.

During this same period, Spain had become increasingly oriented toward Europe. Its trade, commerce, and tourism were now chiefly with the European Economic Community. So, increasingly, were its social mores, thinking (including political ideas), and culture. Because of the association in the European mind of Franco with fascism, Spain could not yet formally be a part of the

European community, but in all other ways Spain was becoming a European country. It wanted to think like Europe, to be considered a part of Europe, to behave like Europe, and to be integrated into Europe—politically and psychologically as well as economically. The Franco regime continued to emphasize Spain's uniqueness, its distinctiveness from Europe; but fewer and fewer Spaniards thought that way any more. Although the process was still incomplete, Spain was a part of Europe long before the formal ratifications of the accords took place, making it an EEC member. Franco was the main anachronism standing in the way; Spanish culture and society were already well on their way to being European.

A personal anecdote may be illustrative of these themes. When one of the authors first did research work in Spain in the early 1970s, he had just come from several years of research and writing on Latin America. He had recently published an article suggesting that Spain, Portugal, and Latin America be treated politically and sociologically as part of a common, distinct, Iberic-Latin culture area, with numerous similar features.[9] That article provoked a storm of controversy in Spain, not all of it scholarly. In fact, Spain did not want to be grouped with Latin America, which it thought of as part of the Third World. Spain no longer considered itself "distinctive" or "unique"—that was considered part of Franco's propaganda. Instead, Spain preferred to be thought of as "European," not "Latin American." The author's article was controversial not just on scholarly grounds but because it rode heavily over these sensitive political, cultural, nationalistic, and psychological issues.

Franco, however, had begun to take steps to continue and institutionalize his rule. His goal was to provide for a smooth transition with continuity—such as what Portugal had experienced in 1968 when Caetano took over from Salazar and the system continued, not a sharp break which Portugal had in 1974. Franco, therefore, had established the position of prime minister, while he himself continued as head of state and de facto head of government. He installed his friend Admiral Luis Carrero Blanco in the office. After Carrero was assassinated, the position was filled by Carlos Arias Navarro. But Arias did not have Franco's confidence in the same way that Carrero did, nor had he as strong and dominating a personality. Yet Arias would be the person who would help preside over the post-Franco transition.

The other main institutional innovation was the restoration of the monarchy. Recall that the monarchy of Alfonso XIII in Spain had been abolished in 1931 upon the establishment of the republic. Later, after the civil war, Franco had talked about restoring the monarchy, but for a long time he had not actually gotten around to doing so. Franco had not wanted to share power with a monarch; in addition, the main claimant to the throne, Alfonso's son Don Juan, was a liberal who had lived abroad for many years and was critical of the

Franco system. So instead Franco turned to Don Juan's young son, Juan Carlos, brought him back to Spain, gave him a solid military education, trained him in Franco's own values, and eventually restored the monarchy. A lot of jokes circulated in Spain at this time about Juan Carlos's alleged thick-headedness, and because everyone expected his rule would be short, they believed he would be known as *Juan el breve* ("Juan the brief"). But, as it turned out, Juan Carlos surprised a lot of people with his acumen, steely determination, and sound political judgment.

Franco died in November 1975 of the accumulated medical problems with which he was afflicted. The two basic political institutions in the country were now the prime minister, Carlos Arias Navarro, and the young monarch, Juan Carlos. The two did not see eye to eye. Arias was a Francoist whose idea of reform was to proceed very slowly. He was like Caetano in Portugal, who wanted to reform the Salazar system but not very much. The king wanted to go faster. A month after Franco died, Arias and Juan Carlos agreed on a limited amnesty for certain political prisoners, but the king had wanted a broader amnesty. In the first several months they disagreed on a variety of other issues affecting the pace of change. Spanish public opinion now clearly wanted to move toward greater pluralism and democracy. The king was known to feel that by proceeding too slowly the prime minister was inadvertently strengthening the arguments of the radicals who favored a sharp, even revolutionary, break with the past.

In the summer of 1976, eight months after Franco's death, the king used his authority to remove Arias as prime minister. He appointed Adolfo Suárez, a young and handsome man, but a political unknown. Suárez, as an official of the only authorized political party, The Movement, had grown up in the Franco system and accommodated himself to it; he had never been in opposition, let alone in exile. Nevertheless, he was known to favor pluralism, liberalization, and democratization. He was also a generation and a half younger than Arias and symbolized the new generations and the new thinking in Spain, which were definitely non-Francoist. Meanwhile, the many Spanish exiles were returning from abroad, the underground was rising to the surface, and the nuclei of the new political parties were being organized.

Now the pace of change accelerated. At this stage the main issues were no longer maintaining fealty to the right (the Francoists), who had very little popular support and had already lost control of some of the country's main institutions; it was opening up to the center and the left. Suárez and the king proceeded to engineer a political opening that was far broader than the one initiated earlier. The young prime minister began holding meetings with the even younger head of the Socialist Workers' Party, Felipe González, who would soon come to fill the prime minister's own chair. These meetings paved the way in early 1977 for the legalization of opposition political parties that had been forbidden under Franco. A few weeks later even the Communist Party was legalized, a step that caused considerable consternation among the old guard. At the same time the government dealt adroitly with the economy and with the desires for regional autonomy.

Meanwhile, the Suárez government and the king had pushed through the Political Reform Act of 1976. It provided for the holding of elections for a new bicameral *cortes*, or parliament, which would also have the authority to write a new constitution. The *cortes* would have a chamber of deputies of 350 members elected by proportional representation and a Senate of 270 members elected by plurality. In an adept political move, Suárez and the king got the old *cortes* to approve the Political Reform Act even though it meant the end of the old *cortes*'s existence. This maneuver established the legal basis for the country's new democratic institutions and furnished them with sorely needed legitimacy. At the same time, the government was negotiating social pacts with business and labor, providing for wage increases in return for a no-strike pledge.

Elections were scheduled for June 1977. Three major groups contested the elections. The Right (the old *Franqustas*) came together as the *Alianza Popular* (Popular Alliance) headed by Manuel Fraga, who had been considered a liberal in an earlier Franco cabinet. The center was brought together under the banner of the *Unión del Centro Democrática* (Union of the Democratic Center, or UCD) headed by Suárez, a loose coalition of a dozen political factions and bureaucratic interests. The main force on the left was Felipe González and the *Partido Socialista Obrero Español* (PSOE—Spanish Socialist Workers' Party). The *Partido Communista Español* (PCE—Spanish Communist Party) headed by Santiago Carillo also contested the election. Suárez and the UCD won the largest plurality with 34 percent of the vote, but augmented by the d'Hondt system of representation, which favors large parties at the expense of smaller ones, the number of UCD seats in the *cortes* was 47 percent—enough to form a governing bloc.

More important legislation followed. A constitutional committee of the *cortes* drafted a new, democratic constitution in 1977–78 that was overwhelmingly approved (over 90 percent) by Spanish voters in a referendum of December 1978.[10] Suárez also called the leaders of all the political parties to his residence, where they hammered out an accord (the Moncloa Pact) providing for an economic stabilization program to be accompanied by increased social programs. Neither left nor right, neither business nor labor, was entirely happy with all aspects of the pact, but they were in remarkable agreement that the economy had to be managed successfully if democracy was to survive, and that served as the basis of the accord. The Suárez government had also enacted major legislation dealing with labor's organization and rights, and had entered into negotiations to arrive at autonomy agreements with the more independent-minded regions, such as Catalonia and the Basque provinces. These impressive accomplishments were later reflected in the March 1979 parliamentary elections, when the UCD and Suárez slightly increased their percentage of votes and seats, and then again in April 1980, when the UCD candidates won twice as many municipal positions as those of any other party.

Despite the impressive policy accomplishments of Suárez and the solid electoral approval for his party, trouble was beginning to mount for the young prime minister. The effectiveness of his leadership was increasingly questioned because of the continuing problem of Basque terrorism, the poor performance of the economy in the late 1970s (when the second "oil shock" hit), the political differences over educational and religious issues, and the increase in crime and immorality. In addition, with the basic accomplishments of the democratization carried out successfully, there was no longer such a strong sense of the need for national unity as there had been earlier, and the political debate now turned more partisan and rancorous. Finally, the UCD was a coalition that electorally had done well so far, but now it began to split up into quarreling factions that often criticized Suárez and would no longer take directions from him.

Apparently fed up with the carping and wishing to build his own political base without such fractious disputations, Suárez resigned abruptly in January 1981. He was succeeded as prime minister and head of the UCD by Leopoldo Calvo-Sotelo. But the economy continued to slide downhill and Basque terrorism continued unabated. These events provided ammunition to a number of reactionary military officers who became disillusioned with the course Spanish democracy was taking. They plotted several coup attempts, the most serious of which occurred in February 1981, when a cadre of soldiers invaded and shot up the *cortes* and appealed to other military forces to join them in revolt. But the king, during a long night on the telephone, rallied his military commanders (many personal friends from his military school days) and urged them to remain loyal. Later, he put on his military uniform, went on national television, made it clear that he was the commander-in-chief and that he supported democracy, and appealed for national calm. The coup attempt galvanized wide sections of the population into demonstrating for democracy and the constitution, the rest of the officer corps stayed loyal, and the coup failed.

Calvo-Sotelo proved to be an unpopular and ineffective prime minister. In addition, González's Socialist Workers' Party (PSOE) had been increasing in strength in recent elections and in the polls. Some Spaniards were convinced their democracy could not be thought of as consolidated until the opposition had actually won and a peaceful transfer of power had taken place. On the left, sentiment was also increasing that while Spain had successfully achieved political democracy, now it was time to take the next step to economic democracy. Only the Socialist party could achieve that, they said. There was an air of Marxist determinism about these arguments that some Spaniards found disturbing, especially if the process had to work the other way. That is, if the Socialists did come to power, would they then be willing to give up power if they were subsequently defeated in an election, or would that same "historical inevitability" previously described imply that they would have to stay in power regardless of the popular vote? The answer proved to be that the Socialists played by the democratic rules.

Actually, the PSOE had been undergoing a considerable transformation. In the 1930s republic, the Socialists had on some issues been more radical than the Communists. In exile under Franco, the Socialists retained their Marxist militancy. But now with Felipe González as their head and with the prospect of democratic electoral victory, the Socialists began moderating their positions. Not without some major fights from the militant wing, the party at its conventions in the late 1970s had excised Marx and the Marxist lexicon from its platform, moderated its foreign policy stands, and came to accept capitalism and private property. The party went from a socialist to a more moderate social-democratic position. On that basis Felipe González and the PSOE decisively won the parliamentary election in 1982, with González becoming prime minister, and then won again—overwhelmingly—in 1987 and 1992.

González proved to be an effective and popular prime minister. Only in his thirties when he came to power, González was handsome and politically shrewd. He recognized the need to give the left wing of the PSOE some positions in his government (for example, in the Foreign Ministry headed by Fernando Moran), but for the most part he governed pragmatically and adeptly. Although his party was on the left of the political spectrum, González moved to occupy the broad center—as had Suárez before him.

González's policies were also prudent and pragmatic. In foreign affairs, where he had little experience, González started by following the advice of the Socialist International, an association of the world's Socialist parties, and of his foreign ministry officials who represented the PSOE's more militant Marxist wing. But this stance earned him criticism from the United States, NATO, and even other Socialist governments in Europe; and hence the flexible González backed away from the left's positions and began following a more centrist course—as in his campaign to have Spain join NATO. In 1986 González ushered Spain into the EEC, which meant vastly increased trade, subsidies, and prosperity for his country. On the domestic front González assured business leaders of his nonrevolutionary credentials, moved to reform the military, backed away from nationalization and socialism, which the PSOE's militants wanted to carry out, and followed an orthodox economic policy—including implementing a strict austerity policy whose incidence fell hardest on the shoulders of González's own followers in the unions and the PSOE. He continued the policy of his centrist predecessors by renewing the social pacts between labor and business under which labor largely abandoned its strike weapons in return for employer-financed benefits. González faced criticism from his own party for abandoning the socialist agenda and following such a centrist course, but the PSOE militants had no one other than González to vote for, and, besides, by this strategy González picked up far more votes in the center than he lost on the left.

González and the PSOE had won elections in 1982, 1987, and 1992. But by the early 1990s his halo—and the party's electoral support—was slipping. In the 1992 election, González had failed to achieve a majority in the *cortes* and was forced to share power with some of the smaller regional parties. There were charges of major and widespread corruption in his government; González himself was tainted because a number of the officials charged were part of his personal political clique from Seville and because of charges he had authorized secret police assassinations directed at Basque separatists. Meanwhile, the conservative opposition had reorganized, posing a new challenge to his continuance in office.

The earlier efforts of Manuel Fraga and the *Alianza Popular* to continue the Franco legacy by electoral means had not been successful; meanwhile, the centrist UCD had broken up in the early 1980s. That left an enormous hole on the Spanish center-right waiting to be filled. That tack was undertaken in the mid-1980s by a low-level government official and Fraga protegé, José María Aznar, who pulled together the various factions on the center and right to form the Partido Popular (PP, which could be translated as either Popular or People's Party). The PP increasingly challenged González and the socialists at the polls, gradually increased its electoral strength, and in 1996 beat out the PSOE by a single percentage point. But the PP gained only a plurality and, hence, like the PSOE in its later years, had to put together a coalition in order to govern.

While Portugal in 1995, after a decade of right-of-center rule, was going back to the socialist left, Spain in this same period was going from left to right. Aznar was not a colorful or charismatic prime minister, but he was careful and prudent. Like Guterres in Portugal, he emphasized his Catholicism, his careful shepherding of the national economy, and an austere lifestyle. While careful to avoid being labeled a Thatcherite, Aznar did follow a neoliberal economic agenda. He emphasized privatization, the need for belt-tightening, international trade and exports, and a streamlined, more efficient government. At the same time, he maintained the Spanish social safety net. In foreign policy he kept Spain tied closely to Europe while distancing himself from Fidel Castro in Cuba. By his careful and generally successful policies, Aznar increased his lead in the polls over González and the Socialists, but the margin remained thin. In March 2000 Aznar won reelection, achieving a majority in the *cortes*.

By this point, the year 2000, both Spain and Portugal have successfully passed the usual institutional tests for measuring whether a country has consolidated democracy. Both countries have strong political parties, regular and competitive elections, and a full and open political climate. In both countries there have been at least two peaceful electoral transfers of power from the governing party to the opposition. The question is not whether Spain and Portugal have the institutional bases of democracy but rather how deep, how profound, and how thoroughly democracy now reaches into the everyday values, beliefs, and operating behavior of most Spaniards and Portuguese.

HOW SOLID IS IBERIAN DEMOCRACY?

Spain and Portugal are old societies, old cultures, at least two to three thousand years by most reckonings. As unified nation-states, Portugal has over eight centuries behind it, Spain over five. Yet in all those years neither country had much democratic experience: Portugal from 1910 to 1926, and Spain from 1931 to 1936, and both countries briefly and episodically in the nineteenth century. So the period since the mid-1970s, a quarter century in time, represents the longest period by far that either country has been democratic. Indeed, the democratic periods seem to pale before the extensive periods and deep traditions of absolutism, monism, corporatism, and authoritarianism. So the question naturally arises of just how strong and consolidated Spanish and Portuguese democracy is.

There are a number of key issues, however, that need to be addressed before a final answer can be reached. Here we raise the issues, subsequent chapters try to answer them, and the conclusion attempts to put the whole picture together.

The "Explosion" of Political Participation

Spain and Portugal have moved quickly from being closed, backward, antidemocratic, "sleepy" nineteenth- (or sixteenth-!) century societies to modern, highly mobilized ones. Whereas Franco and Salazar had run their regimes in part on the basis of citizen apathy, in the postauthoritarian era voter turnout has generally been in the 70–80 percent range—far higher than in the United States. Such citizen involvement is good for democracy but, if participation increases too rapidly rather than gradually as in the British and U.S. experience, it can be destabilizing. Popular demands increase faster than governments can respond to them, and that can be a formula for discontent and instability.

Recently, however, Spanish and Portuguese voter turnout has been decreasing. That may be a negative sign for democracy, but it could also be a good sign for stability. All political systems face tradeoffs of this sort and need to resolve them in their own way.

Has the Political Culture Changed?

Spain and Portugal have all the institutions of democracy: political parties, elections, parliaments. The harder question is: Has the political culture—the underlying beliefs and values of the people—also changed? For Spain and Portugal have long, deeply imbedded traditions of elitism, authoritarianism, and patrimonialism—none of which is conducive to democracy. Establishing the institutions of democracy since the mid-1970s was the easy step; still uncertain is how deeply the core values of democracy, egalitarianism, and civic consciousness have sunk roots in Iberian soil. We will have to weigh carefully (see chapter 5) how much traditional and non- or even antidemocratic Spanish and Portuguese values still predominate; alternatively, the degree to which democratic values have triumphed.

The Socioeconomic Underpinning

A rich literature suggests that there is a close correlation between socioeconomic development and democracy.[11] As the levels of literacy, education, and urbanization rise, as economic development advances and a larger middle class is created, the possibilities for democracy increase. These are not necessarily prerequisites for democracy and one must caution against correlation being equated with causation (education or economic development causes democracy); nevertheless, democracy has a better chance of flowering in developed, literate, middle-class societies than in poorer ones lacking these attributes.

We will, therefore, have to know how successful Spanish and Portuguese economic development efforts have been, how urban and literate their populations are, what the size of their middle class is, and whether they have solved their historically deep class divisions, problems of poverty, and issues of land distribution and inequality. And what about the considerable socioeconomic differences between the two countries? Once we have answers to these questions, we will be in a far better position to assess the prospects for Spanish and Portuguese democracy.

Vestiges of Authoritarianism

Many institutions in Spain and Portugal have been thoroughly democratized since the mid-1970s. The political parties, the parliament, and the electoral machinery are all functioning in a democratic fashion. Other vestiges of the old regimes—the censorship, the prohibitions against political activity, and so on—have been abolished or brought under control.

But other political institutions have lagged behind; democratization has been uneven. These include the judiciary, the police, the Church, the bureaucracy, the elites, the armed forces, the rural peasantry. Over time, however, these institutions have also either democratized, at least in part, or been subordinated to civilian authority.

If we look at underlying social institutions—the family, gender relations, religion, class relations, interest-group activity—a mixed picture emerges. As usual in Spain and Portugal, the rural areas remain more traditional; the urban ones, more liberal. At the same time, social and class relations are still heavily determined by considerations of rank and hierarchy, not egalitarianism. And while Spain and Portugal are more pluralist now than before, neither country has competitive interest group lobbying in the American sense; instead, the state and a modified, updated system of corporatism ("neocorporatism") still predominate. We return to these important themes in subsequent chapters.

Democracy's Consolidation

Scholars distinguish between transitions to democracy (the initial stage) and the full consolidation of democracy (a longer-term process). Clearly Spain and Portugal have transitioned to democracy; the harder question is whether they have fully consolidated their democracies.

By one measure—two successive transfers of power by electoral means—Spain and Portugal have clearly succeeded in consolidating democracy. Another measurement method is to survey attitudes toward main institutions: parties, elections, parliament, and the like. Here the results are more mixed: democracy as a system of government is broadly admired and enjoys widespread legitimacy but the main institutions of democracy—parties, unions, parliament—are held in low repute, down in the 20 percent range. Still another worrisome feature is those institutions—listed above—that are only partly democratic, to say nothing of the nonegalitarian presumptions that still govern most social or class relations.

So let us leave open for now the all-important question of whether Spain and Portugal have shed their past and are fully committed to democracy. At the level of the main political institutions—elections, parties, parliamentary rule—they have, but at a deeper cultural, social, and value level many uncertainties remain. Moreover, after a quarter century of headlong rush by both countries to forget the past, emulate Europe, and embrace democracy, a certain nostalgia for the past can be detected, a desire to rediscover historic roots, a renewed interest in Iberic distinctiveness. These themes are addressed in succeeding chapters.

NOTES

1. Philippe C. Schmitter, "Corporatist Interest Representation and Public Policy-Making in Portugal" (paper presented at the annual meeting of the American Political Science Association, Washington, D.C., September 5–7, 1972), and Howard J. Wiarda, *Corporatism and Development: The Portuguese Experience* (Amherst: University of Massachusetts Press, 1977).

2. Wiarda, *Corporatism and Development,* chap. 9.

3. Among the best studies is that by Neil Bruce, *Portugal: The Last Empire* (New York: Wiley, 1975).

4. The interviews with Caetano took place in the spring of 1973. Professor Wiarda had approached the prime minister to discuss the early origins of the Portuguese corporative system, of which Caetano was one of the architects. But once the interviews began, it became clear that Caetano really wished to talk about current politics. These interviews have never been published, but they are so revealing that they should be.

5. For a report on some of these interviews, see Howard J. Wiarda, "The Portuguese Revolution: Toward Explaining the Political Behavior of the Armed Forces Movement," *Iberian Studies* 4 (autumn 1974).

6. Antonio de Spínola, *Portugal e o Futuro* (Lisbon: Arcádia, 1974).

7. Among the better accounts of the revolution are Douglas Porch, *The Portuguese Armed Forces and the Revolution* (London: Croom Helm, 1977); Lawrence S. Graham and Harry M. Makler, eds., *Contemporary Portugal: The Revolution and Its Antecedents* (Austin: University of Texas Press, 1979); and Kenneth Maxwell, *The Making of Portuguese Democracy* (New York: Cambridge University Press, 1995).

8. Among the many books, see Samuel D. Eaton, *The Forces of Freedom in Spain, 1974–1979* (Stanford, Calif.: Hoover Institution Press, 1981); and José Maravell, *The Transition to Democracy in Spain* (London: Croom Helm, 1982; New York: St. Martin's Press, 1982).

9. Howard J. Wiarda, "Toward a Framework for the Study of Political Change in the Iberic-Latin Tradition: The Corporative Model," *World Politics* 25 (January 1973): 206–35. A Spanish-language version was presented at a conference in Madrid in March 1974.

10. Andrea Bonine-Blanc, *Spain's Transition to Democracy: The Politics of Constitution-Making* (Boulder, Colo.: Westview Press, 1987); also Robert A. Goldwin and Art Kaufman, eds., *Constitution-Makers on Constitution-Making: The Experience of Eight Nations* (Washington, D.C.: American Enterprise Institute for Public Policy Research, 1988), chap. 6.

11. W. W. Rostow, *The Stages of Economic Growth* (Cambridge: Cambridge University Press, 1960); and Seymour Martin Lipset, *Political Man* (New York: Doubleday, 1960).

Chapter 5

Political Culture: The Iberian Melody

What does democracy mean in an Iberian context? Does it differ from democracy elsewhere? What does justice look like in Spain and Portugal? How does one understand leadership in Madrid, government in Lisbon? What does it mean to be a good citizen in these two countries? In order to answer these questions we need to understand the political culture of Spain and Portugal and how it developed over time. Unlike the format of the earlier, historical chapters, here the culture of Spain and Portugal will not receive separate attention. Although they are two separate political units with somewhat different traditions, these two nations evolved from a single political culture.

Anthropologist Clifford Geertz defines culture as "the structures of meaning through which men give shape to their experience."[1] The anthems and flags, the military processions and governmental ceremonies, the legends of heroes, the stories told of the battlefield, all these symbols and narratives help us to understand what is meaningful to a member of a particular culture. Max Weber likened culture to a "web of significance." The spider analogy is important. Not only do we spin our own webs, wrote Weber, but we are suspended in them as well. What we create constrains us as much as it expresses our experience. The spider analogy, however, has its limitations: in nature, spiders inhabit their solitary webs; in politics, we are suspended in a collective weaving. "Cultures," wrote Aaron Wildavsky, "constitute our political selves."[2]

Through participation in a culture we come to understand what good leadership is, what good government looks like, even if it may not completely conform to our cultural ideals.

To better capture the social nature of political culture we might think of it as a popular melody, a song that everyone knows by heart. We know when we are in harmony and when we are out of tune. Even without a vocalist, everyone familiar with the tradition knows the words to the song. When handled as a jazz improvisation, the central melody is still recognizable. The saxophone may run off on some particular riff, but we all know that eventually it will come home to the rules of the song. In a political sense, those rules express the shared values of the dominant tradition. We saw earlier how the first Bourbon rulers were unable to gain legitimacy with the Spanish multitude. Their continental ways were initially out of tune with Spanish customs. Over a period of time, however, some of those continental ideas worked their ways into the Iberian repertoire.

Obviously, political culture is not the only factor affecting political behavior. External aggression, natural disasters, social and class relations, and the political institutions themselves, all play a part in forming a political system. Yet as Geertz points out, culture is also a structure, the structure of political meaning. Cultural factors help explain why certain universal models, such as representative democracy, take on very different characteristics depending on locale. Cultural differences help explain why political values, such as justice and equality, mean very different things in different places. One of the central players in creating and maintaining culture is religion. A Protestant culture will value different elements than one that is predominantly Catholic. Many of the major differences between the political culture of America and that of Spain and Portugal can be explained in terms of religious differences.

American political values are informed by our historic Protestant, liberal tradition. The nuances of that tradition help to explain our reaction to political hierarchies and our relationship to written law. For instance, the Protestant doctrine of *sola scriptura,* scripture alone, privileges individual interpretation over a professional understanding of the word of God as delivered by the priests. Law that needs a professional class to explain it is less American (i.e., less Protestant) than a law easily understood by the literate (which may explain our cultural bias against lawyers). When Americans consider a concept like equality, we are operating within a tradition that values government by consent, free enterprise, and a religion that doesn't require an intermediary to know God's word.

The values Americans glorify are embodied by a president who fought hard in the trenches, that is, George Washington, and philosophers who used household items to discover scientific truths, such as Benjamin Franklin.

Americans take pride in presenting our country as the land of equal opportunity, where birth does not preclude political participation. We value common knowledge, ordinary wisdom. We are suspicious of pomp and circumstance, understanding them as part of the foolishness associated with kings and popes. We understand equality as John Locke would have us understand it: as a component of perfect freedom wherein we order our actions and dispose of our property "as [we] think fit, . . . without asking leave, or depending upon the will of any other Man."[3] Good government is a government that leaves us alone to fulfill our private dreams. The main function of government is to coerce good behavior, not tell us what it means to be good. Virtue in the American tradition is generally regarded as a private affair as was evident in the public indifference to President Clinton's private extramarital affair.

Spain and Portugal operate under a different set of values. The hierarchies institutionalized by the Roman Catholic Church conform to ancient understandings of the order of beings. Equality in this vertical landscape refers to equal honor in one's station, not equal opportunity to do as one thinks fit. Although both Catholic and Protestant political theorists understood the Law of Nature as what a rational man could deduce from the world at large, those deductions reached distinct conclusions.

Locke and other Protestant thinkers envisioned a world of autonomous actors who gave their consent to a limited government. Catholic political thinkers envisioned a world arranged according to complementary functions. The body politic truly was a body with each member operating within a group that served the needs of the greater whole. Some were born to lead, some were born to fight, and some were born to stay home and raise children. The corporeal metaphor corresponded to God's will that people live as social beings, not as self-sufficient and independent individuals, as John Locke would have, but dependent on a variety of people in order to survive.

At first glance, this fixed, hierarchical, functionally specific system may seem antithetical to the very notion of good government. Our cultural values privilege social mobility over a guaranteed place. Freedom in America is delivered in individual portions. We don't understand freedom in terms of a group. Liberal reasoning is built on the belief that we don't need the state to be fulfilled, but only to protect our property and our rights. Catholic political reasoning is built on the belief that the state not only needs good citizens but virtuous people as well. Law should not only be coercive, as is the case with the liberal state, but directive. Belonging to a Catholic nation, in other words, makes one a better person, both in this world and the next.

The term that best describes this Catholic brand of political theory is Thomism, the school of thought developed by the Dominican priest St. Thomas Aquinas. Aquinas is credited with marrying Christian faith to Aristotelian reasoning. A prolific writer, he wrote over eight million words in his fifty years of life. Aquinas synthesized science and faith, reason and analogy, creating extensive material useful both to metaphysicians and kings. Although he is now recognized as a key spokesperson for the Catholic Church, at the time of his death, 1274, many of Aquinas's works were viewed with great suspicion. He was accused of excessive "this-worldliness" and was censured for teaching that truths based on reason were not contrary to the truth of the Christian faith. The Roman Church establishment had to intervene on several occasions to prevent formal condemnations against him from being issued in Paris and Oxford. By the time of the Council of Trent (1545–63), the Church formally accepted his work as "the authentic expression of doctrine." In 1567, Pius V declared him "Doctor of the Church."

The same Council of Trent that endorsed Thomism as church doctrine gave birth to the militant order of Christ, the Jesuits. Along with the Dominicans, the Jesuits were fiercely devoted to St. Thomas Aquinas. Two Dominican priests, Francisco de Vitoria and Domingo de Soto, along with two Jesuits, Luis de Molina and Francisco Suárez, constitute the primary political theorists of the Spanish Counter-Reformation. Both Jesuits attended the University of Salamanca, and all four of them at one time or another lectured there. The University of Coimbra, in Portugal, an equally important intellectual institution, was also a center of Thomism. From distinguished universities across the peninsula, these four philosophers were able to articulate to the Spanish intellectual class the philosophical basis for what the culture already knew to be true, that Iberia was the pure expression of Catholic social and political life.

Questions of state and empire were brought before these learned men. Are the Indians of the New World capable of converting to Catholicism? Must the masses follow an unjust leader? Is unwillingness to convert grounds for a just war? How much is a just wage? Is slavery a natural state of affairs? The Thomists of sixteenth-century Spain spelled out the enduring values of a nation confronted with the schism of Protestantism and the souls of new peoples. They gave meaning to the experience of conquest, tyranny, and heresy. Their writings informed the policies of colonialism and the business of taxation. The problems of bringing an imperial government in line with Christian notions of justice and charity were resolved by the scholastic reasoning of Jesuit and Dominican priests; not that they always agreed on particulars and not that they didn't have vocal opposition from time to time; it wasn't in the *conquistadores'* personal interests to be constrained by Christian niceties of charity and justice. For the most part, however, the values that these philosophers articulated were already accepted within the culture, values established through the battles against the Moors, the practice of *convivencia*, when Christians, Jews, and Muslims lived side by side, the Reconquest, the reign of the Catholic Monarchs, the expulsion of the Jews. These customs found authority not only in Catholic political doctrine, but in earlier sources as well. Two of the key sources for the legitimacy of the Catholic political order are found in the natural sciences of Aristotle and the biblical writings of St. Paul.

EARLY SOURCES OF THOMISM: ARISTOTLE AND ST. PAUL

Aristotle was an empiricist. He understood the world and the nature of its existence by examining the details around him. Unlike Plato, who applied ideal forms to the particulars of life, Aristotle started with the basics and extrapolated to general conclusions. He believed we could better know the truth through observation than through speculation. For this reason, he considered himself more of a scientist than a philosopher. Using reason and observation, he argued, anyone might come to know the truth of his particular situation. Realizing one's potential was specific to one's social status. While some were naturally inclined to philosophy, others were naturally inclined to labor.

When Aristotle looked at the world around him, he saw a well-organized system in which the totality of being was laid out in an ascending order of potential, like the rungs of a ladder. The world was made unequal so that a variety of beings might exist in perfect symmetry. The path to wisdom was the path of comprehending every order of being from the least to the greatest. At the bottom of the ladder were rocks and minerals, things incapable of acting but capable of being acted upon. Above the rocks were plants, things capable of reproduction and being acted upon. Animals included attributes of the lower beings with the addition of sentient experience. Humans added reason to the mix. Each group, each species, in Aristotle's words, was more perfect than those below on the "great chain of being."

Aristotle transposed this natural order onto the political sphere. The ascending order of natural potential became the ascending order of political potential. Slaves were capable of labor; artisans were capable of labor and trade; soldiers were capable of labor, trade, and warfare; philosophers were capable of labor, trade, warfare, and intellectual thinking; kings were capable of all activities. It was assumed that those higher up on the social ladder were capable of performing the tasks beneath them although their level of perfection required they focus on their higher skills. Just as a fox would not spend its life working on a being a perfect turnip, so a king would not devote his time to being a perfect weaver. Potential was specific to one's aptitude, to one's place in the order of things. Fulfilling one's natural potential depended on being in one's natural place. Government was understood as the maintenance of harmony and proportionality in accord with the laws of nature. Those who operated on the highest rung used their powers for the benefit of the lower creatures, directing them where they needed to go. Ruling necessitated comprehending every order of citizen from the greatest to the least.

The Stoic philosopher Seneca, who lived in southern Spain from 2 B.C. until 65 A.D., expanded upon Aristotle's chain of being with the notion of "the Gift." Depending on the social status of the recipient, gifts fell into three categories: necessary, profitable, and pleasant. Those on the lowest social rung were given gifts in order to survive, those in a higher strata received gifts that enabled them to live a better life, and those in the upper echelon of society received gifts purely for their own enjoyment. This ancient system became the basis for patronage politics. Those who had gave to those who had not and the price of the gift was submission and loyalty. Social hierarchy depended on a fluid exchange of gifts for loyalty in order for the system to maintain cohesion.[4]

The social hierarchy of Aristotle and Seneca took on spiritual proportions in early Church doctrine. In his letter to the Corinthians, St. Paul wrote that "there are varieties of gifts, but the same Spirit; and there are varieties of service, but the same Lord; and there are varieties of working, but it is the same God who inspires them all in every one" (1 Cor. 12: 4–6). The political gifts described by Seneca now took on a spiritual dimension. All members of the Christian community had received the highest gift from God, that is, the sacrifice of His son. Honored by such a gift, the members naturally returned a loyalty of equal proportion: an abiding submission to God.

As with Aristotle's chain of being, inequality was natural; indeed, it was the method of God's creation. Paul, however, was interested in distinguishing his emerging community from the contemporary Romans whose repressive regime had taken the Aristotelian hierarchy to a frightening extreme. Replacing the ladder image, which emphasized a social hierarchy, Paul used the image of the human body, a metaphor that privileged coordination over hierarchy.

> For the body does not consist of one member but of many. If the foot should say, "Because I am not a hand, I do not belong to the body," that would not make it any less a part of the body. And if the ear should say, "Because I am not an eye, I do not belong to the body," that would not make it any less a part of the body. . . . But as it is, God arranged the organs in the body, each one of them, as he chose. If all were a single organ, where would the body be? (1 Cor. 12:14–19)

As with Aristotle's inclusive hierarchy, wisdom is predicated on understanding the system as a whole. It is not enough to work on one's own perfection, one must come to understand the perfection of the entire body. The common good requires more than the fulfillment of individual lives. More important is the recognition that without the diversity of functions—of limbs and organs to use

St. Paul's metaphor—there would be no community, no body politic. And lest his audience err in thinking that relative placement in the Christian body holds the same social stigma as in the Roman Empire, St. Paul reminds them of honor:

> [T]he parts of the body which we think less honorable we invest with the greater honor, and our unpresentable parts are treated with greater modesty, which our more presentable parts do not require. But God has so adjusted the body, giving the greater honor to the inferior part, that there may be no discord in the body, but that the members may have the same care for one another. If one member suffers, all suffer together; if one member is honored, all rejoice together. (1 Cor. 12:22–26)

The body is a particularly useful metaphor. It introduces the corporate, organic notion of existence in which different types of people work together in a complementary fashion. It also introduces the notion of a ruling head, an organ naturally created to reason for the good of all other members. It was in the natural order of things for one to rule over the many. Christian faith would not destroy the natural order described by Aristotle, but would perfect it.

Both Aristotle's and St. Paul's models require that law not be applied equally. The law of the foot, to carry the body about, is different than the law of the heart, to move the blood around. All members may have equal honor, but not all function by the same principles and needs. A recognition that different factions require different legal measures is consistent with the natural order of things. One can see how the custom of *fueros* would find political legitimacy in the doctrines established by Aristotle and St. Paul: the law is applied differently depending on one's place in the hierarchy. One can also see how the supremacy of a central monarch, that is, the head, might challenge those corporate rights should they threaten to destroy the sacred unity of the whole.

The tension between *fueros* and monarchy illustrates the internal dynamics of Iberian political culture. Culture, in other words, is not a monolithic entity. It is not just one side of an argument. A culture gives structure to experience, and experience is, within limitations, always up for grabs. These limitations, however, are important to recognize. They are the terms of debate, the framing of the questions, what matters and what is unnecessary. The various sides of the argument are only a piece of the puzzle. What one group sees as the doctrinal basis for self-directed groups, others see as a call for a strict authoritarian system. Various factions within the culture may disagree on how the model should be applied, yet the model itself is above reproach. Although there may be disagreement on their specific application, hierarchy, monarchy, and an organic state are accepted ingredients. They are all part of the natural order, all expressions of natural law.

THE FOUR-TIERED LEGAL SYSTEM OF ST. THOMAS AQUINAS

Aquinas applied the Aristotelian inclusive hierarchy to legal matters. At the top was divine law, the will of God. Because God operated outside of time, divine law was eternal. Because God operated outside of nature, divine law did not conform to the laws of nature. Miracles are examples of divine law in action; they represent God's ability to act outside of the laws of nature. The Ten Commandments are an example of divine law. Revealed to Moses, they illustrate a miracle that conforms to natural law. Left to their own devices, the Israelites might have come up with a similar code of ethic, but God was concerned they might not understand the importance of following these prohibitions. By revealing the Commandments to Moses under miraculous conditions, these laws were given divine status.

The history of Iberian political life is filled with miracles: not of a legalistic nature, as was the case with Moses, but of a military or benedictive nature. One of the turning points in the *Reconquista,* the Battle of Clavijo, which gave the subject Christians a sense of possibility, was won through miraculous means. Santiago (St. James), seated on his celestial charger, rode down from the heavens, lopping Arab heads off by the dozens and sending the nondecapitated running for their lives. Visions of Santiago were reported throughout the *Reconquista* as well as during the conquest of the New World. Conquistadors who didn't see Santiago or another Castilian saint, explained the lack of vision by their own sinful nature. "It was not in my powers to see him," wrote Bernal Diaz de Castillo, the chronicler of the Mexican conquest, "sinner that I am." To those who saw and to those who only were told of his presence, Santiago represented the divine law of God. When Franco won a decisive battle against republican forces, he claimed that Santiago had demonstrated his support for the nationalists and promptly reinstituted him as the patron saint of Spain. Along with brutal visions of military saints, the Virgin also has frequently appeared throughout Iberian history. Visions of Mary were frequent in the conservative Catholic communities of the Basque country during the Second Republic. Children and women received messages from the Virgin decrying the politics of the anti-Christ (i.e., the anticlerical republicans). The Virgin of Fátima performed a similar function in Portugal, warning the Catholic masses of the impending evil coming from Russia, even before the Bolsheviks had revolted. Even in the modern era, political legitimacy may be enhanced or weakened by supernatural forces operating according to divine law.

Divine law is positive law. It is the law that God spoke through the Commandments or that was revealed through supernatural intermediaries, like the Virgin or St. James. Eternal law, the second type of law, is something to be imagined, not actually experienced. Aquinas defines it as "the rational governance of everything on the part of God, as the ruler of the universe."[5] Many medieval thinkers conflated divine positive law with eternal law, and, at times, Aquinas appears to treat them as that. We might think of eternal law as the law written upon God's heart, as a natural law operating on a level that humans cannot perceive directly but only through the process of analogy.

Beneath divine law, both positive and eternal, is natural law, which is what men are able to determine through their reasoning powers. It is the law "written upon men's hearts," what we know to be true naturally or through reason or instinct. Should we never read a statute outlawing homicide, we would still know, rationally, that murder is detrimental to the health of society. The "we" is important here. Aquinas believed that all humans are capable of knowing the law of nature whether or not they've been converted to Christianity. This belief would have important implications for non-Christian subjects and for Iberia's external relations. Thomistic natural law doctrine, as advanced by sixteenth-century Thomists, became the basis of Catholic international law, a doctrine based upon a universal humanity.

Finally, the lowest form of law is human law. This would include laws of custom as well as formally written laws. In order to have authority, human law must conform to natural law which, in turn, conforms to divine law. Human law fulfills two functions, one of which is coercive and the other directive. People may be coerced into good behavior but only if it does not risk the health of faith. Aquinas was very clear on this. He did not believe that people should be forced into conversions as that would only create scandal and bring shame to the Christian faith. "Faith," wrote Aquinas, "is a matter of will." For people who had converted and then slipped back into pagan ways, force and coercion were warranted. "These are to be compelled, even by physical force, to carry out what they promised and to hold what they once accepted." This doctrine became the basis for the Spanish Inquisition.

This three- or four-tiered theory of law, promulgated by the intellectual class and accepted by society, deeply influenced Iberian political development. Political legitimacy depended on adhering to natural law principles, to the law "written upon men's hearts." Political legitimacy, however, did not always depend on following human law, and some interesting tensions developed as a result of this bifurcated thinking. The king, with the advice of his council, might pronounce a law, but he was not necessarily subject to that law. Instead, he followed a higher law, the law of nature and the word of God. For a ruler to be above the written law of the land did not make his rule illegitimate. Actions that were out of step with tradition might be explained as God's will. The complete disregard for domestic matters exhibited during the Hapsburg era, for instance, was justified by the need to maintain the Catholic hegemony abroad. Philip II may have been violating the manmade obligations of his office but he was faithful to the obligations of a supranational faith.

Although a hierarchy of law created problems for Old World citizens, it did provide some relief for the indigenous people of the West Indies. *Conquistadores* who tortured Indians or priests who forcibly converted non-Christians were attacked by Spanish theologians, appalled at the conditions of conquest in the New World. Using natural law as the existing law, these Dominicans and Jesuits ordered the colonialists to desist from their "Godless" way, claiming they would ultimately suffer divine judgment for their sins. It was only when the Inquisition set up its tribunal in Mexico and Peru that the Church had the ability to prosecute these misdeeds.

Natural law theory is not specific to Catholic cultures; it is the basis for Protestant political theory as well. The belief that reasoning powers will lead individuals to a common good is the foundation of Anglo-American law. Yet there is an important distinction in the methods available to the state and to the goals sought. Aquinas and his followers believed strongly in the directive measure. Law could lead one towards virtue, not just enforce moral codes of behavior. Law and lawmakers played a positive role in the moral development of the citizens. Instead of leaving people alone to do things as "they saw fit," the Thomistic state was actively involved in developing a person's sense of fitness. The relationship between state and citizen was much more intimate than we experience in a liberal society. We might bear in mind that intimacy as we consider one of the key components of Iberian political culture: patrimonialism.

PATRIMONIALISM

Patrimonialism refers to the practice of mutual obligation. In a less sympathetic light, it might be defined as "a favor for a favor." In its most unsympathetic rendering, it looks like corruption. In legal terms, patrimony refers to property inherited through the father, or, more generally, inheritance. In political terms, patrimony creates economic relationships based on bloodlines. Patrimonial systems begin as extended families or clans. Membership involves who one knows or who one is married to. Unlike more modern systems, which emphasize merit and personal achievement, patrimonial systems rely on traditional values, emphasizing family connections and social status. Familial obligation, not individual initiative, is the organizing principle of a patrimonial system.

Portugal, perhaps because it is a smaller, more cohesive nation, maintained kinship as the primary constituent unit up through the Salazar regime. Prominent families—the Borges, Fonsecas, de Brito, and de Melo—acted as informal decision-makers for the country. Each family has its own organic structure, with one member involved in construction, another involved with the Church, another enlisted in the military, and yet another engaged in producing a valuable commodity, such as cement. Along with other corporate groups, which were organized on a functional basis, representatives of these families comprised the ruling elite. While a cause for scandal in a liberal system, which would charge them with conflicts of interest, these enmeshed family groups were accepted for most of Portugal's history as a normal state of affairs. That the extended family would include public matters only reinforced the naturalness of the household system. During the Salazar regime, the household unit represented a single vote as suffrage was limited to heads of families who "naturally" represented the family's interest.

It is easy to see how this cultural norm would create a mercantile rather than free market economy, one heavily regulated by personal connections. Although Iberians have been involved in international trade since the time of the Carthaginians, those cosmopolitan practices did not promote a free market. Rather, deals were forged behind the scenes, and restrictive policies dictated who could work with whom. The Jews developed their own patrimonial system, operating quite successfully through family connections that stretched across the Diaspora. Unlike the Christians, they were not as constrained with political obligations or religious restraints. Their expulsion in 1492 denied Spain a valuable example of family connections that contributed to a healthy economy. Instead, Spain and Portugal closed their borders on any heretical ideas. During the Hapsburg era, trading policies were restricted on the basis of religion. Dutch and English traders, corrupted by Protestantism, were not allowed to operate in Spanish waters. Family connections came to be understood as protective, closed systems. Paranoia and fear destroyed a network that might have been efficient and productive.

Although systems based on obligation are clearly susceptible to corruption, other values are at work as well. The directive force of government was understood as an obligation at the top to lead the lesser members toward their potential. Although this system has often hampered a laissez-faire approach to economic development, it has provided a charitable system for the needy. Concern for the welfare of all its members has been a higher priority in traditionally Catholic countries, such as Spain, Portugal, Italy, and Ireland, than in Protestant countries, such as England and the United States, which emphasize a work ethic and individual responsibility over an obligation to help the poor.

A commitment to social and political obligations runs deep through Iberian culture. El Cid, whose cultural stock value has remained high throughout the millennium, embodies a Catholic who honored feudal obligations as well as Christian orthodoxy. Of course, these extended networks of obligation, combined with a high sense of honor, have also resulted in enormous bloodshed. The medieval knights were quick to take up arms to defend the honor of their lords. Chivalry was understood in terms of duels, of fighting to the death rather than shrugging off harmless insults. This deeply ingrained sense of extended loyalty may account for the difficulty Spanish and Portuguese parties have had in forming coalitions. When one is defending the honor of a larger group, it is harder to forge political compromises. Only those whose authority transcended group obligations, who were free to operate on their own without defending anyone else's honor, were in a position to effect social and political change.

AUTHORITARIANISM AND REPRESSION

A commonly held principle in Catholic political theory is that God may, from time to time, change the natural order. Divine will, through miracles and revelation, may intercede and alter social customs and beliefs. What today social scientists might call a paradigm shift, medieval authors understood as the "hand of God." Only the supernatural had enough authority to create change, even to change the law written on men's hearts. Without divine intervention, the natural law would continue just as it had before.

On a political level, this understanding—that change in the system required supreme authority—translated into authoritarianism. Modernization policies were only legitimate when they were enacted from above. A leader who wished to improve the economy or the institutional infrastructure needed to be seen as the supreme leader. In a trend that goes back to the culture of the Berbers, he particularly needed to be seen as the supreme leader of the armed forces. A mere spokesperson for the multitude would not have the legitimate authority to be the leader, let alone to produce change. Portuguese and Spanish voters would be less interested in a "man of the people" than in a leader who wasn't afraid to seize the reins of power. "I need authority for my cattle," said one Portuguese politician out on the stump, "and I will need authority for my people." Rather than take offense, the crowd cheered.

A good leader is one who "commands obedience," wrote Ibn Khaldun in the fourteenth century. He is not "emasculated" by human law but is made strong through serving God's law. The Muslim Ibn Khaldun, like the Catholic political theorists, believed that true authority meant operating above the law of people yet within the law of God. The obedience the good leader commands derives from his directive and his coercive capabilities. He knows what is good for the people and he is capable of using force. Following the tradition of the monks of war, Iberian leaders have had to be both pious and tough.

Many of Spain's leaders have been generals, the two most recent being Primo de Rivera and Franco. Indeed, Franco was the supreme general, *el Caudillo,* who achieved his power *por la gracia de Dios* (by the grace of God). Had he been selected by the people, he would have lost much of his authority. Although Salazar was not a military man, he showed himself capable of fierce, ruthless tactics. Both Franco and Salazar used torture and repression as a way of maintaining social order, going way beyond anything approved by the Catholic political theorists. In a tradition that goes back to the Roman coliseum, the Berber warriors, and the *conquistadores,* Franco and Salazar ruled through fear. They disarmed their adversaries through systematic cruelty, knocking out all opposition, whether real or perceived. The Black Legend of Iberian cruelties found modern expression in their two regimes. Given the culture of violence and an ethos that honored an indifference to suffering, it is not surprising that political dissent took on extremely violent tones. Disagreements with the *Generalissimo* were often expressed through political assassinations. From a liberal perspective, all of this sounds outside of the bounds of political activity, yet from a cultural perspective, these strong-arm tactics have been the basis for political legitimacy.

The importance of a virile leader continued after the Franco regime. When a group of military officers stormed the Spanish Parliament in January 1981, King Juan Carlos, dressed in full military regalia, appeared on Spanish television and ordered the usurpers to desist. His orders were taken seriously in large part because of his decisiveness, made professional through a military career and uniform. He was, after all, the commander-in-chief in a hierarchical system. In a dramatic change from the past, the coup attempt did not become an excuse for a repressive regime. Although he is an orderly and disciplined leader, Juan Carlos is measured in his response to violent affronts, even negotiating with terrorist separatists. When King Juan Carlos speaks as the head of a body politic, the diverse members, for the first time in decades, willingly respond.

The king of Spain and the president of Portugal are symbolic heads of government. The day to day running of the government is handled by their respective prime ministers. Although both the king and the president are largely ceremonial officers, the power of ceremony in a traditionally hierarchical system should not be underestimated. Less involved in partisan squabbles, the Spanish king and the Portuguese president are able to transcend party politics and embody a higher law, one that unifies the entire country and not just that particular moment's majority.

CORPORATISM AND ORGANICISM

Corporatism is a political system in which the constituent units are functionally specific groups. It is the modern version of St. Paul's body politic, in which various members coordinate their activities for the good of the whole. Corporatism suggests a state, that is, a head, that is very involved in the political process. Bargains are negotiated from the top, by the elite members of the various groups, and are imposed on the masses below. Traditionally those elite groups were the army, the Church, and the oligarchy. With the advent of industrialism, business was given a seat at the bargaining table. Unlike a Marxist system, which pitted bosses against workers, a corporatist system assumed that bosses and workers shared a common goal. Rather than work in an adversarial system, Spain and Portugal developed a coordinated system of government. As long as people subscribed to a recognized group, their interests would be represented.

Corporatism is a very different system than those developed by Marxism and liberalism. Class struggle is out of the question, as that would tear the body asunder. The foot, as St. Paul reminded us, could not operate on its own; it needed the other members to survive. Marx's goal of a classless society, a body of feet, was also against the natural order of things. Similarly, liberalism's notion of a limited government was out of harmony with natural law. Separated powers suggested a head at war with itself; rule by the many was an inefficient use of potential. The most efficient system of government, according to Aquinas, was a monarchy. The community's health depended upon a ruler who was holy, wise, and virile, who knew what was best for everyone and could guide each member to their proper place.

The medieval corporate system received legitimacy in the industrialized world through two important papal encyclicals. *Rerum Novarum* (1891) and *Quadragesimo Anno* (1931) urged a natural law solution for the problems of industrialization. Both encyclicals critiqued Marxism and capitalism, the former for its abolition of private property, the latter for its enslavement of the working man. *Rerum Novarum* was responsible for the creation of trade unions in Catholic Europe; *Quadragesimo Anno* strengthened the autonomy of the functional groups. Both Franco and Salazar understood these encyclicals to be the basis of their corporatist systems, primers on how to be modern and Catholic at the same time.

Corporatism is an organic system, organic in the sense of organs (going back to St. Paul), in the sense of a coordinated whole, and in the sense of something fundamental. What developed as a political system developed organically. Although Spain and Portugal suffered enormous internal battles, a clean break with the past never occurred. Unlike the United States, whose early arrivals had the privilege of starting over on fresh soil, Spain and Portugal developed within the constraints of the feudal, medieval past. Startling changes in government generally resulted in a *pronunciamiento* or coup. Each time there was radical change, the organic system reasserted itself.

In all fairness, every political system relies on shared values and common goals, otherwise conflicts would be settled through civil wars and not by political methods. We may value our U.S.–style pluralism but those differing interests do not suggest a major cleavage in the fundamental ideology. Some may vote for a party that supports an active government and some may vote for a candidate who vows to cut back governmental waste, but all agree on rule by the majority. The issues may be handled differently, but the method, for the most part, is above reproach. There exists a consensus on the system as a whole and, in that sense, our democratic liberalism is organic.

With the exception of the civil war period, all political dissent in America has operated within the terms of liberalism. Some recent politicians, Pat Buchanan in particular, have threatened that another moral issue is about to provoke what he calls the "culture wars." With over one hundred years since the last major civil disturbance, Americans, on the whole, do not panic at that rhetoric. Given the health of our economy, our social mobility, and the promises of a new global marketplace, civil war seems highly unlikely, a throwback to an earlier time before e-commerce and cordless phones.

The effects of the Spanish civil war, however, are still visible. Many churches refused to remove the long list of those who died for "God and Spain," the fallen nationalists, although it remains a sore point for families of republican fighters. It is not unusual to find the painting of a young priest, shot by anarchists, hanging somewhere in a quiet chapel. Paintings of the Virgin, punctured by Soviet regulation bullets, hang as reminders to tourists and supplicants that Spanish cultural resources have been as much at risk from native elements as any global forces. Marriages between children of the left and the right make politics an impossible topic at the dinner table and even in the neighborhood café. God forbid that Spanish honor reestablish itself and the blood feuds begin again.

The political fallout from the civil war was exacerbated during the Franco regime. Many people were sent to jail or killed for critiquing the regime. The press was limited to covering events Franco wanted reported and in the way he wanted them reported. So-called "dangerous elements" were rounded up in the middle of the night and sometimes never heard from again. It was smarter to leave the workings of government to the few who were in charge than to risk trouble. This same resigned attitude dominated Portuguese public life as well. Efforts to involve the public during the period of *rotavismo* were complete failures. The public did not want to know about secret dealings and back room politics. Although liberal rulers had been telling the masses about popular sovereignty and the rights of man since the eighteenth century, those values were not always accepted as truth. Part of the explanation for the apolitical nature of the Iberian masses historically may well have to do with the absolute methods that put these liberal ideals in place; democratization, such as it was, was implemented from above. Yet part of the explanation may have to do with the political culture. In the functionally specific natural hierarchy, those on the lower rungs of the social ladder gained no virtue by meddling in the affairs of the top.

In the midst of the Franco regime, when Spaniards were dying of starvation and corruption was rampant, a British hispanophile made a plea to the Allied powers to reconsider their demands for a liberal democracy in Spain. Originally published in 1950, Gerald Brenan's description of Franco's Spain began with a focus on democratic assumptions. If leaders of the free world believed they could bring about the general's collapse through economic means, wrote Brenan, they were mistaken. "Anyone who could survive the past two years of poverty and drought," wrote Brenan, "can survive anything."[6] The second illusion was that the only alternative to Franco was parliamentary democracy. Spain was not suited to a parliamentary democracy, argued Brenan, particularly after the bitter battles of a civil war. Controlled dissent, the ethos of a democratic system, was beyond the capability of a people guilty, on both sides, of blood lust and fratricide. Instead, Brenan proposed a monarchy, one that would not require bribes and terrorism in order to maintain its support, as was the case with Franco. Only a king could rise above the horrors of the past and promote pardon. It took over twenty years for Brenan's solution to emerge, a solution more in keeping with Spanish political culture than anything imposed from afar.

The king Brenan was waiting for, Juan Carlos, is the personification of Spanish political culture. The Spanish constitution identifies him as "the head of state, the symbol of its unity and permanence." Rarely does a day go by without some coverage of the royal couple in the national press, and not, as is the case in England, because of some scandal. On the contrary, the Spanish press, having fallen afoul of public sentiment with allegations of the king's marital misconduct early on in the monarchy, is currently contributing to their prestige. Monarchists appreciate his " long Bourbon nose and his big Hapsburg lips." Socialists note that "the King is the best thing Spain could have invented for its politics."[7] Two-thirds of Spaniards polled during the late 1980s believed that, without the king, "democracy in Spain would not have been possible."[8] Given the weakness of the central state, the monarchy may be what holds the national identity together. In a country with many local but few national holidays and in which the national anthem is rarely played—indeed few Spaniards know it exists—only the monarchy receives national recognition.

The second factor that is reinvigorating national identity, for both positive and negative reasons, is Spain's and Portugal's relationship with the European Union. In a positive light, Spain and Portugal are now recognized as European cultural resources. The European Union sends enormous subsidies to restore the peninsula's Romanesque and Gothic cathedrals, monasteries, and chapels. The medieval pilgrimage to Santiago de Compostela has been completely refurbished, with new hostels and hotels set up for the thousands of pilgrims, and safer pathways laid out away from heavy traffic. The EU named Compostela a European cultural center for the year 2000.

In a negative light, the EU's agricultural policies are causing concern about national sovereignty. EU policies on olive oil production, which favor Italian methods of production over Andalusian, provoked outrage from Spaniards across the regions. The olive oil story claimed the front page of national papers throughout the summer of 1999. Coverage that had focused on Barcelona's discontent with Madrid's domestic policies, or the Basque country's critique of Madrid's criminal policies, shifted to a unified attack on Brussels, the seat of the European Union.

One flyer dramatized the farmers' vulnerability through the use of a well-recognized cultural icon. The famous Goya painting of Napoleon's soldiers executing the citizens of Madrid, *The Third of May, 1808,* was posted on telephone polls with "European Union" scrawled on the backs of the French soldiers. The nappy-haired prisoner stands with his arms spread out, a Dominican priest by his side administering last rites, his nearby comrades covering their faces in horror. The message of the picture was clear. Spain had been invaded by foreigners once again.

This time, however, Spain is being led by a different sort of king. Juan Carlos's royal ancestor, Carlos IV, may have surrendered Spain to Napoleon's forces, but one cannot imagine the current Bourbon turning his back on the Spanish people. Besides, this time the representatives of the imperial power are bringing cultural subsidies, not firing squads. The question remains whether Spaniards will rally around the targeted olive producers or will quietly go about their business in their newly restored medieval cities. Both responses could find legitimacy in Iberian political culture.

MOBILIZATION OF THE MASSES—INFORMAL CATHOLICISM

Up to this point, our discussion of the Catholic aspects of Iberian culture has focused on the Church as an institution. Should we limit the discussion of the Church to its official practices, however, we would miss a large part of the Catholic experience in Spain and Portugal. Alongside the formal institution, a strong tradition of informal or folk Catholicism exists in both countries, a religion that operates outside the walls of the Church. In sixteenth-century Spain and Portugal, the days of the village were structured through venerations of the many local saints. Using somewhat suspect methods, at least according to the Church, villagers lit candles and offered comestibles to the Virgin and other saints in order to protect themselves from disease, fire, and natural disaster. The unification programs, begun by St. Isidore in the fourth century, were constantly operating against these indigenous folk practices. Everyone might know the Credo in Latin but how they used the Credo differed from town to town.

Even with the enormous tide of people leaving the small villages and moving to the cities, these local practices persist. Each town, no matter how small, celebrates its feast days with ceremony and processions. The saint is carried through the streets and candles are lit in his or her honor. A mass is celebrated, sometimes the only mass of the year in the smaller towns, and everyone in the village attends. Family members who may have moved to a nearby city, return to celebrate their local saint. The festivities for the patron saints are magnified in the larger towns and cities. Businesses close, the streets are filled with traditionally garbed dancers and folk musicians, and fireworks fill the night sky. The patron saint is honored with several days of bullfights, speeches by local politicians, and, occasionally, cameo appearances by the king and queen. Cities compete with one another to put on the finest show for their particular saint, yet none compares with the extravaganza put on in Compostela for the patron saint of Spain, St. James.

The feast day of St. James, July 25, is a national holiday, and his official veneration generally lasts for weeks on either side of the day. In the summer of 1999, a holy year, the ceremonies began a month ahead with an outdoor concert by the decidedly non-Catholic Rolling Stones. On the day of the official ceremony, King Juan Carlos, in the company of Prime Minister José María Aznar of Spain and President Jorge Sampaio of Portugal, defended the patron saint's validity as the common protector, asking the apostle's help "to cultivate the honorable distinction of belonging to the same family, no matter what our ideas, preferences and customs may be, and no matter how legitimate and healthy those differences may be." Shown with his arms wrapped around the enormous statue of Santiago, the king used the annual event of the national offering to the apostle to ask for continued understanding "between the many Spains." In a tradition that goes back to the *Reconquista,* Santiago reminds Spaniards, and in that ceremony even the Portuguese, what it means to be part of a nation. A nation of "many Spains" but just one apostle.[9]

The pilgrimage to Santiago de Compostela is something each Spaniard intends to complete in his or her lifetime. Most travel by bus in groups organized by the various municipalities. More and more are traveling by foot and bicycle, and even horseback, thereby earning the privileges of pilgrims. Should they travel far enough, these pilgrims will receive a "Compostela," an indulgence recognized by the Church. The recent numbers of pilgrims making the trek to Santiago are astounding. In 1993, over ninety-nine thousand pilgrims, ninety-four thousand of whom were Spaniards, received a Compostela. Far fewer people walk on a nonholy year, yet even those numbers are increasing dramatically. In the 1980s only four or five thousand people walked or bicycled to Santiago each nonholy year. Since the 1993 holy year, the numbers have risen from fifteen thousand in 1994 to thirty thousand in 1998. The holy year of 1999 broke all existing records with over eight thousand people a day arriving in Santiago, many of them under their own steam.

Around 90 percent of the pilgrims make the journey for religious or religious-cultural reasons. Many pilgrims attend mass at small churches along the way. When asked about the relationship between the pilgrimage and the Church, many of the younger Spanish pilgrims respond that "El Camino," the name for the route to Santiago, is their church; that the Knights of the Templar, a medieval religious order, are their priests; and that the many pilgrims throughout the ages constitute their community of believers.

Not many Portuguese are included in the recent statistics provided by the official Pilgrim's Office web site. Perhaps because of centuries of Spanish aggression, the Portuguese people have not developed a similar devotion to St. James. Instead, the Virgin of Fátima fulfills the supernatural needs of the nation.

According to the legend, the Virgin appeared to three young shepherds in Fátima on May 13, 1917, and told them to return every month on the thirteenth day for further messages. News spread of the Virgin's appearance and, despite official Church skepticism, crowds began gathering in the village of Fátima to await her return. Many claimed to see her and by October 13, 1917, tens of thousands of faithful were awaiting the Virgin's return. This time all sorts of celestial happenings were recorded: the sun blazed more brightly and colored fireballs flashed across the sky. Many people claimed to have been miraculously cured. Only one person, one of the original shepherds, a ten-year-old girl named Lucia do Santos, was actually able to hear the three messages from the Virgin. The first message called for peace, for sinners to repent and pray, and for the faithful to make sacrifices. The second message warned against the spread of Russian "error" should the first message be ignored. The third vision, which was revealed only recently by the Vatican (in May 2000), predicted the 1981 attempt to assassinate the pope.

Over the years, Fátima developed into an important pilgrimage site. By 1951, a holy year, over 1 million pilgrims arrived in the Portuguese village in hopes of being cured. The uneasy relationship between devotees of the Virgin and the Roman Catholic Church demonstrates the limits of formal Catholic power. The Church was slow to recognize this mass movement and, indeed, until the papacy of John XXIII, treated it with a good deal of disdain. After Vatican II, when the Roman papacy moved increasingly toward the world and its spiritual needs, Fátima began to receive official recognition. Pope Paul VI visited the shrine of the Virgin on its fiftieth anniversary along with 2 million other faithful from around the world.

If we want to find mass movements in Iberian political culture, we need only look at these informal, grass-roots religious traditions. Unlike the democratic reforms of the past, which were instituted by the elite, the pilgrimages to Santiago and Fátima represent social movements initiated by the masses. Although the Spanish and Portuguese people have not always responded well to political matters, that does not indicate a lack of interest in public life. While political beliefs have dissolved frequently into internecine warfare, supernatural matters have coalesced the community, not through reasoned discourse but through the social practices of an unofficial faith.

MODERNIZATION

The Catholic, hierarchical, ceremonial, organic system that traces its roots back to Aristotle's inclusive hierarchy and Seneca's notion of the Gift is only half the picture. As noted in chapter 2, the split in the Spanish and Portuguese soul that occurred in the seventeenth century with the introduction of continental ideas by the Bourbons, created a second, more secular, political culture that developed alongside the more traditional one. The social, economic, and political goals of the progressives were completely at odds with the goals of the traditionalists. The Bourbons and the *afrancesados* of Spain, like their Pombal counterparts in Portugal, envisioned a more modern country, a nation capable of becoming more like cosmopolitan Europe. The traditionalists looked at any progress with skepticism; they believed the old Thomistic hierarchy was static, perfect the way it was. Change might come from a supreme, divinely appointed leader, which immediately excluded the French, but not through a slow erosion of values.

Not only did the deep ideological differences between progressives and traditionalists cut across class and regional lines, but generations within the same family found themselves at odds with one another. In the mid-twentieth century, while northern European tourists cavorted on the many beaches of the Iberian peninsula, Spanish and Portuguese young people were forced to follow highly restrictive dating habits. Girls were not allowed to wear makeup or even to ride bicycles. Village priests reported to peasant fathers what their daughters had been up to while they were off working in the fields. Modernity over time became associated not just with economic innovation and continental politics but with sexual expression as well. Progress became known as the Great Temptress, seducing young peasant girls and boys from their traditional villages. Once again, it became the task of the Church to protect the vulnerable masses from dangerous, heretical influences.

In the confusion of the Portuguese First Republic and the Spanish civil war, what had been a split became a total breakdown in the social fabric. As far as the traditionalists were concerned, progress of any sort became identified with the anti-Christ. As far as the progressives were concerned, religion of any kind was incompatible with the demands of social and economic development. Rather than work out a compromise or consider a middle ground, personal honor and political vengeance ruled supreme. Ideological fanaticism displaced any political pragmatism as, particularly in Spain, society set about to destroy itself. Those afraid of lipstick-wearing women joined forces with those who wanted to remain an agricultural economy. Those afraid of the power of the Jesuits joined forces with those who despised the peasant class. Once they had vanquished their enemies, these loosely held coalitions set their suspicious eyes on one another.

Rather than separate itself from this political mayhem, the Church only added to the drama, giving credence to visions of the Virgin that labeled the Second Republic as the work of the devil.[10] Anarchists retaliated and the Church became the target of anticlerical violence; nuns and priests were assassinated and many of Spain's churches were permanently defaced. When the military stepped in to restore order, the Catholic Church gave them its blessing. Protected by the new regime, the Church looked the other way as the restorers of order instituted severe methods of control. Even when the Roman Catholic Church began to take a more active stance throughout the world in terms of social justice, the Spanish and Portuguese bishops remained wedded to their regimes.

At the same time as political methods became more restrictive and authoritarian, economic and social conditions kept pushing Spain and Portugal toward the more open climate experienced by the rest of Europe. The strict economic policies implemented by Franco sent a million Spaniards abroad in search of work. With the influx of tourism to Spain and Portugal in the sixties, the regimes were doubly exposed to "foreign" ideas. Spanish and, to a lesser degree, Portuguese workers brought home politically and socially promiscuous ideas, such as democracy and free love. European tourists modeled more relaxed social norms on Spanish and Portuguese beaches. Despite the efforts of

Franco and Salazar to turn the clock back, increasing numbers of Iberians took on European customs and mores. By the end of the dictatorships, the cities of Spain and Portugal had become more cosmopolitan and less parochial, more interested in becoming a part of Europe and less willing to carry the religious burdens of the Counter-Reformation.

Despite these social and economic trends toward a modern, secular society, a full civic culture, that is, a politicized, involved, and participatory society, has yet to appear. Although the percentage of Spaniards who vote is higher than the numbers that vote in the United States, in terms of European voting behavior, the numbers in Spain and Portugal are relatively low. In some recent surveys conducted in Spain, social scientists discovered that membership in voluntary associations has actually decreased since the Suárez government took power. Fewer people are involved in political parties now than in the early years of the transition to democracy. Some have explained this declining trend in terms of "depolarization."[11] In an effort to leave the bitter disputes of the past behind them, Spaniards have moved away from political activities of any sort. A similar depoliticalization has been noted in Portugal since the mass mobilizations of the revolutionary years in the 1970s. Efforts to institute change through the political process were seen by most Portuguese as being illusory at best.

In a survey conducted in 1990, Spaniards were asked how much trust they placed in fifteen different things which they then ranked in terms of importance. At the top of the list was self, followed by family and kin, with God coming in as the third most popular entity worthy of veneration. National government, unions, and businessmen, on the other hand, were located at the bottom of the ranking with political parties being the least trustworthy of all.[12] The low ranking of political parties, however, does not indicate that political power itself is untrustworthy. In a survey that tested the levels of trust extended to certain public figures, King Juan Carlos was ranked as the most trustworthy public figure. Both the king and Pope John Paul II were deemed more trustworthy than the prime minister, Felipe González. The fact that a democratically elected official was considered less trustworthy than two figures whose leadership did not depend on a democratic process says quite a lot about the relationship between Spaniards and democracy.

While Spain and Portugal are clearly taking on democratic practices, these surveys suggest that the old ways are still essential for maintaining political legitimacy. Even though the Church has lost its institutional status within the Spanish and Portuguese governments, its role as The Legitimator appears as relevant as ever. The place afforded to the pope in the 1990 Spanish survey indicates a strong connection between the formal Church and social and political norms. Even though divorce and abortion became a reality in both countries during the 1980s, fundamental Catholic principles still shape the two nations' societies. The status accorded to Juan Carlos suggests that the Catholic principle of monism, of a strong leader able to pilot the country toward economic and spiritual salvation, is still central to most Spaniards. The presidency of Jorge Sampaio, a prestigious man above the squabbles of party politics, serves a similar role in Portugal.

What we are seeing is a fusion of Catholic beliefs with modern democratic governments. As do most continental Europeans, Spaniards and Portuguese see the government's role as taking care of the needy and displaced; achieving social justice and equality is an important function of government. Following in the corporatist tradition of the past, governments are expected to coordinate interests and promote economic development. Participation in the political process, however, has been significantly less than in France and Germany. Partisan debates do not inspire democratic activity; on the contrary, perhaps because of the turbulence of the past, political debates are generally met with disapproval. Should a Spanish king or a Portuguese president fall out of favor with the pope, for instance, the peoples of Spain and Portugal may be put in a position where they will have to take matters into their own hands. This hypothetical situation might cause the old split in the Iberian soul to reassert itself. As long as the symbols of national unity stay out of politics, however, as long as they are able to maintain their prestige as well as their roles as visionaries, the representatives of fragile democratic procedures will get the protection they need to survive.

NOTES

1. Clifford Geertz, *The Interpretation of Cultures* (New York: Basic Books, 1973), 312.

2. Aaron Wildavsky, "Choosing Preferences or Constructing Institutions: A Cultural Theory of Preference Formation," *American Political Science Review* 81 (March 1987): 40.

3. John Locke, *Two Treatises of Government* (Cambridge: Cambridge University Press, 1988), II§4.

4. Sidney M. Greenfield, "The Patrimonial State and Patron-Client Relations in Iberia and Latin America: Sources of 'The System' in the Fifteenth Century Writings of the Infante D. Pedro of Portugal," Occasional Papers Series 1 (Program in Latin American Studies, University of Massachusetts, 1976).

5. St. Thomas Aquinas, "Qu. 91. The Kinds of Law," in *St. Thomas Aquinas on Politics and Ethics,* ed. Paul E. Sigmund (New York: Norton, 1988), 46.

6. Gerald Brenan, *The Face of Spain* (New York: Penguin, 1987), 13.

7. Jon Lee Anderson, "The Reign in Spain," *The New Yorker,* April 27, May 4, 1998, 110–19.

8. John Hooper, *The New Spaniards* (New York: Penguin, 1995), 86.

9. "Don Juan Carlos exalta 'el orgullo de ser españoles' y denuncia' el odio fratricida,'" *El Pais,* July 26, 1999, 15.

10. William A. Christian, *Visionaries: The Spanish Republic and the Reign of Christ* (Berkeley: University of California Press, 1996).

11. Peter McDonough, Samuel Barnes, and Antonio López Pina, *The Cultural Dynamics of Democratization in Spain* (Ithaca: Cornell University Press, 1998), 145–164.

12. Ibid., 54.

Chapter 6

Interest Groups and the Political Process

One of the defining characteristics of the American political system has been the presence of interest groups. Alexis de Tocqueville, visiting in the early nineteenth century, commented on the number and variety of voluntary associations in America. There were business groups, civic groups, literary groups, agricultural groups, and countless other associations a citizen might join. The number of interest groups has continued to grow, with some thirty-thousand special interest groups now active in American politics. Group participation is still a large part of American public life. In a Harvard University study published in 1995, 79 percent of the respondents belonged to at least one organization.[1] The types of organizations ranged from scientific associations to veterans groups, from women's rights organizations to cultural salons. Political life in America has largely been experienced through voluntary group activity.

A political system built on competitive voluntary associations is known as pluralism, and it indicates a high degree of civic responsibility on the part of its members. Citizens are expected to belong to a number of interest groups, each one acting as a linkage to the state. Membership is understood to be fluid and multiple, encouraging political participation without enslaving its members to a single cause. Competition between the various interest groups is assumed to correct any extreme leanings a particular group may have, thus ensuring a more democratic process.

Pluralism arose out of a very unique situation: the American founding. The homogeneous community of active, civic-minded individuals has not been duplicated elsewhere on the globe. The democratic institutions that developed in this country reflect the conditions of the founding period: a limited government and an active citizenry. When we consider attributes of democratic rule, interest group activity tends to have a large role. Lack of interest groups, therefore, is considered antidemocratic. An important question to consider regarding Spain's and Portugal's development of social groups is how central they were in achieving democracy. How successful were these group interests in curbing the absolute power of the state? What place does pluralism and competitive lobbying hold in Iberian democracy?

Even before Franco made participation in most interest groups illegal, Iberians have had difficulty organizing. "The Iberians," wrote nineteenth-century traveler Richard Ford, "never would amalgamate, never would . . . put their shields together—never would sacrifice their own local private interest for the people's good." Philosopher and intellectual leader of the Spanish Republic José Ortega y Gasset referred to this phenomenon as "invertebrate." Writing in the early twenties, Ortega y Gasset described his country as separated into distinct vertebrae, bending and breaking with no connecting tissue between them. Spain was deeply divided. Lacking the cement of associational life, the country was splitting along a variety of unresolvable cleavages: monarchists against republicans, scientists against theologians, absolutists against anarchists. Eventually these differences erupted into civil war.

Traditionally, the corporatist structure provided the backbone of Iberian society, the Iberian version of "civil society." Membership was of a compulsory and scripted nature, determined by social class, gender, and even one's birth rank. The cement that held the body politic together was never the associational life described by de Tocqueville but belief in the absolute rightness of the vertical nature of things: of the rule of the king over his subjects, the rule of the pope over his bishops, the rule of the general over his lieutenants, and the rule of the boss over his workers. Equality provoked not democracy as in the American conception but an invertebrate situation. Even the great republican Ortega y Gasset never encouraged social equality. In *The Revolt of the Masses,* he likened mass movements to "an invasion from below" and considered the members of these movements to be "barbaric." The philosopher of the republic believed the masses should follow the wisdom of the intellectual aristocracy, those who were trained to think for the benefit of others.[2]

THE TRADITIONAL *INTERESES*

The historical triumvirate of power in Spain and Portugal has been the Church, the army, and the nobility, all of them comprised from the same social class. Under laws of primogeniture, the first son inherited all the family's property, the second son of an elite family often went into the army and became a general, the third son often went into the Church and became a bishop. Bloodlines reinforced political interests. To put it bluntly, the army and the Church worked together to guarantee the property interests of their elder brothers. Family loyalties, however, were somewhat modified by the distinct cultures of the various *intereses.*

The Army

The army developed out of the religious military orders discussed in chapter 2. These orders never completely surrendered their autonomy to the emerging central state, and the army held on to that independence. The warrior ethos added to their autonomy as every king knew that any encroachment on the army's power would result in an armed coup or a *pronunciamiento.* The army, like the king, often claimed to be above human law, following the will of God, existing prior to and above the state. Citing a higher authority, military officers were as likely to disrupt the programs of a reform-minded monarch as a duly elected parliament. Not a servant to the executive or legislative branch, the army has traditionally seen its sacred mission as maintaining the unity of the nation at whatever cost.

The religious military orders, however, represent only half the history of the armed forces. Irregular peasant groups, basically armed militias, carved out petty chiefdoms for themselves during the *Reconquista* as well as during the many civil wars. Politics often took the form of one or more *caciques* (chiefs) gathering up their irregular forces to do battle with other *caciques* and their forces. The prize was national power and a share of the spoils, patronage, and national treasury that went with it. This more brutal form of the military, which was carried over to the conquest of the Indies, was eventually reduced with the bureaucratization of the military during the Bourbon reforms. The men-on-horseback mentality was replaced with a highly structured chain of command, closer to the discipline, if not the passion, of the religious military orders.

During the Franco and Salazar regimes, a change took place in terms of class loyalty. The older, more aristocratic officers, with their ties to the *ancien régime,* were pushed aside as the younger generation demanded more modernization policies, more progress. This shift was particularly visible in Portugal when a

1974 coup toppled the inheritor of the Salazar regime. More to the left than their counterparts in Spain, these junior military officers bypassed the offerings of liberalism and went straight for an army-led socialist solution. The class consciousness of the Portuguese military had swung way to the left.

The army in post-Franco Spain was generally regarded as an instrument of the right. However, when the socialists came into power under Felipe González, the army was able to sell its less honorable methods to a left wing government under the banner of antiterrorism. *Grupos Anti-Terroristas de Liberación* (GAL), a group of military officers with death-squad politics, was linked to the murders of twenty-four people in the Basque country and in southwest France suspected of having ties with the Basque separatist group, ETA. The Spanish independent judiciary called for a full investigation to determine the authority behind the GAL assassinations. Claiming executive privilege, the González administration refused to participate and eventually the judiciary backed down.

The events around the GAL scandal suggest that partisan identity is secondary to the demands of maintaining social control. The army, it would seem, is as willing to protect a socialist government as it was to carry out the policies of the quasi-fascist regime of Franco. The GAL assassinations also point to that enduring political problem of what to do with a highly trained warrior class whose honor comes from decimating the enemy. Had not the cross hairs been trained on political enemies, what damage might they have done to the ruling team? Although many wish to believe that the days of bloodshed were put to rest with the failure of the 1981 coup attempt, the GAL trouble indicates that some members of the armed forces are still operating under the mandates of the past.

The Institutional Law of the State, which was the closest thing to a constitution that Franco had, outlined the armed forces' responsibility as guaranteeing "the unity and independence of the country, the integrity of her territory, national security and the defense of the institutional system." Although Juan Carlos quickly set about to restructure Franco's shock troops, some of this language survived the transition to democracy. Article 8 of the 1978 constitution states that the mission of the armed forces is "to guarantee the sovereignty and independence of Spain, defend its territorial integrity and the constitutional arrangements." *Territorial integrity,* a term found in both the Franco document and the constitution, became, in the minds of some, the constitutional basis for the army to maintain its vigilance with regard to politics, especially against "foreign," that is communist or socialist, ideologies.

In a country where even self-identified royalists cannot agree—up until recently Carlists were challenging Juan Carlos's rule as a usurpation of power—territorial integrity is a fragile state of affairs. Everyone recognizes

Spain's capacity to come apart at the seams. The problem has been who decides when territorial integrity is at risk? The dictator? the parliament? the king? the *cortes*? A socialist government? Traditionally, the barometer of civil unrest has been the army, and it has been slow to surrender that customary right.

Although the last attempted military takeover occurred some twenty years ago, Spaniards discuss the 1981 coup attempt as if it occurred in an earlier century. Indeed, some claim that Spain, the land of El Cid, bull fighters, and *conquistadores* is now a country of pacifists. Around one-third of the young men conscripted into military service object on conscientious grounds; by the early 1990s the government was allowing almost 90 percent of those requests. The American Gulf War during the Bush administration was not approved of in Spain, perhaps because Spain has traditionally been an ally of the Arab states, or perhaps because, on the whole, Spaniards have no interest in going to war. The popular support behind military operations in the former Yugoslavia have had more to do with the idea of "peacekeeping" than any glory associated with donning a uniform.

Whether the Spanish and Portuguese armies are able to improve their approval ratings remains to be seen. The 1981 coup attempt severely tarnished the public image of the Spanish army. Portugal's extended African wars in the sixties and seventies created much the same distrust and discontent with the military as the Vietnam War did in America. Nor are the incentives to join particularly high. With government subsidies available for higher education, young Spaniards and Portuguese do not have to make the same difficult choices as young Americans from lower-income backgrounds do. Being a member of the officer class still brings some social honor, but it is increasingly difficult to find bodies willing to fulfill the duties of the rank and file.

At the same time as the army may be losing some of its popular support, the institution itself has been downsized since the 1970s through budget cuts and layoffs. These troubles have been somewhat ameliorated through membership in NATO, which has both professionalized the military of both countries as well as kept the armed forces' attention engaged in matters other than those of a purely domestic nature, thus reducing the risk of a *pronunciamiento* or a coup d'etat.

The Church

The second member of the triumvirate is the Roman Catholic Church. Catholicism has always been more than just another religion. As discussed in chapters 2 and 5, Catholic values are at the core of the social, political, and economic culture in both Spain and Portugal. During the Franco era, the relationship between state and Church was as entwined as anything seen during the

Visigothic and medieval periods. A Concordat, negotiated with Rome in 1953, gave Franco effective control over the appointment of bishops. Under the terms of the Concordat, the Church was exempted from taxation and was guaranteed subsidies to support capital improvement of its properties. Named the official censor, the Church was granted the authority to remove offensive material from public view. Once again, the Church was in charge of educating the Spanish young and was the sole authority to recognize marriages. Divorce and birth control were out of the question. So complete was the Church's sphere of jurisdiction that Spanish police officers were forbidden to enter religious buildings on official business and members of the clergy could only be prosecuted with the consent of their spiritual supervisors.

Although most of these powers were rescinded when the Concordat was renegotiated by the Suárez government in 1976, the Church has continued to be heavily subsidized by the state. Everyone concerned agrees that both parties would benefit from having a self-supporting Roman Catholic Church, but that goal has been difficult to reach. Originally the government subsidies were supposed to end after three years of transition. Those transitions took an actual nine years to complete. The second phase of the plan gave taxpayers the power to determine how much of their taxes would go to the Church. Filers were asked to check a box on their tax form if they wanted the Church to receive funding. However, this procedure, intended to reduce the bond between Church and state, bore only superficial results. No matter how much was actually allocated to the Church by the taxpayers, the government always made up the shortfall. Some of this continued support is explained by the number of public charities that the Church maintains. Yet secular programs could equally well be established with government money.

The persistent relationship between the state and the Church points to the cultural power of the Roman Catholic Church. Although attendance at mass is down and the number of vocations in Spain and Portugal has dropped sharply since the end of the dictatorships, the Roman Catholic Church still retains its status as a cultural icon. Spaniards and Portuguese may not go to confession, may rarely attend mass, but less than 2 percent of the population identify themselves with some other religion than Catholic. It is one thing not to know your priest's first name and another thing entirely not to have your child properly christened. As a member of a labor union explained when asked why "a bunch of communists" in the late sixties wanted days off for christenings, "You had to believe in baptism otherwise your kids would be Moors, wouldn't they?"[3]

The Church continues to hold considerable influence with regards to education. The constitution may have diminished the Church's authority; however, the article explicating the rights of education has provided the Church with its traditional avenue to power, that is, educating the young. Article 27, Section 3 guarantees that the public powers will assist parents in having their children receive the moral and religious foundations consistent with their beliefs. Since Franco, religious education has been mandatory, with local bishops in charge of any religious pedagogy. After the transition to democracy, public and private schools offered alternative classes, such as ethics, for those parents whose beliefs were not consistent with Catholicism. For whatever reason, few took advantage of the "ethical alternative." Even more disturbing to liberal Catholics, the mere option of a secular alternative was taken as an excuse to teach the catechism in the religious classes. This arrangement was drastically overhauled in 1984 with the *Ley Orgánica del Derecho de la Educación* (LODE), which put education firmly within the control of the state. Although LODE met with huge public opposition, with parents and Church officials protesting in the streets, stricter controls were passed in 1990. In recent years, the Church has begun a campaign to reassert parents' rights as upheld in the constitution. The relevant constitutional language hangs in the entrance to many a small parish church, reminding the faithful of the government's promise to assist Spanish parents in their efforts to provide their children with a moral and religious foundation.

Although the Church complains that Spain is galloping toward secularization, in fact the number of people entering the priesthood is not as low as in other parts of the world. In 1992 there were more than twenty-thousand parish priests, eighteen-thousand monks and no fewer than fifty-five-thousand nuns. While representing a sharp drop from the previous decade—when there were thirty-thousand monks and seventy-nine-thousand nuns—those numbers still represent a fairly healthy institution. What is even more surprising is that Spain's closed religious communities represent 60 percent of the world total.

No numbers are available for what is undoubtedly one of the strongest religious institutions in Spain, Opus Dei. This highly secretive and highly influential group was started by Josemaría Esquivá de Balaguer during the turmoil preceding the civil war. In 1947 Opus Dei (meaning the Work of God) was recognized by the Vatican as its first secular Roman Catholic institution. In 1979 John Paul II recognized it as the Vatican's only personal prelature. In its short history, Opus Dei has grown into an international organization with over seventy-five-thousand members in over eighty-seven countries, many of whom have influential positions in government and education.

It is not unusual to hear of a university being "infiltrated" by Opus Dei. The organization is active on campuses, recruiting new members from the student population, and shaping educational policies through prominent faculty and administration members. Adherents of Opus Dei generally live together in unmarked, communal houses, taking vows of chastity and poverty. Many engage in purifying techniques, such as self-flagellation and the wearing of a *cilicio,* a barbed wire worn around the thigh with the points turned inward. By these methods, members cleanse themselves of impurities.

Although certain of the group's activities may seem positively medieval, the group's collective power is largely derived from influential positions in modern institutions. Along with university appointments, Opus Dei members sit on corporate boards, are members of parliament and financial institutions, run broadcasting networks, and are influential in the film industry. Opus Dei has been credited as a key player in the economic development of Franco and post-Franco Spain. Because of the members' strong work ethic, some scholars have likened Opus Dei to a Protestant version of Catholicism. The lack of hierarchical structure within the organization, the emphasis on salvation in worldly activities, and the universal call to perfection have more in common with the Puritans than the Jesuits. In fact, the Jesuits have been the least sympathetic to the rising success of Esquivá and his disciples, protesting most strongly when Esquivá was beatified in 1992.

The international aspect of the Roman Catholic Church has caused problems for its members in other secular democracies. John Quincy Adams, the sixth president of the United States, went so far as to say that Catholics could not be democratic as they were enslaved to the pope. Similar sentiments have been expressed, since the Reformation, in England and Holland. For most of Spain's and Portugal's history, however, Catholicism was understood as a national activity; there was no conflict of interest. The Church and the state were entwined through the *Patronato Real* in both countries and through the dictatorships of Franco and Salazar. Opus Dei is challenging that symbiotic relationship. Although it was a crucial player in the Franco regime, Opus Dei's legitimacy has come to depend far more on Rome than on any diocese in Spain. Many of the Spanish bishops are concerned about the privileges being extended to this irregular group, privileges denied to the ecclesiastical orders. Because many Opus Dei members are not formal priests, they are able to be involved in politics and business with the blessing of the pope. Indeed, Pope John Paul II has gone out of his way to grant special privileges to Opus Dei, further alienating the movement from the Council of Bishops.

Alongside of this more traditional, disciplined expression of Catholicism, the Church has had to watch some of its social power erode as both Spain and Portugal dismissed papal censure on abortion and divorce. Beginning in the early 1980s, the divorce rates began to rise as Spanish and Portuguese couples found ways to disentangle themselves from their marriage vows. Even abortion laws were relaxed, despite the vehement protests of the Church. In Portugal, 60 to 70 percent of the rural population regularly attend mass, while only 30 percent of Lisbon dwellers get to church on a regular basis. Church attendance in

Spain is similar—rural Catholics get to Church more often than those who live in the cities.

The Nobility

Whereas the armed forces and the church have only recently seen their power erode, the third member of the triumvirate, the nobility, have been operating without political power for quite some time. This is far more true in Spain than in Portugal, where a group of elite families was able to maintain its power up through the Salazar regime. But in Spain, the aristocracy lost all claim to power when the republicans took power before the civil war. Although Franco depended on the political support of the monarchists, he was never a puppet to the exiled king. Instead, Franco kept Don Juan outside of Spanish territory, successfully negotiating for Don Juan's eldest son to conform to Franco's standards rather than those of the Bourbon dynasty.

One might conclude, given the enormous popularity of the current king and queen, that the nobility has made a political comeback in Spain. In fact, King Juan Carlos and Queen Sofía are a quieter branch of royalty, operating at one-half the cost of their British counterparts. Instead of living in the royal palace in Madrid, they have remained in their spacious home just a few miles outside of the city. Although they are both aware of their ceremonial duties, they are not given to pomp and circumstance. For instance, there has been no title of Keeper of the Royal Hairbrushes bestowed upon the country's aristocracy. They are much more a king and queen of the people than of the traditional elite.

For much of Iberian history, however, the elite families held enormous political power. They distinguished themselves from those of lower-class origins through a doctrine known as *limpieza de sangre,* "purity of blood." During the sixteenth and seventeenth centuries, members of elite families produced detailed genealogies to establish that their bloodlines had not been sullied by Muslim, Jewish, or *converso* blood. The Spanish clergy was particularly challenged by this practice. Many of the theologians were in fact descendants of *conversos.* By the end of the sixteenth century, those who couldn't prove *limpieza de sangre* were forced out of the universities and pulpits. These statutes spawned an industry of genealogical fabrications as Spaniards attempted to prove how clean their blood was. Those whose relatives had run afoul of the Inquisition were unable to benefit from these revised pedigrees. The Holy Office kept precise and detailed records of all that took place in their chambers and was easily able to verify any suspect pedigree.

With the end of the Hapsburg regime and the introduction of political reform, the circle of nobility was expanded to include the merchant class. Many merchant families married into the old nobility, thus joining old and new wealth and power. Through the granting of monopolies, many elite families were able to improve their already healthy circumstances. These mercantile practices, combined with a cultural disdain for labor, had a stifling effect on economic development. The aristocratic owners of the licenses took little interest in the day-to-day business affairs, content to let things just plod along at their traditional pace.

Business was, and continues to be, heavily regulated by the state. In order to open a store or a café one still needs a license from the municipality. Historically, those licenses were given out to well-established families who passed them on from generation to generation. Competition was rarely permitted as the recipient of the license, undoubtedly a close relative of the mayor, made sure that his was the only restaurant/green grocer/bodega in the neighborhood. This stranglehold on business development has caused many young entrepreneurs to emigrate to the larger cities or even out of the country.

With the transition to democracy, business leaders have institutionalized their informal connections. Newly formed employer organizations promote modernization and economic expansion policies within the government as well as through support of the far-right party, the *Alianza Popular* (Popular Alliance—AP) and later the center-right party, the *Partido Popular* (Popular Party—PP). Some of these employer organizations were regionally based, some functionally based. In 1977 a majority of the organizations formed the *Confederación Española de Organizaciones Empresariales* (Spanish Confederation of Employers' Organizations—CEOE). This organization now represents most of the large-scale companies in Spain and continues to be a powerful interest group.

Banks have also wielded considerable political power. The Franco regime, aided by favorable loans policies, returned the favor by enacting legislation that favored the banks' interests. From 1936 to 1962, no new banks were permitted to open, further consolidating the power of a few private banks. The economic recession of the 1970s and the democratic government's intervention to free up the banking industry eroded some of the power of the banking industry. Those economic shortfalls have since been made up in the recent times of prosperity.

In both Spain and Portugal, the mercantile practices of the past are being challenged by the demands of the European Union. Banks that hold privileges with the national government are not given the same respect by the EU financial minister. The business practices negotiated in Madrid or Lisbon are not necessarily recognized by the technocrats in Brussels. An example of the encroachment on standard Spanish business practices is the precarious status of the siesta. Historically, businesses and banks have closed for three hours every afternoon, permitting employers and employees alike to enjoy a hot meal, a fine wine, and a good, solid nap. At five in the afternoon, business resumes, closing for the day at eight thirty or nine. This schedule works well with the hot climate of the south and the central meseta. In a land with few air-conditioners, the daily schedule allows for sleep when the temperature demands it.

Lately, the European Union is demanding that Spain follow a schedule similar to her neighbors'. In a recent *New York Times* article, the human resources director for Banco Bilbao, one of Spain's largest banks, made clear his position on the matter: "Those who can take siestas do. But those who are really serious about working do not." In the more competitive environment, many employers feel they can no longer maintain the luxuries of the past. But not all Spaniards agree. The same article points to a recent ban on noise between the hours of three and five instituted by the mayor of Plasencia. Concerned about the increasing commerce being conducted during the prime napping hours, the mayor stepped in and protected the rights of the dozing. Whether the large companies represented by CEOE follow the European Union's mandates remains to be seen. Small business interests are, for the most part, unwilling to make these concessions to foreign powers.[4]

The Portuguese elite was able to extend its reign up through the Salazar regime; however, after the Revolution of 1974, it was completely stripped of its rights and properties. Landholdings were confiscated, and many of its members were either exiled or sent to jail. As of the early 1990s, many of the elite were allowed to return, particularly since the expanding economy demanded some financial advisers, bankers, and business experts with knowledge of the national and international situation. Although since the 1974 revolution their political power has not been able to reestablish itself in the same way as in the past in the national government, these financial advisers and industrial magnates may be in a very good position to negotiate with Brussels. Indeed, technocrats in Portuguese cities, like technocrats in Spanish cities, have often bypassed national politics to negotiate favorable deals within the EU.

Labor

The Spanish labor movement, having enjoyed a brief moment of glory during the Second Republic, 1931–36, was brutally repressed during the Franco regime. Trade unions were outlawed and replaced with vertical syndicates, set up on an industry basis, with bosses representing workers' interests to the state. Under a corporatist model, with strict state controls, strikes were forbidden and collective bargaining was highly scripted. Order depended on everyone accepting the conditions of their place, even if those conditions were dangerous and unhealthy. When miners in Asturias, working in appalling conditions, rose up against the industry, Franco sent in shock troops to restore order. Yet even the *Generalissimo* recognized that he could not cut labor interests completely out of the picture and still maintain a functioning economy. Eventually, the government began negotiating with the illegal unions, all the while declaring they didn't exist.

Labor unions were also outlawed during the Salazar-Caetano era. Using the same corporatist model as Franco, the unions were channeled into functional groups represented mainly by the employers. Labor leaders, who had been instrumental in the First Republic, 1910–26, were either exiled or jailed. Some cooperated within the new structure and some went underground. Eventually, the Salazar regime, like Franco's, began bargaining with these illegal trade unions. One militant, communist-controlled underground labor organization achieved enough political clout that the government was forced to negotiate with it as if it was a legal bargaining agent.

Intersindical, as this group came to be known, expanded rapidly in the Revolution of 1974. Closely connected to the Portuguese Communist Party, it was made the official union during the revolution. For a brief time, it was the only union given government recognition and blessing in Portugal; eventually, the socialist labor organization was able to get its foot in the door, although its membership remained smaller than that of *Intersindical*. Amendments to the constitution in 1982 and 1989 reduced the hegemony of the Communist Party, reflecting a political climate less concerned with ideological stances and more interested in pragmatic solutions. As of the early 1990s, only 30 percent of the workforce was unionized.

The 1978 Spanish constitution guarantees all citizens, except those in the armed forces, the right to join, or not join, a union as well as the right to strike (Article 28). In 1980 the Workers' Statute expanded the rights of workers to include a guaranteed minimum wage and the right to social security. In an explicit rejection of the corporatist methods of the past, the Workers' Statute stipulated that the government would not be directly involved in labor negotiations between unions and management, even while the government was heavily involved in the "social pacts" of the time. Collective bargaining became a statutorily defined, legal practice, with elected representatives negotiating on behalf of the workers. Workers received additional guarantees in the Organic Law on Trade Union Freedom, passed in 1985, which included prohibitions against any form of discrimination on the part of the employers.

As in Portugal, actual union membership in Spain has dropped off in recent years. One study indicates that less than 20 percent of the workforce actually belongs to a union, with even fewer workers paying their dues. Although the unions are financially weak, they retain their political strength through the frequent use of strikes. The González government had to deal with periodic strikes throughout 1987 and 1988 that severely disrupted the day-to-day business of the country. The continued strength of the unions as well as labor's rigidity has made foreign firms reluctant to invest in Spain.

The handling of the general strike of 1988 shows a surprising similarity to the negotiations conducted between Franco and unions in the early seventies. Publicly, the González administration refused to consider the workers' demands, some of which were quite legitimate. Secretly, talks between the government and labor officials went on for some months after the strike was called off; eventually the unions achieved most of their demands. Welfare benefits were greatly improved, although the connection to labor negotiations was never formally recognized. As was the case during the Franco regime, the unions' political power was wielded through threats of social unrest as well as through providing the government with guaranteed social support for domestic programs. Even with diminished financial support and a weakened labor market, the unions still play an important role in state-society relations.

Both Spain and Portugal are contending with EU requirements of reduced public spending that directly contradict many of the statutory guarantees. Entitlements such as disability, unemployment, and pension benefits are at odds with the austerity measures established in the Maastricht Treaty. Multinational firms, who have the option of using Third World labor, have also eroded the Iberian unions' ability to negotiate for better conditions. Spanish workers, however, have a longer tradition available to them than the trade unions. During the summer of 1999, workers in Navarre claimed that their regional *fueros* exempted them from national measures to increase productivity by extending the workday. As the European Union erodes the powers of the nation-state, regions may find themselves relying more and more on their historical privileges as they negotiate workers' needs in an increasingly supranational economy.

ETHNIC INTEREST GROUPS

Fueros provided legal status not only for regional groups but for ethnic groups as well. Jews and Muslims, *mestizos* and *conversos,* each had their own distinct legal status as well as distinct privileges, taxation, and exemptions. Of all the interest groups, ethnic-based groups present the greatest difficulty to the state. Corporatist and statist systems depend on a large degree of cooptation and compulsory association. Outside players, such as the Church, the army, and labor groups, are given insider status in an effort to bring them in line with government directives. Ethnic identities generally refuse such cooptation. Their identity depends on being separate and distinct from the government. Relying on tradition and myths, ethnic enclaves are often able to generate enormous hostility to a bureaucratic government hoping to be recognized as the voice of the general will.

An unwillingness to appear coopted has been most clearly seen with the Basque separatist movement ETA (*Euskadi Ta Askatasuna*, which means "Fatherland and Freedom" in Basque) and its attendant political party HB (*Herri Batasuna*, "Popular Unity"). To counteract this dangerous climate, the central government has attempted to maintain strict controls over the process of devolution. The Organic Law on the Harmonization of the Autonomy Process (LOAPA—Ley Orgánica de Armonización del Proceso Autonómico), approved in July 1981, is an example of such an effort. This controversial legislation laid out often Byzantine methods by which the regions could achieve autonomy. Yet even the grants of limited autonomy were not enough for the ETA, which launched a campaign of violence that lasted through the González government. Airports were bombed and regional ministers were kidnapped, prompting right-wing forces within the military to consider their hand at another coup.

The González government attempted to outlaw HB, but the Spanish Supreme Court declared unconstitutional any effort to remove a political party from its rightfully won seats in parliament. Although ETA has seen a decline in popular support over the past few years, ethnic identification itself is not on the decline. *Fueros*, kinship ties, language barriers, a strong sense of regional identity, and a cultural mistrust of government all contribute to a climate that supports ethnic identification. Just because the government, by 1983, had recognized the seventeen autonomous communities does not mean the ethnic members have any intention of being coopted.

AD HOC INTEREST GROUPS AND NGOs

At the other end of the political spectrum from ethnic groups are ad hoc interest groups and nongovernmental organizations (NGOs). Whereas the former act as if they operate beyond the jurisdiction of Madrid and Lisbon, the latter gain legitimacy through their negotiations with the state. With the transition to democracy, Spain and Portugal have seen a rise in groups that form around a single cause, such as the prevention of AIDS and cruelty to animals, or against a single issue, such as NATO's air strikes in Kosovo. It is not unusual to see peaceful demonstrations in front of government buildings and volunteers out gathering signatures in front of the cathedrals. Street graffiti is often of a political nature, against the central government (and NATO and the EU) and for a particular region. Some of the anti-EU graffiti in Spain has taken on an eerie, nationalist expression, "Franco is not dead," said one. "He is only sleeping."

Often these ad hoc groups and NGOs are coopted by the state. Concerns about domestic violence and child abuse created places for women's advocates within the Spanish government. Rather than lobby for change from the outside, women's organizations took on key policy roles inside of government, often working in tandem with the Church to provide shelter and counseling. The support and funding to prevent domestic violence, interestingly enough, is not unlike the system used in the United States. With the passing of the 1994 Crime Bill, American women's shelters now receive federal funds in exchange for coordinating services with the local states' attorney offices.

However, the shift to more democratic ways, to interest groups and participatory government, has not necessarily made Spain and Portugal less enamored of the older ways, particularly when those ways are being challenged from the outside. We have mentioned the challenge to the siesta. Many thought that bullfighting would also end once Spain entered the modern world, but in fact, interest in bullfighting is on the upswing, despite international efforts to "save the bulls." In 1990 a German member of the European Parliament attempted to ameliorate conditions for the bull by banning the role of the *picadores*, the three bullfighters who implant small spears in the bull's shoulders in an effort to wear him out, through blood loss and frustration, before the *matador* enters the ring. That effort was unsuccessful, but the Spanish members may have a tougher time in the political battles to come.

INTEREST GROUPS IN THE NEW EUROPE

Interest group pluralism has been slow to develop in Spain and Portugal. Except for some brief activity in Portugal during and after the 1974 revolution, peasant groups have not formed a strong political force. Those unhappy with the poverty of the countryside have voted with their feet and left for the cities. Nor have students, a natural power base in many developing countries, created a lasting coalition. Since the end of the dictatorships, student activism has declined in both countries. The middle-class, however, has been steadily growing, and with it various middle-class organizations and associations. Given the trend of depolarization, noted at the end of chapter 5, most of these associations are nonpolitical in nature. A 1990 study ranked the types of voluntary associations in terms of participation. Athletic clubs and neighborhood groups drew the most attendance, student, consumer, and environmental groups drew the least, and political parties fell somewhere in the middle.[5]

Historically, family allegiances and kinship rivalries severely reduced the ability to form associations on anything but a clan basis. Groups that were able to organize, organized on a vertical basis, reproducing the top-down authoritarian structure modeled by the state. Without strong horizontal alliances, it is no wonder that Iberian politics swung between dictatorship and chaos, between a rigid backbone of authority and an invertebrate nation.

Recent studies have shown that an independent, organized society was developing during the final decades of the Franco and Salazar regimes.[6] The labor movement in particular needed to be highly organized in order to survive the repressive conditions in both countries. Business interests, hoping to improve economic conditions, needed to organize outside of the heavily regulated system engineered by Franco and Salazar. Students and intellectuals also organized outside of the regimes. When more democratic institutions were put in place, these groups quickly rose to assert their influence. This was not the case with the groups that had been coopted by these regimes. In Spain, neither the army nor the Church had developed much of an organization outside of the Franco regime. In Portugal, however, the army, dissatisfied with the African policy, had developed a group awareness separate from the ruling regime. This put the army briefly in a powerful position when the Caetano government was toppled.

What we haven't seen in either country are interest group lobbying or groups that maintain their organization as something separate from the state. In both Spain and Portugal, there is a tradition of looking to the state to solve problems rather than to the private sector. This has created a swelling in the bureaucracy, as more administrators are required to implement these new social programs. Indeed this group (government bureaucracy) is now one of the largest and best organized in the country, wielding immense power because of its control of the state machinery. Unfortunately, the civil service does not pay very well, and many of the public officials are vulnerable to bribes or feel compelled to take private sector positions, thus blurring the line between public and private interest. Further, the Spanish and Portuguese civil services are famous for their inefficiency. Offices employ people just to stand in line and fill out the many complicated forms needed in order to conduct business. This inefficiency is most apparent in the legal system, where plaintiffs have been known to wait eight years in order to have their cases heard. It is hard to carry out downsizing and privatization in such a system.

The Spanish and Portuguese states are still bureaucratic and only partially pluralistic. The interest groups tend to deal with each other not directly but indirectly through the state system. The state is still the leading voice in settling labor disputes, despite statutory claims to the contrary. Interest groups are required to fulfill various state requirements before they can be recognized as legitimate, thus adding to the state's influence. These features have led many analysts to conclude that Spain and Portugal are still corporative systems. They are no longer corporative in the old, Franco and Salazar, exclusionary sense, but in the newer, less hierarchical, European, and more inclusive sense of trying to tie all the groups together under the guidance of the state, a system that some have called neocorporatism.

In general, pluralism has not been the experience of European political development. Instead, Western European governments have traditionally taken an active role in coordinating and defining the needs of the various groups as well as limiting who may represent those interests. We have discussed the corporatist policies of the Franco and Salazar regimes, in which the state was the prime actor in a bureaucratic, hierarchical, repressive system. Not only did the state determine who should do what, but the elite representatives were, in turn, responsible for disciplining the subordinate members.

Since the end of the dictatorships, Spain and Portugal have followed a system closer to that found in France, *étatiste* or statism. As in the corporatist system, the government continues to play a leading role in determining the functions of the various political actors. For this reason, the range and number of interests needs to be manageable, as the state cannot keep too many balls in the air at the same time. From a democratic perspective, statism has advantages over the corporatist system as the playing field is more level and less hierarchical. Workers can organize as easily as bosses; consumers receive the same audience as producers; manufacturers are subject to the same governmental restrictions as environmentalists. The primary mode of action of the statist system is regulation. Groups come into existence in an effort to amend existing regulation or to curb proposed ones. Welfare provisions also tie the groups to the central government; in order to qualify for the latest social welfare provisions, the various groups need to be recognized by the state. Italy and Belgium have similarly statist systems.[7]

Spain and Portugal offer a variation on the statist theme. The balance of power between the state and corporate groups has been greatly affected by the tradition of *fueros*. These organic laws delineate the rights and responsibilities between the central government and the corporate group, acting as a restraint on both parties. Because the governing arrangement is more like a contract than a unilateral agreement, we have come to think of Spain and Portugal as "contract states." Rather than one constitution that applies equally to each citizen, Spain and Portugal maintain a plurality of contracts that govern the political behavior of the various corporate groups as well as that of the central government.[8]

The compacts worked out between the state and the Roman Catholic Church in the Middle Ages still carry some legal authority in the twentieth century, which may explain why even the socialist González government, operating under a constitution that guarantees freedom of religion, agreed to subsidize the Roman Catholic Church. The contract between Navarre and the state is still being touted by workers unhappy with government demands for more productivity. Even in modern times, the democratic roots of the peninsula, particularly in the sense of a limited government, go back to medieval soil.

All of these systems, whether defined as corporative, statist, or a contract state, have come under attack since the 1980s. A global economy has promoted deregulation, causing a major erosion in the powers and authority of the nation-state. The labor market has steadily weakened as a result of high unemployment and unstable employment. The European Union (EU) has taken on the role of the supreme regulator; groups which used to protest or promote national policies are now forming international alliances to lobby the bureaucrats in Brussels. And multinational corporations further complicate the picture by conducting much of their business outside of the regulatory arm of the nation-state.

What this means is that Spain and Portugal have been following a very different development program than other European countries. The bans on interest group activity during the Franco and Salazar regimes created a society with little experience in civic participation. With the transition to democracy, both governments not only lacked the necessary institutions but they suffered from a "democratic deficiency," that is, a population with little training in democratic values such as interest group participation. In order to have a responsive government, Spain and Portugal needed citizens who knew what it meant to make reasonable political demands.

Unlike the U.S. Constitution, which came out of a civic-minded society, the Spanish and Portuguese constitutions were drafted before a civic culture was actually established. In its inception, the Portuguese constitution envisioned a socialist society, one that valued workers' rights and universal benefits. The Spanish constitution, on the other hand, envisioned a pluralist society, one that valued political participation and a sense of individual rights. Both Spain and Portugal introduced constitutional guarantees concerning their citizens' quality of life. These guarantees became the basis for demands for an extensive social welfare system, entitlements that most other Western Europeans had taken for granted since World War II and were at risk of losing.

While other European countries have been cutting back on entitlements, Spain and Portugal have been increasing their social programs, with almost half of government expenditures going to education and health. Thanks to these generous national programs, Spanish and Portuguese citizens have begun to develop a sense of individual rights, the social basis, according to some political scientists, for democratic pluralism. Those benefits, however, are being offered at a time when austerity measures from the EU demand a cut in public spending. Without generous social programs will these new democratic attitudes fade away?

Interest groups make up one part of a civil society. Political parties are an equally important component. The third aspect of a civil society has to do with its relationship to the state. The following two chapters consider the development of political parties and the Iberian tradition of state-society relationships.

NOTES

1. David McKay, *Essentials of American Government* (Boulder, Col.: Westview Press, 2000), 273–74.
2. José Ortega y Gasset, *The Revolt of the Masses* (New York: Norton, 1932), 89.
3. John Hooper, *The New Spaniards* (New York: Penguin, 1995), 126.
4. Suzanne Daley, "Spain Rudely Awakened to Workaday World," *New York Times*, December 26, 1999, 1.
5. Peter McDonough, Samuel H. Barnes, and Antonio López Pina, *The Cultural Dynamics of Democratization in Spain* (Ithaca: Cornell University Press, 1998), 151.
6. Soledad Garcia, "The Spanish Experience and Its Implications for a Citizen's Europe," in *The Anthropology of Europe,* ed. Victora A. Goddard et al. (London: Berg, 1996).
7. Colin Crouch and Anand Menon, "Organized Interests and the State," in *Developments in West European Politics*, ed. Martin Rhodes, Paul Heywood, and Vincent Wright (New York: St. Martin's Press, 1997).
8. Howard J. Wiarda, "State-Society Relations in Latin America: Toward a Theory of the Contract State," in *American Foreign Policy Toward Latin America in the 80s and 90s* (New York: New York University Press, 1992); also Howard J. Wiarda, *Politics in Iberia: The Political Systems of Spain and Portugal* (New York: Harper & Row, 1990).

Chapter 7

Political Parties and Elections

Political parties and elections are essential ingredients in democracy, but they are relatively new in Spain and Portugal. Early in the twentieth century, a nascent party system had begun to form in both countries, but it was snuffed out by the dictatorships of Franco and Salazar-Caetano. Both the Franco and Salazar regimes then created a single, official party to serve as an instrument of authoritarian control, but there were no free and democratic elections, and party competition was proscribed. Hence, it was only in 1974–75 with the Portuguese revolution and the death of Franco that a modern, competitive, democratic party system emerged for the first time.[1]

There is more to the issue, however, than retarded party development and dictatorships that eliminated political parties. A long tradition exists in Spain and Portugal that is antiparty, of whatever kind. Political parties have long been seen as divisive agencies, detracting from the unity and integrity of the nation and the state, committed to narrow partisan interests over grander national concerns. This stand is not entirely unique: remember that George Washington warned against "factions" (by which he meant political parties) and that former French president Charles de Gaulle was similarly opposed to the factional divisiveness of parties. In Spain and Portugal, however, antiparty-ism has a philosophical base as well as a practical one. For if one accepts the longtime Spanish and Portuguese notions, discussed in chapter 2, of the need for organic harmony and unity in society, then there is no need or room for political parties; indeed, parties are viewed as negative influences. Attitudes toward political parties historically are thus remarkably parallel to those toward divisive interest groups; and if both of these are viewed in negative ways, that has enormous implications for political party and interest group history, for the pluralist base of society, and ultimately for democracy itself.

Spanish and Portuguese political parties and functioning party systems, therefore, like pluralist interest groups, have only been in existence for about twenty-five years. That is probably too short a time for parties and the party systems to have been fully consolidated and institutionalized as the only legitimate way of presenting candidates, articulating interests, and determining political outcomes. On the other hand, within this relatively short period the parties have been well established, a full party spectrum has come into existence, and democracy and elections have been strongly legitimated as the only avenue to political power. Hence, in this chapter we look at both the emergence of political parties and their strengths, as well as their continuing weaknesses—for to the degree parties are strong, democracy in Spain and Portugal is also strengthened; but to the degree they are weak, disrespected, and disorganized, democracy may also be in trouble.

HISTORY OF POLITICAL PARTIES

Spain and Portugal have long had factions that can be seen as the precursors of today's political parties. During the late Middle Ages, as Spain and Portugal emerged as centralized nations, these factions debated vigorously, and were often at war, over the issues that we have seen as constants in Spanish and Portuguese life: centralism versus regionalism, the power of the state versus corporate group rights, the extent and form of popular participation and representation, and the role of the Church and religion in national life. These intense disputes indicate that Spain and Portugal were not always monolithically authoritarian, that there were rival factions and positions, that the seeds of a Spanish and Portuguese form of democracy were present, that the outcomes were not foreordained.

It was not until the eighteenth century, however, that the factions that would serve as the forerunners of the modern political debate emerged. The issue was the reforms carried out by the new Bourbon monarchy in Spain and by the reformer Pombal in Portugal. The debate divided Spain and Portugal into two rival "families" of interests, two rival "countries." On the one side were urban Spain and urban Portugal, commercial elements, a small middle class, intellectuals, Freemasons, and modernizing elements who favored the reforms, believed in rationalism and the Enlightenment, were European-oriented, and were often antichurch and antireligion. On the other side were rural Spain and rural Portugal, the landed class, the Church, the conservative peasantry, the Counter-Reformation, traditionalists in general, and defenders of Spanish/Portugese uniqueness, anti-Europeans. This split in the Spanish and Portuguese bodies politic deeply divided the two countries and was exacerbated by the French Revolution of 1789, which polarized both nations and persisted into modern times.

In the nineteenth century these divisions seemed to become only deeper. On one side was an emerging nationalism and liberalism (and anticlericalism) that sometimes verged on libertinage (chaotic, anarchic); on the other was a traditionalism that hardened into reaction, seeking to restore the absolutism and orthodoxy of the sixteenth century. The immediate issues varied: the "liberal" (by Spanish standards) constitution of 1812, rival pretenders to the throne, issues like education and industrialization; but the underlying question was the future direction and destiny of the Spanish and Portuguese nations. One group, heirs to the eighteenth-century Enlightenment, favored constitutionalism, a limited monarchy (like the British), representative government, and basic political freedoms. The other group opposed all change, wanted to restore the Catholic Church to its privileged position, and favored absolute monarchy. These differences produced numerous conflicts, civil wars, and military *pronunciamientos* (revolts) throughout the nineteenth century—even though the long-term trend was away from reaction and toward greater liberalism.

In the latter part of the nineteenth century and the early twentieth, some real political parties began to emerge out of the earlier cleavages. Portugal remained a monarchy until 1910 and Spain until 1931, but even under the monarchy parties continued to grow. In the early years the main opposition to the monarchy was led by the republicans, who favored either abolishing the monarchy or limiting it by constitution, but at different times, and usually clandestinely, Marxist, socialist, and anarchist groups also emerged. The establishment of the Portuguese Republic, 1910–26, led to a flowering of new political parties and factions which were often so divided, disorganized, and chaotic that a reaction both against them and the republic itself took place. The founding of the Spanish Republic, 1931–36, similarly led to an explosion of political activity and parties, including the Falange, socialist, communist, anarchist, and other groups. As in Portugal, this explosion of political parties and the chaos, upheaval, and eventually violence (each party had its own armed militia) that went with it produced an equally violent reaction against the parties and against democracy itself. In 1926 in Portugal and in the Spanish civil war of 1936–39, the army rose up to reestablish order, snuff out the parties, and quash democracy. The ensuing Salazar and Franco regimes meant an end to the parties and the emerging party systems for the next forty years.

POLITICAL PARTIES UNDER AUTHORITARIANISM

Franco and Salazar shared the antiparty attitude that had long been present in Spain and Portugal. They believed that parties were divisive, corrupt, and inefficient, that they detracted from the unity and integrity of the nation, and that they should be illegalized.[2] And looking at the chaotic, unstable, violence-prone Portuguese and Spanish republics that constituted Franco's and Salazar's formative learning experiences, it is easy to understand these antiparty sentiments.

Hence, with the coming to power of Salazar in Portugal and Franco in Spain, political parties and the party "system" were eclipsed and illegalized. Many party leaders were jailed, forced underground, sent into exile, or (especially in Spain, in the aftermath of the civil war) killed. The most severe actions were taken against the parties of the left (socialists, communists, anarchists); there was clearly an ideological dimension (right versus left) to the suppression of the parties and the persecution of their leaders. But Franco and Salazar were against all parties, against all factionalism and divisionism, and took action against the right parties as well as the left. Salazar snuffed out Raol Preto's fascist Integralist Party and was not kindly disposed to the monarchists (he never did, despite pressure to do so, restore the monarchy); similarly, Franco coopted the Falange even while isolating the real fascists in Spain and restored the monarchy only late in his rule as a way (which we saw in a previous chapter did not work out as he had planned) of perpetuating his system of government.

To replace the old illegalized parties, Franco and Salazar created or gave their blessings to parties of their own. Salazar created the *União Nacional* (National Union—UN) while Franco took over the Falange, which he then renamed The Movement. Note that neither of these were called "parties," in keeping with their leaders' disdain for such organizations, but were "national unions" or "movements." The two organizations were meant to function as civic associations, rallying agencies to unify public opinion rather than divisive parties in the traditional sense.

Immediately after their incorporation as official parties, it was widely thought the Falange and the *União* would become fascist and totalitarian organizations, as in Mussolini's Italy or Nazi Germany. But that never happened. Neither party ever developed a complete fascist ideology. Nor was much power ever devolved upon them. Neither Spain nor Portugal ever became a party-state, with all power resting in the party, like the Soviet Union. Recall the discussion in chapter 3: it was Franco and Salazar, personally, who ruled their countries, not the parties. The parties were really appendages to their personal dictatorships and constituted just one instrument of domination among several; the parties never were at the core of decision making in these two regimes nor did they ever become party-ruled regimes.

If the parties were not at the heart of these two regimes, what did they do? Here we briefly summarize their functions, remembering that these "parties" did not do what parties do in democratic countries and that some of their functions are still present in current Spanish and Portuguese parties.

First, the parties stood for and symbolized unity, in contrast with the divisiveness of the past. They extolled national togetherness, rejuvenation (after the discouragements of republicanism), and nationalism. Second, they functioned as agencies of propaganda, publishing exhortations to love of duty and country, criticizing regime opponents, and lauding the government's accomplishments. Third, along with the secret police, they helped keep tabs on the population, maintaining files on politically active persons and rooting out dissenters. Fourth (a function not very different from that of democratic parties), the party served as a recruiting agency for young, rising politicians, and as a "resting place" for old or out-of-favor ones. Fifth, the party helped keep the loyalty of the population. Membership in the official party was required for all government and many private sector jobs. Nor could one get a passport, travel abroad, or open a business without a party card. Sixth, the party functioned as a giant national patronage agency. Along with jobs, it often dispensed toys to children, sewing machines to widows, wooden legs to indigent soldiers—to say nothing of government contracts, favors, and access. This system is once again similar to the feudal contract or Seneca's idea of the Gift: favors rendered in return for loyalty and service in a vast hierarchy of patronage that reached from local and regional to national levels. If one has an understanding of big city political machines in the United States and can translate this to national levels, one can then understand how the Spanish and Portuguese official parties functioned as patronage machines based on the principle of a favor for a favor.

Only incidentally, seventh, did the parties do what we in democratic systems think of parties doing: drafting platforms and running candidates in elections. Both countries held elections regularly, but remember that all other parties had been banned, competition was not allowed, and the official party always won. The official party put up candidates who usually ran desultory campaigns and were "elected" without opposition. These were, in short, ratifactory elections designed to reaffirm the ruling party in office but not to provide real choice. The only "politics" occurred (as in the old U.S. one-party South) before the election, when the choice of which candidates would get the official party's nomination was made. Such elections provided limited legitimacy to the Franco and Salazar regimes and also served as indicators as to which way the winds were blowing within the regime, but they were by no means democratic.

Toward the end, both of these long-term authoritarian parties began to open up somewhat to new influences. Within Franco's Movement, one could begin to see left, center, right, Christian-Democratic, and monarchist factions that began to function almost like political parties within the system. In Portugal, Salazar's old *União Nacional* was rebaptized as the *Accão Nacional Popular* (ANP) by his successor, Marcello Caetano, in an effort to revitalize the tired regime. Within the ANP there were similarly liberal, moderate, and ultraconservative factions. But it took the Portuguese Revolution of 1974 and Franco's death in 1975 before a functioning democratic party system came into existence.

THE EMERGENCE OF A NEW PARTY SYSTEM

The present-day party systems in Spain and Portugal had their origins under the old dictatorships. At least four forces were at work. The first was the increasing factionalism already alluded to within the official parties of the old regime. Once the dictatorships ended, several of these factions emerged as separative political parties in the new democratic climate.

A second source of new parties was the "tolerated opposition" that had emerged in the late 1960s and early 1970s in both Spain and Portugal, while the dictatorship was still in power. By this time authoritarianism in Spain and Portugal had considerably softened; opposition political parties were still not allowed, but opposition "study groups" could and did function. They held meetings, issued statements on public policy, and even published their own newspapers. These groups were monitored by the police but no longer persecuted. Moreover, such tolerated opposition was still limited to moderate and centrist groups; socialists and communists were not allowed to function in this way and were still persecuted. Once the Portuguese regime was overthrown and Franco died, a number of these study groups, such as the Portuguese Social Democrats, emerged as regular political parties.

A third source of future political party cadres was the underground. In both Spain and Portugal in the 1960s and early 1970s, socialist, communist, and other radical groups were active in the underground movement, recruiting students, workers, and intellectuals. The underground was especially active in organizing labor unions that fought for higher wages, increased benefits, and improved working conditions. These underground labor groups often challenged the official or corporatist *sindicatos*. And though strikes were illegal and the underground unions had no legal standing or right to bargain, the government sometimes dealt with them anyway as a way of maintaining industrial peace. Later, once the Portuguese dictatorship had been overthrown and Franco had died, a number of these previously underground groups emerged to provide the mass base for the socialist and communist parties that were then formed.

The fourth element important in the formation of a new party system was the exiled opposition. This included mainly the leaders of the socialist and communist parties, plus independents, who had often lived abroad for long periods of time. There were often close but indirect connections between the underground movements mentioned above and these exiled leaders. Once the Portuguese regime was ousted in 1974 and Franco died in 1975, these leaders were allowed to come back to their countries as part of an amnesty arrangement and the general liberalization. A number of the returning exiles then assumed leadership roles in the revived socialist and communist parties being formed.

This view of the later Franco and Salazar regimes shows them as more porous than the usual picture we have of them as monolithic dictatorships. Toward the end of these regimes, a variety of activities was going on that would not have been tolerated before. There were opposition study groups, underground movements, and clandestine as well as openly oppositionist newspapers; sensing the end might be near for these aging regimes, the opposition was mobilizing, planning for the future. These activities help explain why, when the Salazar/Caetano regime was overthrown and Franco died, a full-fledged party system sprang up so quickly. For the nuclei of the parties were *already in place* even while the old regime continued to fuction; and when these regimes collapsed, the new parties, with their leaders returning from exile and the underground swelling their mass base, sprang quickly to life.

THE PARTY SPECTRUMS

The political party spectrums in Spain and Portugal are wide and remarkably similar. In part, this is due to the common culture and parallel histories of the two countries, to the fact that both became democracies during the same time period, and to mutual watching and learning from each other. However, while the party spectrums are parallel, there are interesting differences as well. The party spectrum of the two countries is shown graphically in Table 7.1.

On the far left in both countries are a number of small, often radical, sometimes revolutionary groups. But because they are vocal, they get attention out of proportion to their actual vote count. Often they are centered in the universities and among intellectuals but receive modest support among workers as well. In Portugal the left bloc, consisting of radicals, far-left ecologists and fem-

Table 7.1
The Party Systems of Spain and Portugal

		Spain			
	Left		*Center*	*Right*	
Radical left groups	Communist Party (PCE)	Socialist Party (PSOE)	Union of Democratic Center (UCD)	Popular Party (PP)	Other right-wing groups
		REGIONAL/PROVINCIAL PARTIES			
		Portugal			
	Left		*Center*	*Right*	
Radical left groups (left bloc and Socialist Revolutionary Party [PSR])	Communist Party (PCP)	Socialist Party (PS)	Social Democratic Party (PSD)	Social Democratic Center (CDS)/Popular Party (PP)	Monarchists and other right-wing groups

inists, and members of the Socialist Revolutionary Party (PSR), won two seats in parliament in the 1999 elections, giving it political bargaining power. In Spain the far left was similarly strengthened for a time by the increasing moderation and reasonableness of Felipe González's Socialist Workers' Party.

The main party on the far left in both countries is the Communist Party. Both the Spanish and the Portuguese communist parties have long histories of defiance and martyrdom during the Franco and Salazar dictatorships; their leaders spent long years in jail or exile while the rank-and-file was often the core of the underground opposition. Both parties were orthodox, Moscow-oriented, Marxist-Leninist parties in the Soviet mold.

But after Franco's death and the fall of the dictatorship in Portugal, the two parties diverged. The Spanish Communist Party (PCE) became much more moderate. Led by Santiago Carillo, it espoused the doctrine of "Eurocommunism," which meant respect for democratic elections and freedom. The PCE was somewhere between a Western European (democratic) and an Eastern European (Soviet bloc) socialist party. It wanted socialism but by electoral means. In part, this stance was ideologically driven; in part, it was driven by Spain's circumstances in the mid-1970s, favoring democracy and not revolutionary upheaval.

The PCE won 9 percent of the vote in the first national election (1977) after Franco died; in subsequent elections its vote stayed at around 10 percent or less. The party was hurt by the growing middle classness of Spain, the moderation of Spanish voters, the desire not to refight the civil war of the 1930s, and eventually by the demise of the Soviet Union. It was also outflanked on the left by the Spanish Socialist Party (see below) and spent much of the 1980s and 1990s trying to present itself as a left alternative to the socialists but still within a democratic mold.

The Portuguese Communist Party (PCP) took an opposite trajectory. Its leader, Alvaro Cunhal, was a tough, old-line, Moscow-oriented communist who believed in Leninist revolutionary solutions, not democratic ones. In the confusion that accompanied the Portuguese revolution of 1974–75, he attempted to stage a communist takeover and came close to succeeding, but was eventually thwarted by more moderate military and civilian elements.

The PCP received 17 percent of the vote in the 1975 election, Portugal's first after the overthrow of the dictatorship, and in several subsequent elections stayed in the respectable 12–15 percent range. This high percentage, compared to the Spanish communists' election results, may be attributable to greater Portuguese poverty compared to Spain, the small size of the middle class, the strong organizing efforts of the PCP, and the strong sense of frustration felt by many Portuguese voters. But during the 1980s and 1990s, as Portugal became more affluent and middle class, the PCP's vote percentage dropped to under 10 percent; again, the collapse of the Soviet Union and the PCP's being outflanked on the left by the socialists further weakened the party. New leaders and a more moderate platform seem not to have improved the party's support.

Moving next to the socialist parties of Spain and Portugal, we again find striking similarities as well as differences. Both socialist parties have a long history; both were forced underground or into exile by the dictatorships; and both reemerged following the end of authoritarianism. Both parties have moderated their positions away from socialism and toward European-style social democracy; both have enjoyed electoral success and been tempered by elected office and government responsibilities.

During the revolutionary situation in Portugal in 1974–75, the Socialist Party (PS) was seen as the most viable, moderate alternative to the Communist Party. The right had been ousted and discredited and the center was divided, so the main choice was on the left: socialist versus communist. The PS was, therefore, the recipient of much foreign support as a way of keeping the communists out of power; it also received centrist domestic votes that it would not otherwise have had. Led by the articulate and shrewd Mario Soares, the PS won the elections of 1975 and 1976 with a plurality of 38 and 35 percent of the vote, respectively. It formed the first elected government after the revolution, 1976–78, and participated as a partner in several coalition governments through the mid-1980s, when it was eclipsed for a decade by the PS.

But in 1995, with 44 percent of the vote, and then again in 1999, with 44.1 percent, the socialists emerged once more as the largest party and formed the government. Under the pragmatic leadership of António Guterres, the party was much more moderate and centrist than it had been two decades earlier. By this time, it had set aside its Marxist rhetoric, welcomed foreign investment, and governed as a social-democratic party. Indeed, in carrying out privatization, government streamlining, and budget restraint, the party was not much different from its centrist rival.

The Spanish Socialist Workers' Party (PSOE) went through much the same evolution. In exile and in the immediate aftermath of Franco's death, it remained quite radical—on some issues farther to the left than the Spanish Communist Party. But then it began tempering its positions; losing the first post-Franco parliamentary election in 1977 undoubtedly played a role in the PSOE altering its position. In the late 1970s, now under the leadership of the pragmatic Felipe González, it abandoned its earlier Marxian rhetoric ("class struggle," "dictatorship of the proletariat") and adopted more centrist positions. On that basis, it won the elections of 1982, 1987, and 1992, ushering in a fourteen-year period (1982–96) of socialist rule with González as prime minister.

In office, the PSOE continued its move to the center. With González leading the campaign, Spain's voters opted for membership in NATO, to which the older PSOE had long been opposed. In 1986 Spain joined the European Economic Community. The socialist government expanded social programs while also welcoming foreign investment and offering assurances to domestic capital. The older socialist agenda of nationalizations, land redistribution, and anticlericalism was put to rest. There remained a radical, Marxist wing within the PSOE, but it was now a minority.

The PSOE presided over a period of unprecedented economic growth and modernization in Spain. As in Portugal, it was enormously helped by large EEC subsidies, aid, and construction projects (highways, railways, hospitals, schools) that began to bring Spain up to European living standards. But eventually fatigue with González and his government set in; there were numerous charges of corruption and abuse of power; and the PSOE's popularity slipped. In 1996 it lost power to its conservative rival, José María Aznar, and the People's Party; in 2000 it lost again.

The left (communist, socialist) of the Spanish/Portuguese political spectrum thus exhibits some remarkable similarities, but as we move to the center and right the differences become more pronounced. The immediate post-Franco center in Spain was occupied by the Union of the Democratic Center (UCD). The UCD was the creation of transitional prime minister Adolfo Suárez, who had been appointed by the king in 1976 to lead Spain from authoritarianism to democracy. The UCD had little clear program or ideology but was a loose coalition of fourteen smaller groups (technocrats, bureaucrats,

Christian-democrats, moderates, independents, former Franco supporters, friends of the young prime minister, some monarchists) who were dedicated to keeping themselves in power and the socialists out.

Capitalizing on the popularity of Suárez, the party's control of the government machinery, and the lingering fear in many quarters of the socialists, the UCD won the first post-Franco election in 1977 by 34 to 28 percent over the PSOE; its vote increased slightly in the 1979 election. But after that, the party's various factions fell to quarreling; Suárez, disgusted, resigned as party leader; and the party suffered an inglorious defeat at the hands of the socialists in 1982. After that, it completely disintegrated. At one point, Suárez attempted to put together a new centrist party, the Social and Democratic Center (CDS), but it failed to win significant electoral support. For many of the years that the socialists were in power, therefore, no effective center party was operative in Spain.

In Portugal the situation was similar in some respects and different in others. When the Portuguese revolution occurred in 1974, the center was largely wiped out; the center and right had been so discredited by association with the dictatorship that everyone wanted to be on the left. The communists, socialists, and social-democrats (PSD) outdid each other in seeking to advance reformist and revolutionary positions. The struggle between the socialists and communists received the most media attention, but over time the PSD advanced a more moderate position and in the first post–dictatorship election in 1975 received 27 percent of the vote (to the socialists' 38 percent and the communists' 17 percent).

In the years immediately following the revolution, a young, charismatic leader, Francisco Sá Carneíro, sought to rebuild the democratic center in Portugal. Patterning his movement after Suárez's successful (for a time) UCD in Spain, Sá Carneíro built a broad-based coalition, incorporating various groups, to challenge the power of the socialists and communists. As with the UCD, his coalition consisted of social-democrats, Christian-democrats, moderates, independents, liberals, and monarchists. In this endeavor, Sá Carneíro was remarkably successful: his coalition (called Democratic Alliance—AD) won the 1979 election with 43 percent of the vote. But in 1980 the dynamic Sá Carneíro was killed in a plane crash and, as in Spain during this same period, his center-right coalition began to disintegrate.

The largest party in the AD coalition had been the social-democrats. In the early 1980s, the PSD was torn by factionalism, but by 1985 a new leader, Aníbal Cavaco Silva, had emerged. Under Cavaco Silva the PSD won a plurality in the 1985 election; he then led his party to absolute majorities (unprecedented in Portuguese party history) in both 1987 and 1991. Cavaco Silva reorganized the party as a strong centrist party, which also brought in business and conservative votes. He presided over Portugal's entry into the EEC in 1986 and over the unprecedented prosperity and stability that ensued. The PSD has now taken its place as the dominant center-right party in Portugal, vying with the socialists to control the government. It tells us a great deal about the balance of political power in Portugal since the 1974 revolution that a social-democratic party (usually considered quite liberal in the American context) constitutes the center-right. But in fact, the PSD in Portugal is quite conservative and is now considered the party of business and the middle class.

Now let us move to the right of the political spectrum. Again, there are parallels as well as major differences between the two countries.

Immediately after Franco's death, the right in Spain organized as *Alianza Popular* (AP) under Manuel Fraga. Ironically, when he had served in Franco's cabinet, Fraga had been considered "liberal," but now in the changed context of post-Francoism he was considered far-right. Though one of Spain's foremost intellectuals, neither Fraga nor his party did very well at the polls, receiving 8 percent in the 1977 general elections and only 6 percent in 1979. With the disintegration of the centrist UCD in the 1982 election and the continued discrediting of the right, an immense space had opened up in the Spanish political system in the center-right.

Fraga continued to struggle as leader of the AP during the 1980s, but the party increasingly fragmented and his leadership was questioned. In 1988 the old AP was reorganized as the Popular Party (PP), and the following year a new leader, José María Aznar, a colorless but level-headed lawyer, was named. Aznar began to rebuild the party base and to resurrect the coalition of centrists and rightists that had once formed the UCD and the AP. In 1989 the PP received 26 percent of the vote; in the runup to the 1993 election, it received 34. 8 percent; and in 1996, it received a plurality of votes with 38 percent to the PSOE's 37 percent. As the largest vote-getters, Aznar and the PP formed the next government; they won again and gained a parliamentary majority in 2000.

The PP does not have a clear program; it is more of a catch-all electoral apparatus than an ideological party. However, it has succeeded in bringing together most of the factions and small parties of the center and right that once supported UCD and AP. Aznar was skillful in reforming this center-right coalition, thus filling the vast gap on that side of the political spectrum. In office he followed moderate, centrist policies, privatized some government-run industries but not Spain's elaborate social welfare programs, integrated Spain more closely into the EU and NATO, and followed a policy friendly to business. Aznar's success in first coopting all center-right groups, then moving the entire PP to the center for electoral purposes, means that Spain now largely lacks the right wing movements (Falangists, monarchists, Francoists) that were so powerful in the past.

The Portuguese right experienced a parallel trajectory. Discredited after the 1974 revolution, it virtually disappeared for a period. What remained of the right was largely coopted, first by Sá Carneíro's AD and then by Cavaco Silva's PSD. The small conservative groups remaining were organized at first in the Social Democratic Center Party (CDS) under Diógo Freitas de Amaral. The CDS was a Christian-democratic party but, despite the fact that Portugal is an overwhelmingly Catholic country, it never achieved major electoral importance, falling below 5 percent in both the 1987 and 1991 elections. As more and more of its voters were absorbed into the PSD during the 1980s, the CDS decided to reorganize itself as the Popular Party (PP) under the leadership of Manuel Monteíro. The PP took a more libertarian, Thatcherite direction and in the 1995 election increased its vote strength to 10 percent (surpassing the communists as the third largest party). The PP participated as a coalition partner in both socialist and social-democratic governments, but it seems destined to remain a minor party.

The far-far right, once powerful in both countries, is now all but nonexistent. In both Spain and Portugal there remains far-right, ultraconservative, monarchist, authoritarian, and fascist sentiment, but not enough votes in any of these positions to be significant electorally. The far-right, which based its strength on the army, the Church, and the oligarchy, knew perfectly well that, if democracy ever came to their countries, they would lose their power; now that fear has been borne out: democracy makes a difference.

Finally, both countries have regional parties, but they are far stronger in Spain than in Portugal. Portugal's regional parties are really branches of the main parties that sometimes go their own way—not altogether different from the regional differences in U.S. parties. For example, in the Portuguese islands of Madeira and the Azores, the dominant PSD tends to be more conservative than its mainland counterpart because the islands themselves are more conservative. Separatist sentiment is almost nil, especially after Portugal joined the EEC and was showered with subsidies—but when the mainland ignores the islands or is convulsed in upheaval, as in the 1974 revolution, nationalist-separatist sentiment tends to grow.

Regional sentiment in Spain is far stronger and the regional parties more important as well (for a detailed treatment, see chapters 6 and 8). Some distinctions must be drawn, however, for while regional sentiment is often strong throughout Spain, it is stronger and more politically charged in some areas than others. In the Basque country and Catalonia (northeast Spain), regional and separatist sentiment and even the desire for complete independence are strong. In Galicia (northwest Spain), close to Portugal and far from Madrid, the desire for autonomy is strong but not for separation or independence. In Spain's other regions, varying degrees of desire for autonomy are also present.

Further, within these regions major differences on the autonomy issue exist, which is reflected in the regional political parties. For example, in Catalonia, the Convergence and Union (CiU) is an establishment and centrist party that has been skillful in pursuing a moderate autonomy platform whereas the Republican Left of Catalonia (ERC) is more radical. Even more extreme differences may be found in the Basque country, where the Basque Nationalist Party (PNV) is Catholic and centrist while the Basque Left (*Euzakadíko Ezkerra*—EE), Popular Unity (*Herri Batasuna*—HB), and Basque Solidarity (*Euzko Alkartasuna*—EA) are all on the left.

During the later 1970s and through the 1980s the regional parties in Spain were mainly important within their regions and less so at the national level; but after the PSOE lost its majority and then again with the plurality PP government, the major parties were obliged to seek coalition partners to achieve a voting majority in parliament. Rather than going left and seeking a coalition with the communists, both the PSOE and the PP chose to ally themselves with the major regional parties, the CiU and the PNV. That, of course, gave these two parties major bargaining power to extract further concessions from Madrid for their regions.

BASES OF PARTY CLEAVAGE

Spanish and Portuguese politics are divided not just along partisan and ideological lines but along class, geographic, and religious lines as well.[3] These patterns emerged in the first elections after the end of dictatorship and, though altered somewhat over time, have remained quite consistent.

The patterns are clearest in Portugal. The north of Portugal, dominated by small towns and rural villages, is strongly Catholic, and farmers often own their own small plots of land; the centrist (PSD) and conservative (CDS/PP), parties have tended to be the strongest there. In the south of Portugal, dominated by large estates, less Catholic, and where the peasants do not own their own land, the left parties (socialist and communist) have been strong. The socialists and communists have also been strong in the industrial sector or "red belt" around Lisbon and neighboring Setúbal. The center of the country has been the most volatile electorally, alternating between the socialists, the PSD, and then back to the socialists again.

In terms of class, the patterns have long been similarly clear. Peasants who own their own land tend to vote conservative while landless peasants have voted for the left. Urban and industrial workers tend to vote mostly socialist but may vote communist. The middle class in the mid-1970s during the revolutionary phase of the Portuguese transition voted socialist (as the best alternative to the communists) as often as for the PSD; but as Portugal began to settle down in the late 1970s, the 1980s, and the early 1990s, the growing middle class shifted massively to the PSD. But as the socialists moderated their views, a considerable number of PSD voters shifted to the Socialist Party (PS)—enough for it to win the 1995 and 1999 elections; as the Communist Party declined, the PS also picked up its former supporters. Meanwhile, the PSD has sought to widen its appeal among working-class voters.

In Spain during the early post-Franco elections, the social, religious, and geographic patterns were similar to those of Portugal, although the regional configuration was just the opposite. In Spain it is the south and southwest that tend to be more conservative, rural, and Catholic while the north and northeast tend to be more urban, industrial, and secular. Hence, the centrist UCD of Prime Minister Suárez won strongly in the former while the PSOE won strongly in the north and particularly in the urban industrial areas. This split corresponds closely to the division dating to the eighteenth century of the "two Spains" discussed earlier in the analysis.

In subsequent elections, in the 1980s and early 1990s, the PSOE expanded its base of support, continuing to sweep the major cities but, as it moderated its views, appealing to some peasant and middle-class voters as well. Meanwhile, the UCD had broken up and the rightist AP was tagged with the negative "Francoist" label. Hence, it was not until the emergence of Aznar and the reorganization of the PP that a new center-right coalition began to emerge that also shed the Francoist image and appealed to a broad range of voters. And as in Portugal, the Spanish socialists gradually took votes away from the communists while the centrist PP began to appeal to many PSOE voters.

WEAKNESSES OF POLITICAL PARTIES

The Spanish and Portuguese political party systems have been in existence only since the mid-1970s and, therefore, we should not expect them to be as well established and as strongly organized as those in longer-lived democracies. Actually, the parties in Spain and Portugal in this twenty-five–year period have shown remarkable stability and continuity although they still exhibit a variety of weaknesses. So again the question arises as to whether party politics and the electoral arenas are sufficiently consolidated to be the only legitimate avenue of politics and power in the two countries.

First, the leadership of the main parties remains quite thin. The best-led parties in both countries were the communists; more recently the PSOE and PP in Spain and the PSP and PSD in Portugal have developed solid corp cadres of able leaders. The other parties have weak leadership cadres dominated often by a single person; and even in the larger parties *personalismo* (personalistic leadership) is often more important than program or ideology. However, it should be said that the problem of thin leadership cadres is present in almost all

Spanish and Portuguese institutions; the parties are not an exception in this regard.

Second and related, the parties tend to be highly factionalized. They consist of rival "baronies," almost like medieval fiefdoms. The barons and their retinues vie with each other for leadership within the party; if they lose out in these contests, they often leave the party with their followers to form new parties.

Third, the parties are dominated by patronage. Patronage considerations may dominate at several levels. First, party leaders and members want access to the comfortable government jobs that winning an election affords. Second, once in office, politicians are expected to favor their friends and supporters with jobs, access, favors, and government contracts. Third, lower-level politicians attach their fortunes to higher-ranking politicians; if their man wins, they ride his coattails into higher positions; but if he loses, they may abandon him and find a new *patrón.* That helps explain the baronies and *personalismo* noted above; it also means the entire system is shot through and based on patronage—a very traditional political practice in Spain and Portugal—from top to bottom. One must wonder if such widespread patronage is compatible with democracy.

A fourth and again related problem is great party instability. The parties have remained remarkably constant over this quarter century, but within the parties the situation is one of constantly shifting factions, baronies, and patronage groups. The "barons" pull in and pull out and take their followers with them; the balance of power between the rival factions is permanently in flux. Can political parties—and democracy—thrive or even survive on this basis? Or are we really witnessing classic Spanish and Portuguese feudal politics (baronies, patronage, lord-peasant relations) now covered over with the language and labels of party politics?

A fifth problem lies with the still-weak links between the parties and important socioeconomic groups. Each party, of course, tries to forge such links, now often substituting patronage for a whole group (jobs, benefits, special access, control of an entire government agency or ministry) for the old-fashioned individual, one-on-one patronage of olden times. But often it seems the parties and the various socioeconomic groups are in different orbits, operating in different arenas but seldom meeting or coordinating. The parties perform the electoral and patronage functions, but important economic and social policy is carried out directly, in neocorporatist fashion, between the government bureaucracy and socioeconomic groups without the parties or their elected representatives being involved. Politics and policy are thus bifurcated: the parties doing their "things" on the one hand and public policy toward major socioeconomic groups being handled quite differently and even separately from the party arena. So we have party politics and "democracy" on the one hand and a new form of unacknowledged corporatism (government relations with major business and other groups) on the other, with the two seldom meeting or coordinating.[4]

Finally and related to all of the above is the poor reputations of the parties as well as the parliament. Public opinion surveys tend to rank these institutions low in the public's admiration (as they do parties and the Congress in the United States) with only 15–20 percent approval ratings. Here we have an interesting paradox: strong approval (80–90 percent) in both countries for representative democracy as an abstract principal but very low support for democracy's essential institutions: political parties and parliament. Moreover, while the voters recognize the importance of political parties as essential to democracy, they seem to also ignore or bypass the parties in most of the major socioeconomic issues that impact their lives. So while parties and parliament are acknowledged in Spain and Portugal as important in one arena, other arenas seem to operate quite independently of either the parties or democracy.

These are all major problems. They indicate that, although the Spanish and Portuguese political parties have come a long way in twenty-five years, they are not as well established or as integral to the system as supporters of democracy would like to see.

OTHER "PARTIES" WITHIN THE SYSTEM

Parties and democracy have had a relatively short, sporadic, often uneasy history in Spain and Portugal. At present, the parties-elections-parliament arena, in a context where democracy now enjoys unquestioned legitimacy, offers the only legitimate route to political power. But it has not always been that way.

Recall Spanish and Portuguese history: the deep divisions in the two countries, the authoritarian tradition, the weakness of democracy and civil society on those few occasions when it was attempted, the long history of military coups, sporadic revolutions, and on-again-off-again civil war. During these periods, democracy did not enjoy definitive legitimacy. There were other routes to power. These included the well-executed coup d'etat, the heroic revolutionary uprising, the mass march on the national palace that toppled a minister or even a government, or the use of anarchist violence. Clearly, the oligarchy and the elites, knowing they would be outvoted if true democracy ever achieved unquestioned legitimacy, were unwilling to accept a system that would oust them from power and, hence, used the army and the Church to preserve their power; but note the left-wing groups at times also employed nondemocratic, violent means to achieve their goals. Recall in addition, the importance of rank, hierarchy, place, and position in Spanish and Portuguese society: if one truly believes that people are born unequal, then the democratic principle of one-person-one-vote is not going to enjoy unquestioned legitimacy.

The result in Iberia has been a rather broad definition of the term "party." It is not just actual political parties that have that designation but, in a context of multiple legitimized routes to power, the army or the Church or the oligarchy were often referred to as "parties" as well. While the real political parties operated in their arena, the Partído Militar (Military Party) or Partído Oligárcico (Oligarchic Party) operated in theirs. Obviously, some of these latter arenas were nondemocratic and extraconstitutional. But it speaks to the fragility of democracy in Spain and Portugal historically that there could be these multiple political arenas and multiple legitimate routes to power other than the electoral one.

In present-day Spain and Portugal, democratic legitimacy is sufficiently well established that one seldom sees these nondemocratic, extraconstitutional references anymore. The military in both countries is under civilian control, the Church is less powerful than in the past, and a more pluralist social structure has replaced the dominance of the oligarchy. Nevertheless, this older, organic-unity legacy tells us a lot about Spain's and Portugal's past. And to the extent that political parties, parliament, and party government have such low esteem among the public as they do even now, it provides another potentially worrisome feature concerning the strength and stability of Spain's and Portugal's democracies.

CONCLUSION

Political parties, a party system, party government, and even democracy itself are relatively new phenomena in Spain and Portugal. With the exception of the chaotic and short-lived republics of the early twentieth century, neither country had ever, until recently, had a functioning party system. Some observers even now would go so far as to say that the present parties and party systems are not only weak but mainly concessions to foreign demands, contrived and synthetic organizations created to satisfy U.S. and European insistence on "democracy." In this view, the parties serve to show that Spain and Portugal are as "modern" and "democratic" as their European counterparts, when in fact a deeper examination reveals the parties to be ephemeral and of marginal centrality to the political process. As Spanish writer José Iglesías says, "In Spain there has been a tendency to think of politics much more as aesthetics than as an attempt at the practical manipulation of reality in a positive determined sense. There has been no effort to fit political foundations to the exigencies of reality in its rambling process of change, but to adapt that reality to an a-priori scheme of ideas totally conceived outside its conditions."[5]

The analysis here finds some validity in these assertions, but the actual situation is more complicated and more positive for democracy. It is true that the parties in both countries are still weak, unpopular, and not well institutionalized. To a certain extent they remain somewhat artificial creations, derived from a-priori and often foreign criteria. With some exceptions they are not well organized, leadership is thin, patronage considerations are rampant, and the parties are often dominated by factionalism and personalism. At the same time the real foci of power in both countries often lie outside the party arena, in the banks, the bureaucracy, the large industrial complexes, and powerful vested or corporate interests.

And yet parties and a party system have emerged. Democracy functions—often vigorously. Voter turnout remains high, though declining. The parties perform real functions, and a system of party government is operating. Sometimes reluctantly, the public sees parties as essential to democracy, even while holding them in low repute. The parties support valid programs and ideologies and have developed a mass base. A climate of freedom, debate, and viable competition between the parties exists. The parties articulate programs, present candidates for election, and the winners then form governments. The parties alternate in power, depending on their electoral mandates. Respect for the ballot box has gained new legitimacy—indeed, it is the only source of legitimacy. At this stage other routes to power—revolution, coup d'etat—would be unthinkable.

The balance in Spain and Portugal has, therefore, tipped. The old dual power structures—democracy, on one side, nondemocratic army, Church, and oligarchy, on the other—no longer really exist. Of course, there are still many decisions in Spain and Portugal that are made outside the party and democratic arena although that is probably true of all political systems. But in Spanish and Portuguese politics it is democracy that now rules and the parties are essential to it. Overwhelmingly Spaniards and Portuguese prefer democracy to any other alternative. Authoritarianism of left or right is out.

All the institutions of democracy—parties, public opinion, elections, *cortes*—have become firmer and better consolidated. Moreover, while the social base of democracy—higher literacy, greater affluence, a larger middle class, integration into Europe, a political culture of pragmatism and centrism—has been growing, the base and support for authoritarianism—poverty, backwardness, militarism, social extremes—has been shrinking. The older authoritarian tradition is in the process of being vanquished. It is conceivable that the applecart of Spanish and Portuguese democracy could still be upset, but that looks increasingly unlikely as democratic Spain and democratic Portugal continue to be strengthened. Have Spain and Portugal, therefore, become "normal countries"—safely democratic and, maybe because of that, a little boring politically? It is a theme to which we return in the conclusion.

NOTES

1. Tom Bruneau and Alex MacLeod, *Politics in Contemporary Portugal: Parties and the Consolidation of Democracy* (Boulder, Colo.: Lynne Rienner Publishers, 1986); Thomas Bruneau, ed., *Political Parties and Democracy in Portugal* (Boulder, Colo.: Westview Press, 1997); Richard Gunther, Giacomo Sani, and Goldie Shabad, *Spain after Franco: The Making of a Competitive Party System* (Berkeley: University of California Press, 1986); and Howard Penniman, ed., *Spain at the Polls* (Durham, N.C.: Duke University Press, 1987).

2. Juan Linz, "From Falange to Movimiento—Organización: The Spanish Single Party and the Franco Regime," in *Authoritarian Politics in Modern Society,* ed. Samuel P. Huntington and Clement Moore (New York: Basic Books, 1970); Howard J. Wiarda, *Corporatism and Development: The Portuguese Experience* (Amherst: University of Massachusetts Press, 1977).

3. Richard Gunther, ed., *Politics, Society, and Democracy: The Case of Spain* (Boulder, Colo.: Westview, 1993); Peter McDonough, Samuel Barnes, and Antonio López Pina, *The Cultural Dynamics of Democratization in Spain* (Ithaca: Cornell University Press, 1998); and Bruneau, *Political Parties and Democracy.*

4. Martin O. Heisler, *Politics in Europe: The Corporatist Polity Model* (New York: McKay, 1974).

5. José Iglesías, *The Franco Years* (Indianapolis, Ind.: Bobbs-Merrill, 1977).

Chapter 8

GOVERNMENT AND THE ROLE OF THE STATE

The United States is a country with strong interest groups and a comparatively weak central state. By contrast, the former Soviet Union was a country with a strong central government and a weak civil society. These two systems are often represented as polar opposites on a spectrum of state-society relations. The United States is depicted as a society-led government; the former Soviet Union weighs in as a government-led society. Where to place Spain and Portugal on this hypothetical spectrum raises some interesting questions.

First, when we consider the role of the traditional *intereses,* do we see them as state or society actors? Did the Roman Catholic Church lead the state? If so, does that make Spain a society-led government? Alternatively, did the army lead the society? If so, does that make Portugal a government-led society. Questions about state-society relations are predicated on the assumption that state and society are two different entities. However, political practices and institutions of Spain and Portugal were developed within a Catholic model that envisioned state and society as one, complementary, organism.

A second factor that further complicates the role of the government is the question of which government is being considered, the regional government or the central government? Particularly in Spain (although Portugal has had to deal with separatist movements in the Azores and Madeira), the central government has had a difficult time gaining legitimacy. Regional pride is often stronger than national pride. Even when Franco maintained absolute control, the public support for the central government was tepid at best. The population was kept in line by repression and police-state methods, not through loyalty and good will. National sentiments were often expressed as xenophobic nationalism and rarely as a positive expression of patriotism. The devolution policies put in place after the Franco regime formalized the societal preference for regional governments. No longer able to use force to legitimize its authority, the central government has seen an erosion in political power.

Centralized power, such as it is, has been institutionalized through the development of an extensive bureaucratic system. As with many European countries, economic development and modernization have taken place under the firm hand of an absolute ruler. The reach of that hand was extended through the development of a centralized bureaucracy. Both Spain and Portugal, under their respective dictators, experienced a "revolution from above." What follows is a look at the economic and social conditions currently existing in Spain and Portugal and how the state contributed to these conditions. Next we explore the various political institutions created during the democratic transition. Finally, we consider how these vastly enhanced state structures are dealing with the budgetary demands imposed by the European Union.

SOCIAL AND ECONOMIC DATA

So far our analysis has been light on statistics. We've been more interested in considering patterns and themes than in engaging in a more quantitative investigation. When it comes to comparing the economic realities of living in Spain and Portugal, however, statistics offer a precise means of comparison. Although both countries have developed within a similar culture and with similar political institutions, when viewed through the lens of social and economic indicators, some startling differences emerge. For instance, Portugal has only one-fourth of the population of Spain, and around one-fifth of its landmass. With a total area of 35,552 square miles, Portugal is slightly smaller than the state of Indiana. The estimated population for the year 2000 is just under ten million with a density of 280 people per square mile. Spain's total area is 194,885 square miles, making it twice as large as the state of Oregon. The estimated population for the year 2000 is over 39 million with a density of 203 people per square mile.

Along with obvious disparities in size and population, Spain and Portugal report widely different unemployment rates. Spain has the highest unemployment rate in Europe, a little over 15 percent; whereas Portugal has one of the lowest, under 7 percent. (By comparison, France and Germany have an unemployment rate around 11 percent.) A second economic disparity between

Spain and Portugal involves per capita income. In 1998, the total value of goods and services produced in the country within a year (known as the gross domestic product or GDP) divided by the number of citizens was only $10,690 in Portugal compared to $14,080 in Spain. By comparison France's was $24,940 for that same year, Italy's per capita GDP was $20,250, and Germany's per capita GDP was $25,850.[1] Although both Spain and Portugal continue to see an annual increase in the per capita GDP, their respective per capita GDP is only 80 and 70 percent, respectively, of the European average.

Because these figures are lower than the rest of Europe, Spain and Portugal have been entitled to something known as "cohesion funds" to bring them up to speed with their richer neighbors. Members of the European Union are engaged in a massive redistribution program in which richer nations pump money into poorer nations' economies in order to raise them to an agreed upon economic standard. Currently the standard per capita GDP is 90 percent of the EU average. Spending countries, such as Germany (who is also suffering from a rising unemployment rate), are beginning to balk at this significant obligation. When Germany attempted to drop the subsidy line beneath 90 percent of the EU average, Prime Minister José María Aznar threatened to veto EU expansion into central and eastern Europe. In the meantime, as long as the Iberian per capita GDP is less than 90 percent of the EU average, those cohesion funds will continue to benefit both economies.

These European subsidies are building on an economic recovery begun during the dictatorships. Portugal's economic recovery began earlier than that of Spain, growing at an annual rate of 5.5 percent between 1960 and 1974. Kept out of NATO and the early formation of the European Community, Spain did not benefit from the same international aid that Portugal received. Yet Franco was not to be outdone. He pushed for economic policies that favored foreign investment over domestic labor. Although 500,000 Spanish workers were forced to emigrate in order to find jobs, international investors took advantage of the economically freer climate. Eventually these policies paid off. Foreign investment increased the country's capital, and the money sent in from the now one million émigrés increased the home population's spending power. When Spain finally was allowed into the European organizations, it was showing an impressive growth rate of 5.2 percent a year. Although both economies slowed down during the recession of the early 1980s, they have since shown dramatic recoveries. In 1998, Spain had an annual growth rate of 3.6 percent, higher than any other European country. The United States experienced a growth rate of 4.3 percent during the same period.

All EU countries are moving within economic guidelines established by the Maastricht Treaty. This treaty, signed in 1991, commits the participants to an open market economy that prohibits wage and price fixing as well as any type of monopoly. Using monetary instruments and budgetary restraints, member countries are expected to reduce their government deficit, limit their public spending, and keep inflation rates down. Unemployment figures are not regulated by the Maastricht treaty; however unemployment benefits are limited through the percentage allowed for public spending.

Portugal has responded well to all these subsidies, creating public works projects such as the Expo '98 project outside of Lisbon that has helped keep unemployment down and government deficit within the Maastricht-approved 3 percent of the GDP. Although Spain receives more subsidies than just about any other European country (with the exception of Ireland), those massive infusions have not forestalled the largest unemployment rate in Europe. Whereas Portugal is experiencing an infrastructure boom, Spain's public works projects have often been mismanaged with allegations of corruption. Nonetheless, Spain is still largely within the guidelines established by Maastricht with an inflation rate hovering around 2 percent (1 percent lower than Maastricht) and allowances made for the public debt ratio of 68.2 percent of the GDP (8.2 percent higher than Maastricht).

Neither Spain nor Portugal is showing much resistance to converting to the European monetary note, the Euro. Whereas the rest of Europe shows a low approval rating in terms of monetary conversion (around 15 percent approving of the monetary conversion), Spain records the second highest with 52 percent in favor of switching over to Euro notes. The Spanish treasury is making plans to replace pesetas with Euros. The 1998 edition of *The Europe Review* reports that seven hundred trucks, carrying three tons each, "will be needed just to transport the Euro notes around Spain." Portugal is equally enamored of the possibilities of switching to the Euro. *The Europe Review* quotes Portuguese Prime Minister António Guterres in an updated version of the Gospel of Matthew, "Thou art Peter, and upon this rock I will build my church." The socialist prime minister declared, "Thou art Euro, and upon which Euro we will build Europe's future."[2]

Social indicators have more in common than the economic indicators. The demographics from the two countries indicate that both have a growing, healthy population. The population of Spain rose from 33,876,000 in 1970 to 39,820,000 in 1999. During a similar period, Portugal's population rose from 9,044,000 to 9,927,000. Life expectancy increased exponentially: for Spanish males, from 69.6 years to 76.1 years projected for the year 2001; for Portuguese males, from 64.2 years to 75 years. Spanish women now enjoy a life expectancy of 81.8 years of age rather than the 75.1 years of 1970. A similar increase in life expectancy gave Portuguese women almost ten years of statistical advantage: from 70.8 years in 1970 to almost 80 in 2001. For all their love of tobacco and wine with the midday meal, Spaniards and Portuguese have some of the highest life expectancies in Europe.

There are many more doctors per capita in Spain than Portugal. In 1998 there were 277 Spaniards for every doctor in Spain, as compared to 480 Portuguese for their professional counterpart. The rate of AIDS is higher in Spain than Portugal with 16.0 per one hundred thousand as compared to 5.1 per one hundred thousand. Birth rates have dropped off significantly in the two countries. In Portugal, the birth rate in 1970 was 19.1 per thousand. Spain had a similar birth rate in 1970: 19.5 per thousand. By 1995, those rates had dropped to 10.5 and 10.0 respectively. Although in subsequent years Portugal has shown a modest rise in the birthrate (11.4 for 1997), Spain's birth rate has continued to drop with a provisional birth rate of 9.2 recorded in 1997. What this means is that Spain and Portugal, like many other industrialized countries, will be facing a period when a significant part of its citizens will be retired and out of the job market. Because Spain has not addressed the politically unpopular but economically necessary issue of pension reforms, economists predict that Spain will suffer a severe "cash crunch" around 2015 as fewer working young people are obliged to pay the pensions of more old people.

Spain has been much more successful than Portugal in wiping out illiteracy. By 1998, the illiteracy rate for men was 1.8 percent of the population, 3.9 percent for women. In 1998, Portugal still had a 13.0 percent illiteracy rate for females and a 7.5 percent for males. The difference in literacy rates may be explained by Franco's insistence on compulsory education; many private schools were subsidized in order to create places for the numerous young people needing to be educated. Since then, the government has continued to make educational reform a priority while, at the same time, following the traditional program of state subsidies for private and religious schools.

In general, Spain has a more educated, more affluent society with all of the attendant advantages and disadvantages. The higher rate of AIDS and the higher rate of crime (2,286 per 100,000 as compared to Portugal's 968 per 100,000) suggest that some of the benefits of modernization have come at a certain cost.

BUILDING THE MODERN NATION-STATE

Although the power of the central state was largely due to the personalities of the two dictators, not all of it disappeared upon their passing. Both Franco and Salazar expanded the political and military systems, establishing extensive single-party systems, a secret police and paramilitary units, and modernizing the armed forces and national police forces. Not only was the coercive apparatus of the state vastly enhanced but so was the administrative branch. New civilian ministries were created that handled labor and social welfare issues. The traditional ministries were also enlarged, creating a sizable growth in the extent and functions of the public bureaucracy.

The state also played a leading role in the economic sphere. During the early years of each regime—in the 1930s in Portugal and during the 1940s in Spain—the state regulated prices, wages, production, and working conditions. Both labor, and, to a lesser extent, business were subject to extensive controls, further increasing the power of the central state. This situation changed somewhat in the 1960s, when the state took on the role of economic development. Roads and bridges were built, ports and other transportation facilities were upgraded, and massive amounts of public money went into improving the infrastructure. Through negotiations with banks and other lending institutions, both governments were able to engineer astounding economic growth rates beginning in the mid-1960s, further consolidating the powers of the central state.

The third area in which state power expanded under Franco and Salazar was in terms of social programs. Beginning in the 1950s and expanding considerably through the 1960s, both regimes initiated a vast range of new social programs. The state initiated new programs in social security, unemployment insurance, medical care, welfare, and other public assistance. Many of these programs did not function very well and had extremely limited funds and personnel. Some of them existed purely on paper and not in reality. Nevertheless, the structure of the modern welfare state was put in place, creating a societal expectation of the state's social responsibilities.

By the end of the Franco and Salazar regimes, the state had become politically more powerful, economically more activist, and socially more involved. The state's greater economic power gave it greater political power and more levers of control. By the mid-1970s, with the immense expansion of state power, these were no longer simply private enterprise economic systems but, increasingly, systems of state capitalism or updated, modern mercantilism. Meanwhile, the infrastructure of the modern welfare state had also been established.

In the last days both the Franco and Salazar regimes opened up somewhat and allowed for a measure of openness for civil society. With the collapse of the two regimes, the floodgates opened and civil society reasserted itself. In Portugal, that reassertion was abrupt and in complete opposition to everything that had come before, a complete *ruptura* (rupture) with the past. In Spain, the change came one year later and involved far more gradual changes, a *reforma* (reform) of the past. These two processes gave birth to very different economic policies.

Shortly after the 1974 revolution, the Portuguese MFA moved to nationalize large sectors of the economy that had previously been in private hands. Its primary targets were the banks and *grupos,* consisting of eight or ten of Portugal's leading families who were now referred to derisively as "the oligarchy." When the Portuguese government nationalized the banks, it discovered they were not just involved in the banking industry but in construction, transportation, insurance, tourism, mining, manufacturing, publishing, and real estate (including large holdings in Portuguese Africa). In an effort to nationalize the banking industry, the Portuguese government became the directors of a huge share of what had been the private sector. The percentage of GNP generated by the state shot up from 30 percent, where it had been under the dictatorship, to about 75 percent. Almost instantaneously, Portugal became a predominantly state-run or socialist economy.

Following a policy of *reforma* rather than *ruptura,* Spain largely avoided the nationalization of private industry. The new government did not want to disrupt the economy, antagonize the private business community, or discourage private investment. Even when the socialists took power under Felipe González, there was no move to nationalize, somewhat to the consternation of his more militant followers. Even without nationalization, the Spanish government and bureaucracy continued to grow. The share of the GNP generated by the public sector went from about 20 percent, where it had been under Franco, to about 40 percent in 1990. Although less dramatic, perhaps, than what occurred in Portugal, it still represents close to a 100 percent increase in the size of the state sector over a period of twenty-five years.

A culture of patronage politics is one explanation for the rapid increase in Iberian bureaucratization. Democracy, in this regard, means rewarding friends and supporters for their support in a political campaign. As the number of friends increased, so did the number of public offices. Another factor is a result of implementing vast new public programs in the areas of health, housing, education, and public works. In order to administer these programs, new bureaucracies were created. A third factor, particularly applicable to Spain, has to do with the mechanisms of government for a predominantly regulatory state. As mentioned earlier, Spain has moved closer to France in their statist policies using regulation as a means of controlling the economy without actually nationalizing industries.

All of these factors have contributed to very large administrative states, so large that democracy itself may be at risk. If the public sector grows too large, it may become a state almost to itself, may become corrupt and self-serving, not to mention lose all sense of democratic responsibility. Both the Spanish and Portuguese governments have recognized this dilemma. Both have taken significant steps to ensure that its regulatory arm functions fairly and well, without the handing out of sinecures or the making of corrupt political bargains, and that the state sector remain in good standing with the electorate. Nevertheless, corruption, cronyism, and special favors for friends and fellow party members remain as problems in both countries.

Domestic approval ratings aside, the Maastricht Treaty also monitors the growth of the public sector, using concrete economic indicators to test for liberalization and privatization. Portugal has had to privatize many of its holdings and break up state-run monopolies. The telephone monopoly, Portugal Telecom (PT) opened up to competition and the state has, bit by bit, been selling off its holdings of the telephone company. The state also sold off its holdings in Cimpor, the largest cement producer, the Banco de Fomento e Exterior, and in Electricidade de Portugal.

These privatizations have resulted in enormous proceeds—$3 billion in 1996 and more in 1997—that have gone to retire the public debt, bringing it further in line with the provisions of the Maastricht Treaty. Improved methods of tax collection have also contributed to a fiscally healthy government. All of this privatization has helped the private sector. The Lisbon stock market rose 35 percent in 1996 and 66 percent in the first nine months of 1997. In recognition of this bullish market, Morgan Stanley, in 1997, reclassified the Lisbon market as "developed."[3]

Because it never did nationalize to the same extent as Portugal did, Spain is not able to reap the same rewards of privatization. Committed to a statist or *dirigiste* system, neither of the main political parties has been eager to privatize extensively, although Aznar has taken some significant steps in that direction. Instead, the Spanish government is being pushed to attack politically sensitive programs such as labor entitlements and pensions. Other EU countries, such as Germany, the UK, and Italy, shifted the burden of retirement pensions to the workers by attaching benefits to payments made over the course of a worker's life. Spain, during the socialist administration, protected the "pay as you go" system and committed the government to indexing state pensions to inflation. These programs are not regarded well in Brussels and may threaten Spain's status as a recipient country. In compliance with Maastricht regulations on public spending, the Spanish government instituted a pay freeze on the public sector in 1997. When those regulations were met, the pay freeze was lifted and Spain immediately overspent in the following year, forcing the government to consider instituting another freeze on wages and hiring in the public sector.

Along with the creation of an administrative or bureaucratic state, there are other institutions that have helped formalize the central state. The powers of the heads of state, the prime ministers, and the members of parliament are defined in both countries in their postdictatorship constitutions.

CONSTITUTIONAL STRUCTURE

The Portuguese constitution was written by a Constituent Assembly, elected in 1975 on the first anniversary of the revolution. Finally approved one year later, the constitution provides for a democratic, parliamentary system—with political parties, elections, a parliament, and a prime minister—as well as an independent judiciary. The Portuguese constitution is one of the longest in the world, heavily laden with Marxist rhetoric with numerous references to "the means of production" and the "exploitation of workers." There are two unique characteristics of the Portuguese constitution: the role of the military and the dual presidential-parliamentary system.

Given the role of the military in the 1974 revolution, it is not surprising that the constitution institutionalized its status through the granting of some extraordinary powers. Under the constitution, the Armed Forces Movement (MFA) was given a special institutional role as the Council of Revolution that effectively made the MFA a separate and almost equal branch of government. The council acted as an advisory board to the president and was given the right to review all laws passed by the parliament, thus giving it the restrictive powers of a constitutional court. The council was also granted the authority to act as the prime decision-making body for the armed forces. These enormous powers were welcomed by the left who, through the MFA, sought to ensure their dominance of the legislative process even when they lost seats in parliament.

The enhanced role of the president was also supported by the left. Portugal has long maintained a dual executive structure in which the prime minister effectively governs and the president, often a military person, provides a more ceremonial function in many ways similar to the Spanish king. The Constituent Assembly gave the office of the president far more power in order to avoid the dangers of an excessively strong prime minister as epitomized by Salazar.

The Portuguese constitution reflects the conflicting desires of the assembly. The parliamentary sections had the support of the socialists and Christian democrats; the Marxist rhetoric had the support of the communists and their allies. Even when the articles were finally approved, many politicians felt that some of them needed to be amended. As the country began to elect more representatives from the center-right, from the social democrats and the Christian democrats, much of the ideological and restrictive economic language was challenged. In 1982, four amendments were approved: the Council of the Revolution was replaced with the Council of State, a similarly consultative body but one that was more representative. The powers of the president were reduced, much of the ideological language was taken out, and language restricting private investment and business was removed. Subsequent amendments removed still more ideological language, increasing business interest in Portugal. The Portuguese constitution still reflects its Marxist origins yet enough changes have been incorporated to encourage economic growth.

The Spanish constitution reflects an entirely different set of circumstances. Drafted by the Committee on Constitutional Affairs of the Cortes, the document espouses the centrist values of Prime Minister Adolfo Suárez and his Union of the Democratic Center Party (UCD). On at least two occasions, the socialist (PSOE) delegates walked out in protest and it was only through the diplomatic skills of Suárez that compromises were eventually reached. Only the Basque Nationalist Party failed to support the constitution, largely because of dissatisfaction with the articles concerning regional autonomy. In October 1978, both houses of the *cortes* overwhelmingly approved the new constitution, and in December 6, 1978, the constitution received its final vote of approval with 87.8 percent of the voters endorsing the new document. The king signed it into law on December 27.

As with any document created through consensus, the constitution was delivered through enormous compromises. In order to gain the approval of opposing parties, some of the language is vague and, at times, contradictory, causing problems in interpretation. Given the difficulty in moving through the Spanish legal system, many of these gray areas have yet to be sufficiently clarified by the courts.

Besides the thorny issue of regional autonomy, abortion also complicated the process. Article 15 guarantees the right to life and to physical and moral integrity. Included in this article is the right to be free of torture or degrading treatment and the abolishment of the death penalty except for military reasons in times of war. The article currently reads, "Everyone has the right to a life . . ." but for a while the committee considered substituting "a person" for the more general *todos*. Worried that the more general language might be construed to include bulls, which would create problems for the *matadores,* the "person" contingent took on some momentum until someone pointed out that the use of "person" might not include an unborn child, thus opening the door to legalize abortion. Few could politically afford to take that position and the article was approved using *"todos,"* bullfighting concerns to the contrary.[4]

The constitution defines Spain as a parliamentary monarchy. The king is the head of state and "symbol of its unity and permanence" and "is the highest representation of the Spanish state in international relations" (Article 56). The parliament, or *cortes,* is bicameral, and there is an independent judiciary. The first article declares Spain to be a social and democratic state that advocates liberty, justice, equality, and political pluralism. Sovereignty resides in the people and from them all state powers derive.

The constitution achieved compromise on many of the issues that have torn Spain apart in the past. For example, although Catholicism no longer enjoys the status of being the official state religion, Article 16 does recognize the need to "maintain a continuous, cooperative relationship with the Catholic Church." The Church is also indirectly supported through language in the provision on education that guarantees that the state will support parents in their efforts to provide their children with a religious and moral education. This document is a far cry from the anticlerical positions mapped out in the 1931 constitution.

The military's power was also somewhat reduced in the constitution. Article 149 gives the state the exclusive control over the armed forces. However, language in an earlier article, concerning the military's mission to defend the territorial integrity, might be construed as granting the army its historical role of protecting the unity of the country against any internal disorder.

GOVERNMENT INSTITUTIONS

Portugal

The president of Portugal is the chief of state and, like the Spanish monarch, the symbol of national unity. Although the 1976 constitution was vague about the duties of the office, and the 1982 amendments did not add much clarity, the practical powers of the office are apparent whenever the parliamentary branch is in crisis. Even when the parliamentary system is running smoothly, with a clear majority and a popular prime minister, the president is able to exert considerable influence behind the scenes.

According to the terms of the 1989 revised edition of the constitution, the president's powers and duties include acting as supreme commander of the armed forces, promulgating laws, declaring a state of siege, granting pardons, submitting legislation to the Constitutional Court for approval, making many high appointments, and, when needed, removing high officials from their posts. The president also calls elections and convenes special sessions of the Assembly of the Republic, the title of the Portuguese parliament.

The presidency is intended for a national figure of great prestige and ideally one above partisan politics. Portugal has had three presidents since the revolution of 1974–75. General Ramalho Eanes was elected in 1976 and reelected to a second term in 1980. In 1986 longtime Socialist Party leader Mario Soares was elected to the presidency and then reelected in 1991 for a second five-year term. In January 1996, Jorge Sampaio, also of the Socialist Party, was elected with 63.8 percent of the vote; he is also in his second term. All three presidents have been genuinely popular candidates.

The prime minister of Portugal is the effective head of state and governs the country in its everyday affairs. He (to date there has been only one woman in this office) is not elected on a direct, popular basis, as is the president, but is chosen because he is the leader of the largest party in parliament. The prime minister's term may last up to five years—although if he senses an advantage he may call elections before that time. Similarly, he may be ousted by a vote of no confidence in the parliament.

The period following the 1974 revolution up until 1985 was only consistent in its inconsistency: prime ministers were short-lived, cabinets came and went, and seventeen governments formed coalitions before giving way to the next political reconfiguration. The most prominent and successful of the early prime ministers was Mario Soares of the Socialist Party (PS) who carefully guided the country in the years of postrevolutionary turbulence in the 1970s. The leader of the social democrats (PSD), Francisco Sá Carneíro also showed promise, but he was killed in a plane crash while campaigning. Soares came back to power briefly but lost to the PSD again in 1985. The PSD still had to govern in coalition, however, until 1987 when it became the first party with an absolute majority in parliament since the 1974 revolution. From 1985 until 1995, the Social Democratic Party's Aníbal Cavaco Silva ran the country as prime minister. In 1995, when the PSD lost to the PS in the October general election, the socialist party took over control of the government. António Guterres, the leader of the PS, became prime minister as a result of those elections. He was reelected in 1999.

The principal organ of executive power within the government is the Council of Ministers, or cabinet, which is responsible to the Assembly of the Republic. It consists of members of the prime minister's own party who are chosen to help him administer some fifteen to eighteen ministries. Members of the council must also be elected members of the parliament.

The Portuguese parliament is a one-house legislature with 230 members, each of whom is elected directly in a popular election to serve for four years. Neither the Council of Ministers nor the parliament garners much prestige. Surveys conducted in the early years of the democracy reveal that most Portuguese felt that power resided primarily in the offices of the president and the prime minister and only marginally with the cabinet officers or members of parliament. The functioning of the parliament is hampered by low salaries, lack of adequate resources, and a poorly developed infrastructure of committees and subcommittees. Given the poor salaries, public officials are often employed in the private sector as well, creating opportunities for patronage and corruption.

The Portuguese frequently vent their political frustrations regarding the country's lack of progress and efficiency on the parliament. To the public, the parliament personifies all that is wrong with democracy. It is considered inefficient, quarrelsome, splintered, and patronage-dominated. The members are perceived as putting their own interests ahead of that of the nation and of using their public positions to enhance their private careers and fortunes. In newspaper editorials and cartoons, parliament is often portrayed as buffoonish, silly, and irrelevant. That same skepticism does not apply to the more noble offices of the president and prime minister.

Spain

Spain is a parliamentary monarchy. The king is a hereditary and constitutional monarch. The constitution provides that the line of succession will follow the line of primogeniture, making no privileges for a male heir over a female. Like the Portuguese president, the king serves as head of state, but unlike the Portuguese president, he is not an elected official. Although not elected, the current king enjoys enormous popular approval. As a symbol of the nation, King Juan Carlos I has been able to bring together the various *intereses* under the traditional institution of the monarchy.

Although the king's functions are largely ceremonial, he has his share of institutional powers. The king formally convenes and dissolves the *cortes*, calls for elections and referenda, ratifies civil and military appointments, signs decrees promulgated by the cabinet, appoints the prime minister after consultation with the *cortes*, and serves as supreme commander of the armed forces. The importance of these functions becomes clear when the political apparatus threatens to fall apart, as was demonstrated during the attempted coup in 1981.

Because of a reorganization of Spain's political structure, the king has seen his power enhanced. With the devolution of power from Madrid to the seventeen autonomous regions, the central state has seen its power eroded, leaving the king as the only institution to represent the interests of the state (the prime minister being more a partisan figure). The king has risen to this challenge, proving himself to be a master at forging connections between rival interests, making friends with socialists as well as monarchists. In this regard, holding a hereditary office may have increased his political prestige; not subject to the demands of the electorate, he is truly able to hold himself above politics.

The prime minister, on the other hand, is deeply embedded in politics. He is the leader of the dominant political party in the *cortes*, directing the government's programs in both domestic and foreign affairs. With the king's approval, he chooses the cabinet ministers and is generally responsible for the everyday affairs of the central government. The prime minister may ask for a vote of confidence from the Congress of Deputies, may propose the dissolution of the parliament, and may call for new national elections to strengthen his legislative position. The constitution calls for elections every five years, but they may be held before then if the prime minister loses a vote of confidence in the *cortes* or if he thinks he can gain electoral advantage by having an earlier vote.

The current prime minister, José María Aznar, leader of the center-right Popular Party (PP) was first elected in May of 1996 as the head of a minority government depending heavily on the Catalan and Basque regional parties to achieve a majority coalition. Aznar's reelection was secured by enough votes to avoid a second coalition government. In March of 2000, Aznar garnered 183 seats in the 350–seat parliament, an increase of 27 seats from the 1996 election and enough to give him a majority in that legislative branch. Although one of the few conservatives in power in Europe, Aznar has maintained popular support by dropping unemployment from 23 percent to 15 percent and by successfully guiding Spain into the new economic era of the Euro.

The Cabinet or Council of Ministers is the state's highest executive institution. Headed by the prime minister and appointed by the king, the council must win an investiture vote in parliament in order to be approved. Members of the council include the prime minister, the deputy prime minister, and the other ministers of state, all of whom are also members of the *cortes*. The Council of Ministers has both administrative and policy-making functions, including the running of national security and defense.

Each council member is responsible for the administration of a particular ministry. The ministers have considerable discretion in the running of these departments, yet all of them are accountable to the prime minister and the council as a whole. Although some cabinet ministers have proved to be poor administrators and a few have fallen out of step with the prime minister, in general, the Spanish cabinet has enjoyed greater prestige than its counterpart in Portugal.

The *cortes* or parliament is, according to the constitution, the highest governmental institution in Spain. It is here where sovereignty ultimately resides. Spain has a two-house parliament consisting of a Congress of Deputies and a senate. The congress, with 350 deputies, is the most powerful and democratic of the two houses. Its members are elected by proportional representation.

The Congress of Deputies may ratify or reject decree laws promulgated by the government. A vote of support from the congress is also necessary before a prime minister may be sworn in. A majority in the congress must approve all legislation proposed by the prime minister. This procedure is largely pro forma when both the prime minister and the majority of deputies are from the same party. However, in the final years of the González administration and throughout the early Aznar administration, loosely held coalitions have made this process more complicated. Congress also holds the authority to vote a censure or an expression of no confidence in the government, in which case new elections must be held.

The senate mainly ensures territorial representation from Spain's sometimes separatist-leaning regions. It consists of 208 members elected on a provincial basis and an additional 49 appointed as regional representatives. The latter have little influence. Either the congress or the senate may initiate legislation, but the congress has the power to override a senate vote by a simple majority. Many Spaniards question why it is necessary to have a senate since its role is so circumscribed. The two chambers may also meet jointly as the General Cortes (*Corteses Generales*). In that event, the president of the congress presides, again attesting to the superior power of that house.

Spain also has a Council of State that functions in an advisory capacity. The members are appointed by the Council of Ministers and are representative of the country's main corporate groups: the armed forces, civil service, the Catholic Church, universities, professions, farmers, business and industrial groups, and the autonomous regions. The council is a broadly consultative group, a throwback to an earlier Spanish and Portuguese concept of corporative or functional representation. Although the Spanish constitution defines it as the supreme consultative organ of the government (Article 107), it is only rarely called into existence.

DEVOLUTION

The role of the central government has been significantly altered since the mid-1970s. What was once a rigidly centralized state under Franco and Salazar has been considerably decentralized. The process of devolution has reduced the central government's powers, far more in Spain than in Portugal, with a handing over of regulatory and other matters to the autonomous regions. In a sense, this is a return to the government system of pre-Hapsburg Spain. After five hundred years of centralization, rights and privileges are being reextended to the various regions. Spain's traditional instruments of democracy, the *cortes* and the *fuero*, are being reanimated in a more modern context.

International monetary constraints, such as the Maastricht Treaty, have further reduced the national governments' discretionary powers. The price-fixing and mercantile practices of Franco and Salazar are not permitted as long as Spain and Portugal want to stay a part of the European Union. Given their expressed commitment to the Euro as well as the obvious advantages of being recipient countries, it is hard to imagine that Spain and Portugal will not abide by those constraints, even if they do erode the power of the central government.

Even in Portugal, devolution is a political issue. Although Portugal is one of the few EU countries that, so far, has not devolved any power to the regions, the socialist party is making moves in that direction. In an effort to fulfill a constitutional mandate to further the "direct and active" participation of citizens in political life, the socialists are pushing for the development of regional administrations. Unlike Spain, in which the regions have long promoted their separation from Madrid through distinct languages and customs, Portugal is, in a sense, attempting to create regional identity from above. Not everyone is behind this program to promote political activity. Social democrats are against any devolution and stormed out of parliament in 1996 when the socialists pushed through a draft proposal. With the socialists again in firm control of the parliament, more devolutionary legislation may be expected.

The goal behind all European devolution is greater efficiency, a democracy that is closer to the people, and a reduction in public spending. Whether that comes to pass remains to be seen. Both Spain and Portugal have bloated central administrative agencies. That the regional offices will be any less bloated seems contrary to the political culture of patronage. However, the creation of regional administrations should promote more political activity outside of Lisbon and Madrid. Whether that political activity encourages democratic accountability or patronage politics as usual is still an open question.

Regional administrations are able to deal directly with the EU, developing economic programs that completely bypass the control of the central government. Already, bureaucrats in Catalonia and Galicia have negotiated impressive development plans with Brussels. There is no reason to think that other regions will not make similar international bargains, further reducing the need for a national government. Basque separatists, long antagonistic to the national government, may find it less distasteful to negotiate with a European government than their old adversaries in Madrid. The presentation of the European Union as the "Europe of the Regions" is very appealing to a country in which regional identity has long trumped any loyalty to the central state.[5]

The issue of regional autonomy in Spain has long been sensitive and divisive, and it continues so, for Spanish society is unique in Western Europe in the depth and extent of regionalist sentiment. The country includes ethnic/regional groups—most particularly the Basques, Catalans, and Galicians—that are culturally and linguistically different from the rest of Spain and from each other. Even Portugal is sometimes referred to by Spaniards, not as a separate and sovereign country, but as a "lost province" that somehow went astray. Someday—presumably with its own autonomy statute—Portugal should return to its "rightful" fold: Spain.

The 1978 constitution reached a compromise on the regional issue by guaranteeing the rights of regional autonomy, some of which date back to the medieval *fueros*, while, at the same time, maintaining the unity and coherence of the nation. Castilian Spanish is the official language of Spain, but other languages are recognized as co-official in their respective regions. Flags and emblems of the regions may now also be displayed alongside the Spanish flag. None of these provisions were permitted in Franco's day.

There are two procedures by which a region may achieve autonomy: one fast, the other slow. The fast route was applied to those regions—Galicia, the Basque provinces, and Catalonia—that had sought autonomy during the 1930s; these were also the areas where the regional pressures were coming to a head in the 1970s, potentially threatening to break up the nation. Once approved by the Constitutional Committee of the Congress of Deputies, all that was required for autonomy was a vote of approval in a regional referendum. The slow procedure, by contrast, required an initiative on the part of municipal and provincial governments as well as final approval by the *cortes*; the degree of autonomy was also less for those employing this route. In 1981, a new organic law, or charter, was approved by the *cortes* governing these procedures in detail, and, in 1983, the process was essentially completed when elections were held in thirteen new autonomous communities. Andalusia received its autonomy under a compromise procedure that represented a mixture of these two routes, thus making a total of seventeen communities in Spain with varying degrees of autonomy.

Each regional entity has its own capital and a unicameral legislative assembly whose members are elected by popular vote. The assembly selects a president from among its members who then represents the community; there is also a regional Council of Government headed by the president and responsible to the assembly. The regions may also have their own courts, although they are ultimately subject to the Supreme Court sitting in Madrid. With the increasing prestige of the European Court of Justice, litigants in the various regions are beginning to appeal national decisions, which at one time were considered final, to an international tribunal.

Although the national government retains exclusive jurisdiction in areas such as defense, foreign affairs, civil aviation, finances, public safety, foreign trade, economic planning, justice, and criminal, commercial and labor legislation, the increasing power of the European Union is encroaching on that jurisdiction. Eroded from within and constrained from without, the governments of Spain and Portugal may eventually find themselves—with only a little exaggeration—as either administrative agents of Brussels or as transregional coordinators of the autonomous regions. Neither of these conditions would have been tolerated by Franco or Salazar. Some argue that the winners in this power shift will be the more ceremonial offices of the king and the president. If national politics becomes more symbolic than functional, then the symbolic offices will play a greater role in national politics.

CONCLUSION

Spain and Portugal are administrative or bureaucratic states where virtually all policy-making and interest group activity are channeled through the central government. They are not pluralist political systems in the American sense nor do they believe in American-style separation of powers or lobbying. Unity, cohesion, integration, and harmony are emphasized, not checks and balances. In part, this stems from Iberia's historic integral, organicist and Catholic past, which emphasized order and unity at all costs, but in part it also comes from the European continental tradition of parliamentary democracy where the executive and legislative branches are united. In this, as in so many other areas, Spain and Portugal have preserved powerful traditions from their histories and culture as well as adapted to the modern European currents of integral and organic, social democracy. But as shown, this system may at some point be challenged both by internal regional pressures and by the requirements of operating within the larger European Union.

NOTES

1. Figures provided by the World Bank. Available at www.worldbank.org (September 15, 1999). Downloaded: January 30, 2000.
2. William Chislett, "Portugal" and "Spain," in *The Europe Review,* 11th ed. (London: Walden Publishing, 1998), 268 and 226.
3. Chislett, "Portugal".
4. Gregorio Peces-Barba Martinez, *La Elaboracion de la Constitución de 1978* (Madrid: Centro de Estudios Constitucionales, 1988), 222ff.
5. Philip Thody, *An Historical Introduction to the European Union* (New York: Routledge, 1997), 59.

Chapter 9

PUBLIC POLICY: DOMESTIC AND FOREIGN

Foreign policy and domestic policy represent mirror images in Spain and Portugal. For long decades and even centuries, Spain and Portugal were extremely isolated internationally. They were also, until the mid-twentieth century, very poor countries, underdeveloped, closer to the Third World than to the First World of prosperous nations; and their social programs—education, health care, social security—also lagged behind the rest of Europe. Because they were poor and underdeveloped, they could not afford to exercise a very vigorous foreign policy; at the same time, their very isolation from Europe and the world's mainstreams of trade and commerce kept them from progressing. It was a vicious circle that only began to change in the 1950s and then accelerated in later decades.

Societywide poverty, as in other Third World countries, meant for most people concentration on the basics, on eking out a meager subsistence, on surviving; there was little time or inclination to participate in the "luxury" of foreign policy. These twin problems—poverty and international isolation—served to retard Iberia's development and to keep the peninsula's people locked in place domestically as well as immune to beneficial outside ideas. Geographically, Spain and Portugal were a part of Europe but, hemmed in by the Pyrenees, as well as by poverty and long distance, they remained economically, politically, culturally, and even psychologically apart from Europe.

In recent decades, Spain's and Portugal's condition has altered dramatically. Both countries are booming economically, and greater affluence is spreading; poverty and illiteracy are being eliminated; and Spain and Portugal have left the Third World and joined the First World. Spain's living standards have now reached approximately 80 percent of the European average and Portugal's about 70 percent (compared to 50 percent or lower four decades ago); Spain's gross national product (GNP) is now the tenth largest in the world; both countries are ranked by the World Bank as "industrial market economies" and no longer underdeveloped. Greater prosperity in turn has enabled them to play a larger foreign policy role. Foreign policy and domestic policy are thus still interrelated but in ways that are the reverse of the past: both more affluent and more closely integrated into European and global currents.

Hence, in this chapter we treat domestic and foreign policy as closely interrelated, tied to developmental programs. As compared to the treatment in earlier chapters of what are usually called "input factors" (history, culture, religion, interest groups, political parties), and the treatment in the previous chapter of "process variables" (the state, bureaucracy, government institutions), here we consider political system "outcomes": the public policies and programs that come out of the system and in turn have their impact on it. We begin with a survey of domestic economic and social policy in each country and then move on to a discussion of each country's foreign relations.

DOMESTIC POLICY

The economies of Spain and Portugal had long been closed and autarkic. The dominant economic philosophy in both countries was mercantilism, a system of political economy that developed in Europe upon the decay of feudalism but before the onset of capitalism. Indeed, Spain, Portugal, and their former colonies in Latin America remained locked into the mercantilist pattern for centuries and never did, until very recently, develop more free market enterprises. Under mercantilism a strong state sought to maintain a favorable balance of trade, did so by protecting native industries and trading monopolies while keeping out foreign competition, regulated virtually all economic activities, and sought to build up its bullion reserves.

This picture of a centralized, monopolistic economic system, which was closely related to absolutism in the political sphere, clearly fits Spain and Portugal during their three centuries of Hapsburg/Bourbon and colonial rule in Latin America from the late fifteenth through the eighteenth centuries, but what is surprising is that an updated, somewhat modernized, system of mercantilism, or autarky, survived into the nineteenth century and even into the regimes of Franco and Salazar—at a time when most other developing, industrialized nations of Europe were already moving toward a system of open markets with a modern, mixed economy. The continued practice of mercantilism in Spain and Portugal way beyond the time when such a system might have been beneficial served to retard Iberia's economic development and for centuries consigned these nations to the category of less-developed. It may be recalled that Roman Catholic Church doctrine and, therefore, Spanish and Portuguese political culture, strongly undergirded by religious principles, was also anticapitalism and an additional reinforcing factor in their backwardness.

Paradoxically, while under mercantilism the state was supposed to be strong, directing, and authoritative, in fact in Spain and Portugal the state's actual role in the economy was usually weak and indecisive. A strong, organic, forceful state both economically and politically in Iberia represented an ideal to strive for rather than an actual, operating reality. The Spanish and Portuguese states from the seventeenth century on generally provided confused, indecisive, and incompetent direction to the economy rather than real leadership as the mercantilist system called for. In the social sphere, the Spanish and Portuguese states also lagged way behind in providing services for their people. Both countries failed miserably to provide the education, health, housing, and social programs that these countries needed.

In the late-twentieth century all this turned around. The changes began with Franco and Salazar when both dictators, tardily, abandoned mercantilism and autarky in favor of a more open market system. They did not, nor did their successors, entirely abandon statism; but they did make room for a more modern economy. The change triggered a boom in both countries (more so initially in Spain than Portugal) that helped dramatically raise living standards and gave rise to greater prosperity and a middle class for the first time. The economic takeoff also enabled Spain and Portugal to expand social programs in ways they could not afford before. Their entry into the European Economic Community in 1986 and their first-round admission into the European Monetary Union (EMU) in 1999 accelerated their drive toward development and all but guaranteed their status as stable, growing economies. Spain and Portugal are no longer to be identified with the poverty and hopelessness of the Third World but with the prosperity, affluence, and settled status of the First World. Iberia has, therefore, turned a major corner, not only to democracy but to prosperity as well; and the two are closely interrelated.[1]

Spain

Spain's economic decline relative to other nations began as early as the sixteenth century. At that time, in order to raise money for the dynastic ambitions of the Hapsburg family as well as to launch the Catholic Counter-Reformation to quell rising Protestantism, the Spanish monarchy began the practice of selling public offices on a large scale, cut off trade with the more productive and dynamic countries of Europe, drove out its small entrepreneurial class (Jews, Muslims, Protestants, free thinkers), taxed agriculture and commerce so heavily that these economic sectors were ruined, and retreated into the closed, autarkic system of mercantilism. Even at the height of Spain's imperial glory under Philip II, 1556–98, the seeds of economic devastation were already sprouting. The next several centuries were almost all downhill.

When at last Spain began to industrialize in the late-nineteenth century, already lagging far behind Britain, France, Germany, Italy, and the "upstart" United States, it did so slowly and unevenly. The lateness of Spain's industrialization helps account for the extreme poverty of its urban workers, and their attraction to such radical political philosophies as Marxism, anarchism, and syndicalism. When industrialization finally came, moreover, it was concentrated in a few areas: the Basque provinces, Catalonia (Barcelona), and Madrid. The relative economic prosperity of the first two of these compared to the rest of Spain helps account for the rise of separatist movements in these provinces. The Basques and Catalans have long thought that they were contributing more to the national treasury in taxes than they were getting back in programs.

Social programs in Spain also lagged behind the rest of Europe. Spain remained a poor country and could not afford the advanced social programs that other European countries and the United States enacted in the 1930s and afterward. In addition, neither the monarchy nor later the Franco regime had much interest in implementing programs they saw as "socialist." A third reason for the lag in social programs was that the government and most Spaniards thought of these programs as the responsibility of the Catholic Church or of individual families. Families were expected to help or take in those members who were sick or fell on hard times; the Church provided alms to the poor and indigent, cared for orphans, and was the major provider of education and health care. Such arrangements were not so bad when Spain was a rural, traditional, strongly Catholic, and family-centered nation; but as it became increasingly urban, secular, and impersonal in the early twentieth century, these private-centered services became inadequate. Spain had the worst of all possible worlds: private services were breaking down, yet the government was very slow to fill the void.

Meanwhile, Spain's economic troubles continued to mount. The land was terribly unevenly distributed, concentrated in the hands of the elite class, and was inefficiently used; most agriculture was unmechanized even into the 1950s. Industrialization lagged way behind and conditions for the workers seemed to confirm Marx's worst predictions; hence, the emergence of the underground socialist and communist labor organizations. Business, banking, and commerce were woefully inefficient and dominated by an interlocking oligarchy of elite families. Spain, which had lagged since the sixteenth century, fell farther behind the rest of Europe. More and more Spanish left the country for jobs elsewhere.

For a long time Franco had pursued the same autarkic, mercantilist, and ruinous economic policies as his predecessors. The breakthrough came in the late 1950s, when he brought a new group of economic reformers into his cabinet and they began to open up and liberalize the economy. Heretofore, Franco had avoided such an opening because he feared—rightly as it turned out—that economic liberalization would ultimately mean social and political liberalization, and that would be the end of his regime. The new program included an opening to foreign investment, liberalized trade, and the removal of many restrictions on free economic activity. Franco gambled that he could introduce economic reform without it producing the usual social and political concomitants: pluralism and democracy.[2]

The Spanish economy responded magnificently. All during the 1960s and early 1970s the economy boomed ahead at 6, 7, 8 percent per year; this growth became known as the "Spanish miracle." The Spanish GNP doubled within the decade, and then doubled again. After stagnating for centuries, the economy took off. At the same time, the new prosperity enabled the Franco regime to expand or initiate a considerable array of social programs, such as welfare, unemployment insurance, health care, child labor, maternity care, and paid vacations, which had been neglected before.

Other factors besides Franco's economic opening contributed to the growth. Tourism flourished as Europeans flocked to Spain's magnificent beaches on the Costa del Sol; tourism became Spain's second leading industry, attracting forty million tourists annually (the same as the population of Spain) and providing badly needed foreign exchange. Even though it was not yet a member of the EEC, Spain benefitted from its proximity to a newly prosperous Europe that had money to spend and was looking for new investment opportunities. In addition, all those millions of Spaniards who had emigrated earlier continued to send a large share of their salaries (remittances) back to their families in Spain, providing a further impetus to the economy. These factors developed largely independent of government policy, yet the government had the good sense not to stand in the way and followed policies designed to encourage such economic growth activities.

Inevitably, the rapid economic growth produced important social and political consequences despite the Franco regime's efforts to prevent them. Socially, rising affluence stimulated urbanization, led to greater literacy, gave Spaniards the means to travel, created a large middle class for the first time as well as a larger working class, and in general undermined traditional, conservative values. Politically, the changes resulted in the widespread adoption of European ideas and lifestyles (including the desire for greater freedom and democracy). The political culture of Spain was transformed as the older values of authority, discipline, hierarchy, fatalism, and acceptance of one's God-given station in life gave way to the newer concepts—dynamism, change, mobility, and individualism. Even while Franco was still alive, thus, the political culture of Spain was changing underneath him; increasingly, Franco was seen as an anachronism, dinosauric. In short, the transition to democracy in Spain was led by socioeconomic modernization and changes in the political culture that made the post-Franco institutional changes possible; Spain's leaders after Franco largely ratified and built a democratic institutional structure that reflected the even deeper changes that had already occurred in Spanish values, political culture, and society.

Post-Franco Spain was marked by far fewer changes in the economic system than in the political. The political sphere saw a quite remarkable transition to democracy, but economic policy showed surprising continuity. All post-Franco governments have continued the liberalizing policies that began in the 1950s even while keeping in place a large, paternalistic, statist regime. In this respect Spain and Portugal are closer to the French or continental political economy tradition than to the American.

While continuity in economic policy was the rule, several "surprises" of the transition merit mention. The first of these was the smooth and peaceful (given Spain's earlier violent history) political transition to democracy after 1975; the result was that investor confidence remained high, there was almost no capital flight, and the economy continued to grow virtually without interruption. The second "surprise" was the continuity in economic policy even after a socialist (PSOE) government was elected in 1982 and continued in power until 1996. After all, the socialists had a history of radical militancy, but by this time the party had largely abandoned its Marxist rhetoric, pragmatic Prime Minister Felipe González calmed down the hotheads in the party, and the government continued a probusiness policy. It recognized that a flourishing economy was good not only for the country but also for the PSOE and its reelection possibilities, so González banished all talk of nationalization, met with and reassured the business community, urged restraint on the part of the unions, even privatized some state-owned enterprises, and presided over a booming free-market system—even while using the increased tax revenues from the new prosperity to vastly expand social welfare programs. And that was the third "surprise": how well the Spanish economy continued to perform in the early 1980s even while the United States and most of Europe were locked in recession and "stagflation."

With Spain's formal ascension to full membership in the European Economic Community (EEC) in 1986, the economy received a new stimulus. Initially there were problems of adjustment and some dramatic clashes at the border between French farmers and Spanish truckers carrying agricultural products. But these problems proved insignificant compared to the benefits that flowed into Spain. As one of the EEC's poorest members, Spain qualified for a variety of subsidies and special programs which helped build new highway systems, high-speed trains, and a large number of other infrastructure projects. Accession to the EEC also meant a large new influx of European and U.S. capital and the building of vast new factories that brought jobs and prosperity to previously neglected areas of the country. Middle- and upper-class Spaniards complained because they could no longer find maids; they were all working in the SONY factories! Other side effects included inflation and price increases that made traditionally "bargain-basket" Spain nearly as expensive as other countries in Europe. But the overall picture was one of rising affluence and prosperity.

The boom years lasted from 1980 to 1990; then a slowdown occurred, though mild and of short duration compared to the recession elsewhere in Europe. The slowdown brought to the surface other problems that had been simmering for years: the low level of skills and education of many Spanish workers, lagging technology, poor housing, inadequate energy sources, uneven development, vast inequalities, and pockets of extreme poverty. But note we say "pockets of poverty", Spain no longer exhibited a societywide "culture of poverty" as in the 1950s.

Under Prime Minister José María Aznar and the Popular Party, which succeeded the PSOE in 1996, Spain's economy continued to grow at over 3 percent per year, considerably above the European average. Aznar was more conservative, closer to the business community, and carried out a series of privatizations that reduced state size and got rid of losing or marginal state enterprises—surprising given Spain's strong statist tradition. Aznar was determined to continue Spain's modernization, part of which involved a strong commitment to freer trade and more open markets. Meanwhile, Spain continued to qualify for more European subsidies while at the same time meeting the tough budget standards for a first-round entry into the EMU. The continued prosperity means that Spain has closed the gap with the rest of Europe, now reaching 80 percent (as compared with 70 percent a decade ago) of the average European living standard. The usual (and unjust) rule is that the gap between rich and poor countries only continues to widen; Spain is a major exception to that rule.

The result is that Spain has taken its place as one of the world's major economies. It ranks tenth in the world in GNP. It is no longer "developing" or "emerging" but a modern, industrial economy. Its economy revolves around two cities, Madrid and Barcelona, as well as a number of regional centers. Its banks and major industries are competitive on a global basis, vying with other multinational companies (MNCs) in Latin America and elsewhere. It believes that it deserves inclusion in the Group of Seven of the world's major economies, but—and this tells us a lot about the new Spain—it is not angry or bitter about the issue.

Spain has to be considered one of the world's great success stories of the last third of the twentieth century, both politically (democracy) and economically (growth and development). Yet a number of important social problems remain. Pockets of illiteracy still exist, especially among the older generation left over from the Franco regime, which believed an illiterate, apathetic people would better accept authoritarianism. The current unemployment rate, at 15 percent, is too high, the highest in Western Europe, in part a reflection of an unskilled, not well-educated, nontechnologically trained labor force that has been slow in adapting to globalization. Housing remains a vast problem, especially in the cities where slums or ugly, poorly built apartment buildings provide few amenities. Spain's welfare system still lags behind the more advanced European countries, again a product of the country's past poverty. And health care is often inadequate for some groups, although Spain's life expectancy has now reached North American/Western European levels. All of these are long-standing problems; what is perhaps even more striking are the enormous strides Spain has taken to overcome them in the last quarter century.[3]

Among the newer social problems in Spain are drugs, pollution, divorce, product reliability and enforcement, environmental protection, family conflict and violence, AIDs, rising crime, and lawlessness. Spaniards sometimes take a perverse pride in some of these problems, saying that they prove that Spain is as "modern" as anyone else. And indeed many of these problems are the products of modernity. But what is also striking about Spain, perhaps because of its religious values, its strong family tradition, and the continued importance of many traditional ways, is the relatively low incidence of many of these problems as compared to the United States or other Western nations. Equally impressive are the strenuous efforts being made by Spain to solve these problems. For that, too, in Spain's eyes, is part of being "European."

Portugal

Portugal's economic and social trajectory has been roughly parallel to Spain's—except that it started at a considerably lower level (Spain has far more resources and a much bigger market) and is still today at 70 percent of the EU average, versus 80 percent for Spain. But that is an immense improvement over

Portugal's condition thirty years ago, when its per capita income was less than half the European average.

Like Spain, Portugal reached the height of its power and wealth in the sixteenth century, when Portuguese ships explored vast, heretofore unknown areas of the globe and the Portuguese empire encompassed immense colonies in Asia, Africa, and Latin America. But after that early spurt, it seemed to be all downhill for Portugal. Even more isolated from Europe's main centers of wealth and commerce than Spain, Portugal was for centuries the poorest, most backward country in Western Europe.

When Portugal, like Spain, began its belated industrialization in the late nineteenth century, the process was slow and irregular. Portugal lacked resources, capital, infrastructure (bridges, highways), and markets (a significant middle class). Hence, industrialization was incipient, small scale, concentrated in only one or two areas of the country, and dominated by often inefficient, family-owned firms. Social change was also slow, although during the First Republic, 1910–26, a small middle class, a nascent trade union movement, and a new entrepreneurial class, based on interlocking elite families, came into existence.

Under Salazar/Caetano, 1928–74, the country continued to be dominated by mercantilist, autarkic policies, much like Spain under Franco. Salazar was a traditional, pre-Keynesian economist who pinched pennies, imposed austerity, and insisted on budget surpluses. Exploiting the resources of its African colonies, Portugal, in mercantilist fashion, built up some of the largest bullion reserves of any country in the world. To accomplish these goals, Salazar used strict price-and-wage controls that were largely administered through the corporative system.[4] Once again we see that Portuguese corporatism, which began with strong social justice motives, was corrupted into being an instrument of dictatorial controls and socioeconomic oppression.

Portugal remained exceedingly backward economically and socially compared with its neighbors. The depression years of the 1930s, then the years of World War II, when Portugal as well as Spain were subject to a German U-boat blockade, and the period after the war, when Portugal received no Marshall Plan or other aid, were particularly hard years. Poverty, malnutrition, and malnutrition-related disease, and even mass starvation and stunted growth were widespread. The poor conditions persisted after the war, prompting millions of Portuguese to emigrate to Europe, the United States, or the colonies in Africa. There was almost no foreign investment and the country could not afford many social programs. What the Church or a supportive family could not provide in the way of social services, the state was also unable to provide. Portugal stagnated. Salazar, a medievalist in his thinking, for a long time acquiesced in these terrible conditions, believing that poverty was good for the soul and that modernization would bring even worse evils, such as liberalism and socialism.

The breakthrough for Portugal came in 1953, a few years earlier than Franco began his economic liberalization. Salazar adopted a succession of five-year plans that opened the economy to foreign investment and greater trade. Portugal also benefitted from rents paid by the United States for use of air base rights in the Azores, from the ripple effect of European prosperity, and from a U.S. decision to grant Portugal Marshall Plan aid as part of an arrangement that brought Portugal into NATO. But Salazar's reforms, though helpful, were tepid compared to Franco's and produced far less dramatic results. On into the 1960s and 1970s, reflecting the earlier traditions of mercantilism and autarky, most production, wages, and prices were set by the state, not the marketplace.

The economy, however, did begin to expand in the late 1950s and 1960s, though at rates of 3–4 percent compared to Spain's 7–8 percent. And, as in Spain, economic growth accelerated urbanization, increased the size of the middle class, and stimulated new expectations. It also enabled the Salazar regime to begin a number of new social and welfare programs, although relatively few persons were covered and the programs sometimes existed more on paper than in reality.

Meanwhile, in an effort to hang onto its African colonies, Portugal had gotten bogged down in three major counterguerrilla wars in Angola, Mozambique, and Guinea-Bissau. The first uprisings against Portuguese colonialism occurred in 1961; over time, the guerrillas got stronger and eventually acquired from the Soviet Union such modern weapons as surface-to-air missiles (SAMS), which they used to devastating effect on the Portuguese forces. This conflict was equivalent to the United States fighting three Vietnams at the same time. The Portuguese held their ground for a considerable time and were quite confident of their position, but by the 1970s the conflicts were proving a severe drain on the Portuguese economy (over 40 percent of the national budget) and the cost in lives was felt to be unacceptable. Indeed, it was in large measure for the purpose of ending the African wars that the young Portuguese military officers launched the revolution against Caetano in 1974. And once the old regime was toppled, they quickly granted independence to their African colonies, unfortunately doing so in a precipitous and unplanned way.

Whereas the Spanish transition to democracy in 1975 had been smooth and peaceful, the Portuguese revolution a year earlier was chaotic and destructive, with devastating effects on the economy. Investment stopped; capital fled; factories and farms were taken over by their workers; economic activity all but ground to a standstill. Banks and industries were nationalized; the business class was driven out or hampered in its activities; and Portugal adopted a new constitution that was so socialistic that it had to be almost entirely rewritten in the 1980s to attract foreign investment and allow business to operate freely. Other factors were also involved in the economic downturn: fears of a communist power grab, skyrocketing oil prices in the 1970s, and the return of hundreds of thousands of Portuguese settlers from the former African colonies who added to the competition for jobs and social services.

From 1974 (the year of the revolution) to 1985, Portugal followed uncertain, inconsistent, "stop-and-go" economic policies, related to the continued political instability and rapid changeovers of governments of that period. External imbalances and a severe general downturn in the mid- to late 1970s and early 1980s was followed by an International Monetary Fund (IMF) austerity program that led to a depreciation of the Portuguese currency (the escudo), high inflation (29 percent in 1984), and negative growth rates (minus 6 percent between 1982 and 1984). Ironically, it was a progressive socialist party that had to carry out the belt-tightening measures, resulting in the party's loss in the next election and for the following ten years. An entire decade, 1974–84, was thus lost to economic development, with the country experiencing negative economic growth.

Since the mid-1980s, the picture has turned brighter, and most Portuguese have never had it so good. While the austerity was politically devastating in the short term to the government that carried it out, it undoubtedly benefitted the economy in the long run, to the advantage of the Social Democratic Party in power from 1985–95. Inflation came down, the escudo was stabilized, and real growth accelerated to 4–5 percent per year. A huge shot in the arm was provided by American and European assistance (to keep Portugal from going communist), and then beginning in 1986, when Portugal joined the European Economic Community (EEC). As the community's poorest, most vulnerable member, Portugal qualified for massive European subsidies aimed at bringing it up to general EEC levels. New bridges, hospitals, schools, highways, water systems, and housing projects were built on a massive basis. The previously "quaint" (meaning impoverished) countryside received new infusions of jobs and modernization while Lisbon and other cities sprouted new middle-class suburbs. The "sleepy," "backward" Portugal of the past is giving way; the country is almost unrecognizable from what it was thirty years ago. In addition, the government moved to amend the constitution to make it less hostile to business and investment, achieved a balanced budget, and succeeded in presenting a picture of stability and confidence which was also attentive to investors.

The expansion and growth of the Portuguese economy has continued at a record pace. It managed to absorb and find work for all those returning refugees from its Africa colonies; and, unlike Spain, Portugal has all but eliminated unemployment. There is a dynamism in Portugal that was absent before, a great deal of construction and *movimento*. A country whose social and bureaucratic rigidities seemed to belong to the pre–World War I era is on the move, its economy booming, and its whole way of life changing.

In 1998 Portugal was able to qualify as one of the founding members (although still the poorest) of the Euro currency zone. It did so after strenuous budget streamlining, fiscal reform, and economic housecleaning that marked a sharp departure from many earlier Portuguese fiscal practices—that is, lack of transparency, cronyism, patronage. Significantly, these reforms were carried out by a socialist government that, while emphasizing social justice, continued the privatization policies, state downsizing, and free market programs of its predecessors. Although Portugal's main parties continue to disagree on a range of specifics, on the broad, main direction of economic policy they seem to have arrived at a consensus. Moreover, in both Spain and Portugal these policy directions are closely in accord with broader European Union (EU) policy and with globalization trends.

Of course, many problems remain. Portugal is still poorer than the other wealthier countries in Western Europe but, like Spain, it is closing the gap and far ahead of the Eastern European countries whose poverty it once shared. Portugal is also poorer than next-door Spain: both countries have had impressive economic growth in recent decades, but Portugal started from a lower base and also experienced a ten-year interruption brought on by the chaos of its 1970s revolution. Pockets of poverty, illiteracy, and malnutrition still exist in Portugal, like Spain, mainly among the older generation. The European subsidies will eventually run out but, under an agreement Portugal reached with the EU, not until at least 2006. And certainly equity, the maldistribution of wealth, is a problem: Portugal has a dynamic middle class and entrepreneurial element and its working class is better off than before, but income is terribly unevenly distributed and there are many Portuguese—in the rural areas and Lisbon's slums—who have not benefitted from the new wealth. How to blend growth with equity is a burning question. But then, the same could be said for many other industrialized nations, including the United States.

FOREIGN AFFAIRS

The Iberian Peninsula has long been isolated and remote from Europe and from the mainstreams of modern Western life, psychologically as well as geographically. Check the map: Iberia is virtually surrounded by sea and ocean on four sides and is connected to Europe only through a narrow neck of land traversed by the rugged Pyrenees Mountains that are themselves passable in only three or four places. The isolation of the peninsula and the natural barriers provided by water and mountains have historically kept foreign armies and influences out, and the Spaniards and Portuguese locked in. Seven centuries of Moorish rule followed by several centuries more of Counter-Reformation marked Spain and Portugal as "different," unlike their European neighbors.

Spain and Portugal roared in the sixteenth century; their explorations and conquests of Africa, Asia, and Latin America vaulted them to the forefront of European powers. Importantly, the success of those colonial ventures appeared to confirm in Spain and Portugal that their already-outmoded medieval and quasi-feudal institutions were the correct ones and ought to be perpetuated, even though it was already apparent that the rest of Europe would soon pass Spain and Portugal by. Readers will recall from chapter 2 that this authoritarian, top-down, Hapsburgian model remained in place for centuries and that, in the process, Iberia rejected and was therefore unable to benefit from the Renaissance, the Enlightenment, capitalism, the industrial revolution, democratization, and all the great transformations we associate with the modern age. Spain's and Portugal's isolation deepened; during the seventeenth and eighteenth centuries, both nations fell from the ranks of the major powers.

In the early nineteenth century, both countries were humiliated by Napoleonic occupations; and for most of the rest of the century, torn by conflict between liberal and reactionary forces, they continued a downward slide. They lost most of their colonies in Asia and Latin America (although Portugal hung onto its African colonies while Spain had Morocco and some small enclaves on the North African coast); in 1898 Spain suffered the utmost humiliation when it was defeated by the "upstart" United States, losing Cuba, Puerto Rico, and the Philippines in the process. These losses triggered strenuous soul-searching in Spain as to why the nation had fallen so low and what its future held, but the immediate effect was to increase Spain's sense of inferiority and led it to withdraw even further into itself.

Both Iberian countries stayed out of World War I and in World War II their official status was "neutral" and "nonbelligerent." Both regimes had some fascist aspects but neither was fully fascist in the sense Italy and Germany were. Their neutrality helped prevent a German army from crossing the border of occupied France to occupy the peninsula; neutrality was the compromise they reached to keep the Germans out. Their neutral status also enabled Spain and Portugal to serve as conduits by which Jews and others fleeing Nazism could escape the continent. In truth, one could find in Spain and Portugal during this period both strong supporters of fascism and strong supporters of the Allies, with their governments skating in between. In the first years of the war, when the Axis Powers seemed to be winning, Spain and Portugal tilted in that direction; later, when it appeared the Allies were going to win, they tilted—pragmatically (or opportunistically)—in that direction.

Because of the widespread sense in Europe that Franco's and Salazar's regimes were "fascist," the two countries were ostracized and isolated after the war—Spain (because of Franco's crushing of the republican forces in the 1936–39 civil war) more than Portugal. Spain was excluded from participation in the Marshall Plan, NATO, the United Nations (until 1955), and the EEC. Portugal was similarly deprived of Marshall Plan aid immediately after the war and kept out of NATO (until 1955), and the EEC. Both countries were treated as outcasts, pariahs, which only increased their sense of isolation, bitterness, and desire to go it alone in the world. It was a familiar pattern in Iberian history; when Spain and Portugal were accepted by European "normal" countries, they then also thought of themselves as European; but when they were rejected by Europe, their reaction has been to withdraw, thumb their noses at Europe, complain they didn't want to be part of Europe anyway, and pursue an independent, nonaligned, even Third World foreign policy.

All this is prelude for understanding the present. For since Franco and Salazar/Caetano, both countries have been thoroughly integrated into Europe. They have emerged as leaders and enthusiastic members of Europe and the European Community (now European Union), sometimes more enthusiastic and more "European" than the rest of Europe. And they have both joined NATO and other pan-European bodies, pursuing peacekeeping, budget-balancing, and other NATO/EU activities more vigorously than older members of the European "club." Once again, it is a new Spain and a new Portugal we are seeing for whom "Europe" is as much an idea as a geographic entity: democratic, economically developed, socially and culturally modern. Indeed, in recent years, as the following analysis makes clear, Spain and Portugal, both domestically and in their foreign policies, have been thoroughly transformed.

Spain

Spain is nearly five times bigger than Portugal, four times more populous, and with a GNP eight times as large. Spain's voice in international politics is, therefore, considerably greater than Portugal's. Spain also borders on the Mediterranean which Portugal does not, and is two-to-three-days driving time closer to Europe's main centers. Spain is, therefore, somewhat more integrated into European trade, tourism, and mores, and now thinks of itself and wants to be thought of as thoroughly European. EUROPE writ large, in both a physical and a psychological sense, has been the main driving force in Spanish foreign policy over the last thirty years.[5]

Europe, the EEC/EU and NATO. During Franco's rule Spain had sought to have closer ties with Europe, but it was consistently rebuffed on grounds that the regime was "fascist." Once Franco died, integration into Europe became Spain's primary foreign policy goal. Spain wanted not just to join Europe economically (the EEC), however, but to become a European country politically, culturally, and psychologically as well. To Spain, Europe symbolized democracy, progress, and modernization after hundreds of years of isolation and backwardness.

The negotiations to join the European Economic Community were difficult and protracted; Spain and Portugal were finally admitted together in 1986. The main issues included Spain's economic underdevelopment and the amount of European aid that could be provided by the other countries; France, whose farmers feared being undersold by cheaper Spanish products; and Spain's wide-ranging fishing fleet, which impinged on other countries' waters. Over time these issues were resolved or brushed under the rug; Spain learned that it was better to join first and then negotiate from the inside. The late 1980s was a period of recession ("Euro-pessimism") and Spain's membership in the EEC got off to a slow start; but during the 1990s, in terms of both trade and aid, joining the EEC proved to be enormously advantageous for Spain. Its economy took off once again and Spain moved rapidly toward closing the gap with its wealthier European neighbors. In a few years Spain was thoroughly integrated into Europe, so that today it would be unthinkable for Spain to separate from Europe as it had done frequently and for lengthy periods in the past.

Spain's economic and political successes in the 1990s enabled it to qualify as one of the founding members of the EMU in 1998. Spain's (and Portugal's) accession in the first round came as a surprise because initially it had been thought that only the most prosperous countries in the core of Europe would be eligible, but Spain worked hard at achieving economic viability. Its admission was a badge of approval bestowed on Spain by the rest of Europe, a sign that it had "made it" and was fully accepted as a responsible European partner. Membership in this larger community (the world's largest and richest free trade region) meant added economic advantages for Spain, though the demands for probity, transparency, and balanced budgets that came with membership meant it would be harder for Spanish (and other) governments to practice in the future the politics of patronage and special favoritism.

While Spain had vigorously and enthusiastically campaigned to join EUROPE, the EEC, and the EMU, its attitudes toward Europe's military army, NATO (which also includes the United States and Canada), was more ambivalent. The issue had a long and controversial history in Spain going back to Europe's postwar efforts to isolate the authoritarian Franco regime and not allow it into either the EEC or NATO. Spain was admitted to NATO as a Cold War ally—but not to the EEC. The policy rankled with many Spaniards, and particularly those on the left, who saw the U.S. policy as bolstering Franco when they were trying to overthrow him and as riddled with hypocrisy: Franco was anticommunist but his regime could hardly be considered part of the "free world."

Spain joined NATO in 1981 through a treaty negotiated by the centrist (and unpopular) UCD government of Calvo-Sotelo, but it did not come into full force until it was approved in a referendum in 1986, by which time the socialists were in power. The issue was a difficult one for the PSOE for the reasons already discussed, but moderate Prime Minister Felipe González had changed his mind on NATO and lobbied strenuously for the treaty's passage. He had been persuaded by other European leaders that he couldn't accept Europe's advantages (the EEC) without taking on Europe's responsibilities (NATO), too. He was also frightened by a military coup attempt in 1981 that almost overthrew Spain's democracy and would have kept the PSOE from coming to power; González came to believe that integrating the Spanish military into NATO would help professionalize it, give it something to do (plush assignments at NATO headquarters in Brussels), and thus keep it out of politics. Spain approved the treaty by a decisive margin although it still hedged its bets (like France) by joining in the political functions of NATO but not its military arm and by obliging the United States to remove some of its bases from Spain. Over time, however, Spain became more integrated into NATO's military functions and was a strong supporter of NATO's peacekeeping activities in Bosnia and Kosovo.

France. France lies just over the Pyrenees from Spain and a long history of rivalry, competition for empires, invasions, and occupations exists between the two countries. Spain enjoyed the upper hand in the sixteenth century, but France has been the dominant power since then. France was strongly critical of the Franco regime and allowed many Spanish political exiles to use it as a base for anti-Franco activities; to Spain's consternation, France has also sometimes allowed Spanish Basque terrorists to find sanctuary across the border in France; and it was France, whose farmers feared they would be undercut by cheaper Spanish products, that was most opposed to Spain's entry into the EEC. The relations between France and Spain have seldom been friendly though with both of them in the EEC, NATO, and EMU and agreeing on many policy issues, their relations have become cooperative rather than poisonous.

Germany. Germany is further distant from Spain, is not a "Latin" country, has never sent its armies into Spain (although it threatened to do so during World War II), and has never been so deeply involved in the peninsula as France. But Germany as a major economic power has growing trade and commercial relations with Spain, and its parties, labor unions, and government were instrumental in assisting Spain on its route to democracy. Though their relations are not close, by its power and importance Germany has become a major factor in Spanish foreign policy.

Portugal. Spain's relations with next-door Portugal are exceedingly complex. Although the two neighbors share the Iberian Peninsula, Portugal has always been worried by Spain's superior size and power (captured in the expression that "neither a good wind nor a good marriage ever comes from Spain"), while Spain tends to look on Portugal as its poor stepchild, its "lost province" that should by all rights have been united with Spain. Portugal is small and has long been poor, so there was not a lot of Spanish investment in Portugal (and the Portuguese actively sought to keep Spain out to keep from being swallowed up economically); most Spaniards view Portugal as quaint and old-fashioned (compared to themselves), a place to vacation and to purchase inexpensive handicrafts, but not an equal partner. In addition, Spain's main orientation, its major cities, highways, trains, commerce, and ambitions are toward the northeast, toward Europe, and not toward underdeveloped Portugal or Spain's own southwest.

Recently these attitudes have begun to change. New cooperative relations have developed between the two countries: new highways to connect them, a high-speed train line, joint commercial ventures. Their prime ministers meet regularly to discuss issues of common concern. Spanish tourists go to Portugal in greater numbers, there is considerable Spanish investment in Portugal, and Portuguese now travel to Spain more frequently. Nevertheless, Portugal remains sensitive and wary of its larger neighbor while Spain is often condescending toward Portugal.

The Mediterranean. Although in the larger European context Spain is not among the leading countries (behind Germany, France, Great Britain, and Italy), within the Mediterranean region Spain is an important actor. It has a strong interest in securing peace and stability in the region and has been actively involved in trying to resolve the Greek-Turkish-Cyprus disputes, securing a peace agreement between Israel and the Palestinians, assisting development and democratization in North Africa, and restoring stability in the Balkans, including sending Spanish forces as peacekeepers to Bosnia and Kosovo.

Quite a number of these issues are very complicated. For example, Spain's policies in the Middle East are strongly shaped by its lack of petroleum, and thus its policies are dominated by its need to remain on friendly terms with oil-producing Arab states. In addition, because of the Moorish occupation during the Middle Ages, Spain likes to present itself as a bridge to the Muslim world. Spain has tilted toward the Arab states in most Middle East conflicts. Nor did Spain recognize Israel until 1986, the same year it joined NATO and the EEC, since it would not be acceptable for an EEC/NATO member to avoid normal diplomatic relations with Israel. Because of its tardiness in establishing relations with the Jewish state, to say nothing of the Inquisition, Spain's expulsion of the Jews in 1492, and Franco's wartime alliance with Nazi Germany and the widespread perception his regime was "fascist" (even though Franco's Spain served as an escape route for many Jews fleeing Nazi-occupied France), Spain was often viewed as an anti-Semitic country. Now these attitudes are beginning to change, and in 1986 the first synagogue since 1492 was opened in Madrid, but the legacy of ill will remains which Spain is trying strenuously to overcome, even while remaining close to its Arab oil suppliers.

A second difficult issue is the Maghreb or North Africa: Egypt, Libya, Algeria, Morocco. Compared with Western Europe, the Maghreb is a woefully underdeveloped area where democracy has never taken firm root; and Spain is (across the Strait of Gibraltar) the closest European country to North Africa. Plus there is that seven-centuries history of Moorish occupation of the peninsula. Because of geography and history, Spain likes to argue that it understands North Africa and the Arab states better than other Europeans; on the other hand, the strait also provides the shortest route of illegal immigration from North Africa into Europe, and Spain often tends to blame its problems of rising crime, drugs, and AIDS, on the North African immigrants. The issue is complicated by the fact that, while many of the immigrants stay in Spain (and there are new mosques in major Spanish cities), many others use Spain as a "port of entry" and merely a waystation on their way to wealthier European countries.

Another problem in the area is the remaining vestiges of colonialism. Gibraltar ("The Rock"), which lies at the southernmost tip of Iberia, has been a British colony and military base since 1713. Its thirty thousand residents mainly speak English, want to remain British citizens, and Great Britain hangs onto the outpost for historic and nostalgic reasons as one of the last remaining colonies in its once farflung empire. On the other hand, Spain claims Gibraltar as part of its mainland and historic Spanish territory, puts restrictions on travel between the enclave and Spain itself, and insists that the colony be returned to Spain. The issue is complicated by the fact that both Spain and Great Britain are NATO members.

Across the strait exists just the opposite problem. There Spain controls two small cities, Ceuta and Melilla, located in Morocco, which are the last vestiges of Spain's previous imperial glory. The two cities are mainly Spanish-speaking and want to remain part of Spain, while Morocco claims them as part of its territory. So in the case of Gibraltar, Spain rejects the British argument of history and self-determination in favor of an argument for territoriality; while in the cases of Ceuta and Melilla it champions self-determination and rejects Morocco's claim based on territoriality. The issues are emotional and nationalistic for all the countries involved, made more complex now for Spain by rising Islamic nationalism and fundamentalism in the two cities and increased clashes between their Arab and Spanish populations.

Russia and Eastern Europe. During the Cold War, Spanish relations with the Soviet Union and its Eastern European satellites were complicated. On the one hand, Spanish public opinion and the Franco regime were strongly anticommunist; on the other, many Spanish exiles (socialists and communists) were sympathetic to "socialism" and/or had taken refuge in the socialist countries. At the same time, both the Franco regime and its successors flirted at times with "third way" foreign policies, presumably somewhere between socialism and capitalism and between the Soviet Union and the United States.

But since the collapse of the Soviet Union, Spain cannot play the game any more of balancing off the two great superpowers, following its own way, and in the process achieving what's best for itself. It has now cast its lot inexorably with the West, with Europe, and (whatever its lingering reservations) with NATO. In addition, it has almost no trade, commerce, or reasons for extensive relations with the countries of the former Soviet Union. Spain wants a peaceful, stable, democratic Russia, of course, and it wants the same in Eastern Europe and has even sent peacekeeping troops to the former Yugoslavia to help ensure peace in the area.

Spain's relations with Eastern Europe are interesting for two other reasons. First, Spain likes to present itself as a model for democratization, development, and European integration for the Eastern European countries to emulate. Second, once some of the Eastern European countries join the EU, then they will be the poorest countries in Europe and eligible for the subsidies that Spain (and Portugal) have long been receiving. Spain and Portugal have misgivings about this potential loss of aid; nevertheless, they have been supporters of EU expansion.

Latin America. Because of common ties of history, language, and culture established over three centuries of colonialism, Spain thinks of itself as having special ties with Latin America.[6] Further, it likes to contrast its traditions of humanism, spiritualism, and strong interpersonalism with the supposed crassness, materialism, and pragmatism of what it calls the "Anglo-Saxon world," mainly the United States There is certainly something to this "special relationship" although it is doubtful if many of the stereotypes above still apply: Spain seems just as materialistic and consumption-oriented as any other country and perhaps no more humanistic or spiritual.

For a long time in the nineteenth and twentieth centuries Spain lacked the financial and diplomatic capacity to back up its rhetorical claims. And in trying to preach to or lead Latin America, Spain often incurred the resentment of Latin Americans, who didn't feel they needed any lessons from the often-hated former colonial power. But the defeat of Spain by the United States in 1898 aroused sympathy in Latin America, particularly as the U.S. military repeatedly intervened in the area, and brought Spain and its former colonies closer together.

The Franco regime elaborated a philosophy of conservative *Hispanismo* based on the principles of authority, discipline, corporatism, and Catholicism, and sought to link Spain with Latin America that way; but while that ideology had many adherents in Latin America, Spain still lacked the resources to strongly implement it. Later, as Spain undertook its transition to democracy, it sought to offer a new model to Latin America based on democracy and human rights.

Spain is now a wealthier country than before and, hence, has concrete programs of trade, commerce, tourism, and cultural exchange with Latin America that it lacked before. Spanish banks and companies now have major investments in the area, and Spanish prime ministers and the king regularly visit Latin America. Spain gives special priority to Latin America in its foreign relations and has established special semiprivate institutes to advance its interests there. On issues like the Central American conflicts of the 1980s or on Cuba policy, Spain seeks to present itself as more progressive and enlightened than the United States. And in organizing the series of Ibero-American summits—which now meet regularly and include all the Latin American countries including Cuba and which pointedly exclude the United States—Spain is serving notice that it is an important influence in Latin America. Spain will not by any means supplant the United States in Latin America and its main priority is still Europe, but Spain is a significant actor there and sees itself as a bridge between Latin America and the EU.

United States. Spain's relations with the United States are generally good although often touchy, and there are many undercurrents of resentment. First, the United States is often seen by the Spanish right and nationalists as pushy, arrogant, and preachy—and it is resented for having defeated Spain in the War of 1898. Second, on the part of the Spanish left, the United States is often disliked because of its long support of Franco during the Cold War and by alleged CIA machinations against leftist parties and unions; more recently the left has resented U.S. policy in the Third World and feared President Ronald Reagan's confrontational policies toward the Soviet Union. But it is not just the extreme left and right that harbor issues; virtually everyone in Spain has suspicions about the United States, resents its interference in internal Spanish affairs, still harbors anger over the Spanish defeat by the United States in 1898, and still believes the Spanish values (although vaguely defined) are superior to those of the United States.

Anti-Americanism in Spain thus comes from both left and right as well as the broad center; it is pervasive and it is widespread. Most often this takes the form of simmering resentments, hostility at America's superiority tinged with jealousy, and a certain inferiority complex with regard to the United States successes, rather than any overt hostility. In this respect, Spain is not unlike France or other European countries, where the same, often vague resentments and jealousies coupled with grudging admiration apply. As Spain has democratized, however, become more wealthy, more mature and self-confident, many of these resentments and complexes have begun to fade.

Spain's relations with the United States are now more or less normal and regularized. The United States no longer treats Spain as a backwater country subject to U.S. pressures and manipulations, and has put the relationship on the same mature basis that it maintains with the rest of Europe. Since the end of the Cold War, the United States has greatly decreased its military and diplomatic presence in Spain and no longer tracks internal Spanish politics with the same scrutiny that it once did. A new era has also opened up in terms of trade, two-way tourism, investment, and student and other exchanges. Indeed, one could say that for Spain, as for other countries in the post–Cold War era, private investment and private interchanges are replacing in importance official diplomatic relations.

These are the normal relations of two nations associated on a friendly basis at multiple levels of interchange. One would not describe these relations as warm, fuzzy, and "special" (as is the relationship of the United States with Great Britain), but they are proper, quite friendly, and eminently pragmatic

Portugal

For a considerable period after the 1974 revolution, Portugal was preoccupied with domestic politics. In the midst of the revolution, it precipitously and without any preparation granted independence to its African colonies, thus helping precipitate the chaos and bloodshed that still engulfs them, but for the most part Portugal simply abandoned foreign affairs. The revolution, street demonstrations, political machinations, rapid government changeovers, the birth of democracy—it was the internal politics that concerned Portugal, not foreign policy. Only after the revolution had run its course did Portugal begin to reconstruct its foreign policy.[7]

Africa. Portugal was once (the sixteenth century) one of Europe's largest colonial powers with vast territories in Asia, Africa, and Latin America; but by the early 1970s this huge empire had been greatly reduced. Brazil had become independent in 1822, only a few small enclaves (Macão, East Timor) were left in Asia, and in Africa, Portugal was struggling to hang onto Angola, Mozambique, and Guinea-Bissau in the face of Marxist-led, anticolonialist, guerrilla movements in all three colonies. Some Portuguese viewed the colonies as symbols that Portugal was still a great power; others had land, commercial, and mining ventures there; still others believed the colonies and their guerrilla wars were too great a burden in terms of costs and lives for a small country like Portugal to bear.

General Antonio de Spínola, whose 1974 book *Portugal and the Future*[8] had helped launch the Portuguese revolution, proposed negotiating an end to the wars and granting independence to the colonies, but tying them, Portugal, and Brazil back together in a Portuguese-speaking confederation that would function like the British Commonwealth. But this was rejected by the young, radical Armed Forces Movement who had taken over the revolution, were strongly influenced by the Portuguese Communist Party, and favored the immediate granting of independence to the guerrilla groups. In Guinea-Bissau this meant the African Party for the Independence of Guinea and Cabo Verde, in Mozambique the Front for the Liberation of Mozambique, and in Angola the Popular Movement for the Liberation of Angola. All three were Marxist, Marxist-Leninist, and allied with the Soviet Union. Portugal had simply abdicated any responsibilities for its colonies or for what followed.

The haste with which independence was granted and the simple turning of power over to the very Marxist-Leninist groups Portugal had long been fighting, without any preparation or guarantees, proved to be a disaster. First, it left hundreds of thousands of Portuguese settlers, many of whom had farmed and lived in Africa for generations, completely stranded, without homes, jobs, land, or even a country. Second, it was a disaster for the former colonies, who were left without teachers, a middle class, professionals, and technicians of every kind, a functioning economy, bureaucracy, or government, and who were plagued by chaos and civil war for decades to come. Third, by turning power over to Marxist-Leninist elements, it guaranteed that southern Africa would continue to be caught up in larger Cold War conflicts over which it had no control.

For many years Portugal's relations with the former colonies remained severely strained; they resented Portuguese colonialism and exploitation and at the same time felt Portugal had left them abandoned and in the lurch, completely unprepared for independence. However, by the 1990s relations had begun to normalize. Trade and diplomatic relations were resumed; Portuguese educators and technicians were welcomed back; and some Portuguese investment—now that Portugal had become more prosperous—began to flow in. Along with the United States, the UN and others, Portugal served as a useful intermediary in resolving some of the interstate conflicts in southern Africa as well as interlocutory among the contending forces in the Angola and

Mozambican civil wars. Portugal will continue as a player in Africa but not a large one.

Europe. Portugal's relations with Europe are now closer than they have ever been; indeed, Portugal has taken a leadership role within the European Economic Community and the EU. Because of geographic (and psychic) distance from Europe's main centers, because it borders on the Atlantic and not the Mediterranean, and because of location at the farthest western point on the European continent, Portugal has long been isolated from Europe—even more so than Spain. But perhaps because it was a small nation without great pretensions, or perhaps because it faced the Atlantic and reached out to Africa, Asia, and the Americas, Portugal did not have such a burning ambition to become European as Spain did. Portugal is now well integrated into Europe and happy to be there, and its trade, diplomacy, commerce, and politics are now predominantly tied to Europe; but for a long time (and this was also true for Spain earlier on) the Portuguese attitude toward Europe was "take it or leave it." It is sometimes said in Portugal that Europe was the last continent to be discovered.

Since 1986 Portugal, like Spain, has benefitted enormously from its admission to the EEC and, more recently, its first-round qualification for the EMU. In the early years after the 1974 revolution it was the EEC whose economic and diplomatic aid helped cement Portugal to the community of democratic European countries; after 1986 European subsidies helped build highways, bridges, housing projects, and other sorely needed institutions that helped transform Portugal from a poverty-ridden, politically precarious country to a dynamic, developed, middle-class society. Those who remember the morose, underdeveloped, class-ridden, pre-World War I society of the past will not recognize Portugal today, particularly if one gets out of the old centers of Lisbon. Even more than Spain, Portugal is a quite different country than it was thirty years ago, and the old indifferent attitude is neither prevalent nor possible.

In the past three years Portugal has hosted a high-level NATO conference, opened a world exposition, won a coveted seat on the United Nations Security Council, and served as president, on a rotating basis, of the European Union. The joke about Portugal is that five hundred years ago it was at the center of world discovery and trade; then it went to sleep for half a millennium, only to be awakened again in the last decades of the twentieth century. Today, the country is very dynamic, alive, and closely attuned to modern European currents. Along with Spain, its qualification through hard work, budget balancing, and strict fiscal controls for admission to the EMU as a founding member was a welcome surprise and a source of immense pride to the Portuguese. Overcoming past handicaps vis-à-vis Europe and flirtations with Third Worldism, Portugal is now thoroughly European and First World. Indeed, it has no other options at this stage, happily so from the Portuguese point of view.

Spain. Portugal's relations with Spain are good and normal but tempered always by the need to keep its large neighbor at a certain distance. As a smaller, weaker, and comparatively poorer country, Portugal continues to fear being overwhelmed by larger, richer Spain. It is not that Portugal fears military conquest, although that was a preoccupation in earlier centuries, but that the stronger Spanish economy will simply absorb Portugal into its orbit—much like the United States simply swallows the smaller, weaker economies of Central America and the Caribbean. Portugal's relations with Spain are thus cordial at the political and diplomatic level and there are increased economic ties between them, but a main tenet of Portuguese foreign policy has always been to maintain a system of alliances that serves to hold off Spain and gives Portugal maximum independence.

France, Great Britain, Germany. The main countries that Portugal uses to counterbalance Spain are France, Great Britain, and Germany. Portugal often emulates France culturally; the French newspaper *Le Monde* is often displayed on Portuguese coffee tables; many Portuguese intellectuals have lived or studied in Paris; and many Portuguese laborers have gone to France to work. Portugal cultivates these ties both for their own sake and because it wishes to have a strong ally right on Spain's northeastern border.

Portugal's ties with England are also historic, reaching back to a treaty signed in 1373, making it the oldest alliance in the Western world. Britain has long seen Portugal as its point of access to the European continent when other avenues are closed (as during World War II); Portugal sees England as a protector, first, against Spain and, second, against France, which occupied the entire peninsula under Napoleon. In addition, Portugal has long admired England, its strong currency and banking, its strong navy and empire, and its strong parliamentary institutions. In turn, British capital has invested heavily in the Portuguese wine industry and more recently has built manufacturing plants there; and many British pensioners retire to Portugal, where they have long been able to live well because of the low cost of living.

Portugal has not had a lot of contact historically with Germany, though in the nineteenth century they were rivals for African colonies. But in the 1960s and 1970s West Germany developed a major commercial and diplomatic presence in Portugal as it did in Spain; and, next to France, West Germany became the second largest recipient of Portuguese emigration. West German foundations, parties, and unions were extremely helpful to Portugal as it struggled for democracy in the 1970s and has been the major subsidizer of the Portuguese economy since that time. However, now with the unification of the two Germanies and with Germany's interest in the stability and prosperity of its Eastern European neighbors, its interest in Portugal has diminished.

Asia. Portugal is no longer a significant power or even presence in Asia, but three issues there require brief mention. First, Portugal once had three outposts—Goa, Diu, Dimão—on the Indian subcontinent which were retaken by Indian armies in the 1960s; but in these cities as well as scattered throughout the world one finds, because of the Portuguese influence, Indians who are strongly Catholic and shaped by Portuguese culture. Second, is Macão, another former Portuguese trading outpost, this time on the coast of China, which, like neighboring Hong Kong a short time earlier, was in 1999 turned back over to China. Third, is East Timor. This former Portuguese colony was, like the Portuguese colonies in Africa, precipitously granted independence in 1975, and was subsequently overrun militarily and absorbed into Indonesia. However, after Indonesian dictator Suharto's fall, rebellion and conflict broke out again; and in 1999 East Timor achieved independence but without the economic or institutional base to assure future stability.

Latin America. As a smaller, poorer country, Portugal has far more limited interests in Latin America than does Spain. Recognizing its limits, Portugal sees its role not as competing with the world's major political and economic powers but serving as an intermediary or interlocutor in those areas (mainly its former colonies) where it can be useful, such as Angola, Mozambique, or East Timor. Brazil, Portugal's former Latin America colony, is part of this calculation as well, except that, like the relations of the United States to Great Britain, the former colony of Brazil has far surpassed the former mother country in population, GNP, and international clout. Hence, while there is something of a "special relationship," because of common history, culture, and language, to Portugal-Brazil relations, it is Brazil that aspires to be the leader in this partnership. Portugal has invested in Brazil, but there is even more Brazilian investment in Portugal. While Portugal seeks to maintain its role as interlocutor in Southern Africa, Brazil is a larger presence there than is Portugal. And while Portugal has advanced the notion of a Lusitanian confederation of all the Portuguese-speaking nations (like France and its former colonies), it is Brazil as much as Portugal that would like to claim leadership in that group.

The United States. The United States has long considered itself a friend and ally of Portugal; the feeling is, generally, mutual. These sentiments have been reinforced by increased American investment in Portugal as well as by the large number of Portuguese immigrants, both from the Azores and from the mainland, who have come to the United States and, like other ethnic groups, are gaining economic and political importance.

During both World Wars I and II, the United States and Great Britain were granted the right to use naval and air bases in the Azores islands, the only islands in the mid-Atlantic and, therefore, a major strategic asset. During the Cold War, U.S. interests in Portugal were mainly strategic: continued use of the Azores bases in return for military assistance and Marshall Plan aid to Portugal. Relations were strained in the 1960s because the United States took an anticolonialist stand regarding Portuguese Africa and imposed an arms embargo on Portugal; Portugal retaliated by refusing for a time to renew the bases agreement.

The United States was not worried initially by the Portuguese revolution in 1974, assuming that Spínola, the military, and the historically conservative and anticommunist people would steer the country in a centrist, democratic direction. But as the revolution lurched to the left and it appeared possible the communists might seize power, the United States became concerned and launched a campaign to prevent that from happening. The U.S. embassy in Lisbon, then under Frank Carlucci, began vigorous diplomatic and covert activity, including foreign aid, assistance to noncommunist groups, cooperation with NATO allies, and financial and strategic support to the Portuguese Socialist Party as the best alternative to the communists. The United States also sought to rally the moderate elements in the military and throughout Portugal. The period 1974–76 was tense, but over time the U.S. effort paid off as Portugal returned to the democratic fold.

During the late 1970s, U.S. assistance remained high and the United States built a new, fortresslike embassy in Lisbon's outskirts, replacing the cramped embassy building in the city center, which had often been subject to hostile protests. But as Portugal settled down in the 1980s and the communist threat receded, the embassy staff's size and assistance program were greatly reduced. Meanwhile, with Portugal's accession to the EEC in 1986, European assistance and subsidies replaced the American aid. The U.S. presence and assistance returned to what it had been before 1974: low level, low key, and modest.

As Portugal has prospered and firmly established its democracy, U.S.–Portugal relations have returned to normalcy. There are still issues: for example, as the Cold War ended, the United States signaled a determination to terminate its lease arrangements for the Azores bases, costing Portugal jobs and income. On the other hand, the United States has welcomed Portuguese intermediation in such problem areas as southern Africa and East Timor. Meanwhile, to advance its international interests like other foreign embassies in Washington do, the Portuguese embassy has begun to mobilize the Portuguese ethnic community in the United States to vote and get more actively involved in politics. Overall, U.S.–Portugal relations are thus good, friendly, and "normal" but not "special."

Other relations. The Middle East, the Maghreb, and particularly the Arab states are especially important to Portugal, as they are to Spain, because of its need to import virtually 100 percent of its energy supplies, although Portugal has sought to diversify its sources of oil and other raw materials through agreements with former colony Angola. Like Spain, Portugal is distant from events in Russia and the former Soviet Union, although it also wants peace, stability, and democracy in the region and, with its new prosperity, is not averse to EU subsidies being channeled in the future to Eastern Europe. Like Spain, furthermore, Portugal is a member of the United Nations, the Organization for Economic Cooperation and Development (OECD), and other international organizations. It is preparing for globalization but its business firms and bureaucratic infrastructure are less prepared for this twenty-first century new wave than are Spain's.

SUMMING UP

Spain and Portugal have made some remarkable strides economically and socially as well as politically. Poor and long isolated from the modern industrial world, Spain and Portugal lagged behind the rest of Europe. But since the late 1950s and accelerating today, both countries have blosomed economically. Their economic takeoffs, fueled by both enlightened domestic policy and massive foreign aid and subsidies, have enabled them to carry out the beneficial social programs they could not afford earlier. Their economic growth and the modernization of Iberian society to which economic development gave rise in turn enabled Spain and Portugal to put their democracy on a firmer basis. Indeed, if one were looking for a model of how a successful foreign assistance plan should work (relevant for the United States in Latin America, for example), Spain and Portugal would be it. Nowhere else has foreign aid so well accomplished the goals it set out to achieve. Being charter members of the EU should also help the Iberian nations not only to continue their economic and social modernization but to further consolidate their democracies as well. It bears repeating in this context that, while both countries have progressed impressively, Spain is still 30 percent more affluent than Portugal and with a far larger and more solid economic base. But both countries are on their way to becoming modern, middle-class, consumer-oriented societies; both are en route to becoming "normal" countries.

In foreign affairs, too, both Spain and Portugal have broken out of their historic isolation and inferiority. Greater affluence has enabled both countries to pursue a more activist foreign policy than they had followed in decades, even centuries—again with larger Spain doing considerably more than smaller Portugal. For both countries, their entry into the EEC, now the EU, did wonders for their self-confidence; that plus the growth of democracy means they are no longer pariah states, outcasts on the world scene. As both countries have democratized, settled down, and solved some of their historic antagonisms, they have also been able to carry out a more vigorous foreign policy; in turn, they are now treated by others as "ordinary countries." For Spain and Portugal, that is a major, even historic step forward.

NOTES

1. The best studies are by Eric Baklanoff, *The Economic Transformation of Spain and Portugal* (New York: Praeger, 1978).
2. Charles W. Anderson, *The Political Economy of Modern Spain: Policy-Making in an Authoritarian System* (Madison: University of Wisconsin Press, 1970).
3. An excellent survey is John Hooper, *The Spaniards: A Portrait of the New Spain* (London: Penguin, 1987).
4. Howard J. Wiarda, *Corporatism and Development: The Portuguese Experience* (Amherst: University of Massachusetts Press, 1977).
5. A useful overview of Spanish foreign policy may be found in *Spain: A Country Study* (Washington, D.C.: Government Printing Office, 1991).
6. Howard J. Wiarda, ed., *The Iberian-Latin American Connection: Implications for U.S. Policy* (Boulder, Colo.: Westview Press, 1986); Howard J. Wiarda, *Iberia and Latin America: New Democracies, New Policies, New Models* (Lanham, Md.: Rowman and Littlefield, 1996).
7. Eric Solsten, ed., *Portugal: A Country Study* (Washington, D.C.: Government Printing Office, 1994).
8. Antonio de Spínola, *Portugal and the Future* (Lisbon: Arcadia, 1974).

Chapter 10

CONCLUSION: ROOTS AND FLOWERS

The weight of tradition, history, and the past has long hung heavily over Iberia. Shaped not only by the Roman and Christian traditions which made them Western, but also by the Islamic and North African invasion which marked them as non-Western, Spain and Portugal were seen as "different" from other European nations. Then, isolated, withdrawn, and cut off from the main currents of modern Western life, Spain and Portugal remained locked into the structure of the sixteenth-century Counter-Reformation. Their subsequent development, or the lack thereof, was shaped by a cosmology and political culture at variance from that of the more modernizing nations of Europe. Instead of being influenced by John Locke (limited, representative government), Adam Smith (a market economy), and the egalitarian, democratic-pluralist conceptions of Thomas Jefferson and James Madison, Spain and Portugal were powerfully shaped by the hierarchical great chain of being of Thomas Aquinas, by the idea of absolutist, state-building authority as set forth by sixteenth-century Jesuit Francisco Suárez, and by the organic, corporatist, and top-down traditions of Iberian medieval history.

As a result, Spain and Portugal were bypassed by all the great, revolutionary transformations we identify with the modern age: the Renaissance, the Enlightenment, the scientific revolution ushered in with Galileo and Newton, the Protestant Reformation, the emergence of capitalism and the industrial revolution, the English revolution of political reform, the French Revolution of social change. Instead, Iberia maintained a closed, hierarchical, absolutist, traditionalist, mercantilist, authoritarian, and rigidly orthodox system of society, culture, economics, religion, and politics. Earlier in the book we called this the Hapsburgian model (after the dynasty in power in the sixteenth and seventeenth centuries), a shorthand way of saying that Spain and Portugal remained essentially feudal, medieval, and premodern.

It should not be surprising that Spain and Portugal were organized on this basis in the fifteenth and sixteenth centuries; those were the prevailing practices and institutions of the time. What is remarkable is that so many of these features lasted so long. They lasted through the seventeenth and eighteenth centuries of Spanish-Portuguese decline, in partially modified form in the conflicted nineteenth century, and on into the twentieth century in the form of the Franco and Salazar regimes: updated versions of the sixteenth-century authoritarian model. Some of these traditional traits and institutions are still present in Spain and Portugal today; the ancient cosmology and political culture lives on, although now greatly attenuated.

In the mid-eighteenth century a form of enlightened liberalism and reform (the Bourbon monarchy in Spain, Pombal in Portugal) although still highly centralized and autocratic, came to power in both countries. In carrying out its reform agenda, this movement gave rise to the phenomenon of the "two Spains" and the "two Portugals"—two "nations," two societies, wholly separate and apart, coexisting within the same country. The "old" and the "new" in Spain and Portugal were so far apart that they represented two separate "worlds," two distinct sociologies and lifestyles, so distinctive as to be all but uncompromisable: feudalism versus modernism. This split in the Spanish/Portuguese "soul" or political culture produced almost continuous conflict and civil war throughout the nineteenth century and on into the twentieth, leading to the reactionary Portuguese revolution of 1926 and the Spanish Civil War of 1936–39.

But these were not just ideological and cultural conflicts; at their base they were socioeconomic as well. Feudal or traditional Spain and Portugal had their base in the Church, the army, the monarchy, the landed class, and the countryside. Modern and liberal Spain and Portugal had their base in the emerging middle class, among intellectuals, among commercial and trading elements, and in the big cities. Between these two diametrically opposed conceptions and ways of life, there could be no compromise; the "two Spains" and "two Portugals" were almost always in conflict, quite literally at each others' throats. Hence, Spain and Portugal alternated between a reactionary traditionalism that by the early twentieth century no longer seemed appropriate, and a form of liberalism that, as exemplified by the First Portuguese Republic, 1910–26, and the Spanish Republic, 1931–36, seemed to degenerate into libertinage, chaos, and anarchy.

But if in the modern age traditionalism and reaction were no longer viable, liberalism didn't seem to work ("good for the United States and Britain," argued many in Iberia, "but given their history and political culture not good for Spain and Portugal"), and Marxism-Leninism was unacceptable, what else was left? The answer in the 1920s and 1930s was corporatism, for corporatism seemed to offer a new option, a "middle way." It stood for a strong state and a strong central authority, seemingly necessary to hold the divisive Spanish and Portuguese political systems together. Corporatism protected the traditional wielders of power, the Church, the army, and the economic elites, even while it incorporated newer professional groups and the working class. In other words, corporatism presented a way to combine traditional and modern; it seemed to provide the best of all possible worlds. Tradition, religion, and authority would all be preserved while at the same time Spain and Portugal adapted to the modern world. Corporatism would enable Spain and Portugal to retain order, authority, and the existing structures of society as well as to harness both capital and labor for integral national development. Historic institutions and the basics of the sociopolitical status quo could be preserved while the powerful forces of a modern industrial economy could be accommodated. What could be better than that? It is clear why in the interwar period corporatism appealed to a wide range of Spaniards and Portuguese.[1]

Unfortunately for Spain and Portugal, corporatism did not work very well either. The supposed balance that was meant to be achieved between labor and capital gave way to a system where capital and business elites dominated while organized labor was suppressed. What was supposed to be a harmonious and pluralistic "corporatism of association" yielded to a dictatorial "corporatism of the state." Authoritarianism, secret police, repression, censorship, and strict controls over all political activity were the realities of the Salazar and Franco regimes, not free activity or a flowering of cultural life. Franco used the corporatist ideology and phrases to rally support behind his regime, but he quickly ignored them, set them aside, and ruled as a military dictator, thus restoring traditionalist and reactionary Spain. Salazar was more of an ideologue and had a stronger philosophical and moral commitment to corporatism, but he too shunted it aside and ruled as a traditionalist dictator.

For some forty years, Spain and Portugal remained under dictatorial rule. This was a crucial time in both nations' history; for most of this period their development was warped and perverted by authoritarianism. Time stood still as a pair of old-fashioned regimes continued to hang onto power beyond their time. These regimes, however, were not entirely stagnant: economic reform in the 1950s paved the way for vast social changes in the 1960s that stimulated immense cultural and political changes in the 1970s. Even while the old, "dinosauric" dictatorships were still in power, the post-Franco and post-Salazar eras had already begun that would lead to liberalization, Europeanization, and democratization.

Since the mid-1970s, Spain and Portugal have embarked on a democratic course. The transitions to democracy in both countries have been bold and inspiring. Overcoming major structural, institutional, and political-cultural obstacles, as well as great uncertainty, Spain's and Portugal's democratization have served as models to other countries. Democracy has now been established and consolidated in Iberia for a quarter century. But given the sad and rather pathetic history of republicanism and liberalism in Iberia, we need to ask how firmly established are these new democracies? Can they last? How much has really changed? How firm is democracy's socioeconomic base? Will Spain and Portugal revert in the future to a new form of authoritarianism? Are the recent changes permanent or merely cyclical, bound to lead later on to impatience and disillusionment with democracy and to renewed calls for the discipline and order of authoritarianism? That cyclical process after all, based on the alternation between the two Spains and the two Portugals, has been the history of the two countries for over two centuries.

In fact, the changes in Iberia since the mid-1970s (actually since the late 1950s, thus encompassing the last fifteen years of the Franco and Salazar regimes) have been little short of phenomenal. Illiteracy has been all but eliminated. Health and nutrition have improved to the point where life expectancy is as high as in the rest of Europe. Industry, manufacturing, commerce, services, and tourism are the dynamic sectors of the economy; the "old world" of traditional agriculture and poor villages is disappearing. Urbanization has accelerated and vast social changes leading to modernization are under way. The middle class in both countries is far larger, more secure, and has been a rock of stability and democracy; the trade unions can freely organize, are recognized as legitimate political participants in economic and political life, and their members share in their countries' new affluence. Business and industry are well established and, in this new era of globalization, are among the most dynamic elements in society.

Spain and Portugal have joined NATO, were admitted to the EEC, and are founding members of the EMU. Both countries' international connections and foreign policies are stronger than before; their traditional isolation has broken down. Economic growth over a forty-year period has been close to miracle levels; affluence has increased and spread, and quite a bit of it has even trickled down. Spain and Portugal, like other nations, have, for good or ill, been caught up in the modern world culture of materialism, secularism, and consumerism. Traditional attitudes and beliefs are giving way to a changed, freer morality. Indeed, the changes in both countries over the past thirty years are so great as to render them all but unrecognizable. In a relatively short time Spain and Portugal have joined the modern world. These changes also provide a much firmer social, economic, political, cultural, and institutional base for democracy than was true when republicanism and democracy were tried, with tragic results, in the past.

Although democracy has now been firmly established in Spain and Portugal, there remain some pockets of resistance to it. In Spain, immediately after Franco died, support for democracy was at a high 85–90 percent of the population; subsequently, the figure dropped off to 75 percent, where it has held quite steady. Among the remaining 25 percent, 11 percent are critics of democracy; about 7–8 percent are antidemocratic; and 6 percent are indifferent.[2] In Portugal, the chaos that accompanied the 1974 revolution and the years of political instability and economic downturn that followed meant that support for democracy was lower than in Spain; democracy's popularity in Portugal later increased as the country became more prosperous and stable. In both countries, democracy is closely correlated with prosperity, stability, and "good times." But if the good times end, would democracy also lose support? Enough to make it precarious?

In both countries there are groups and institutions that are not yet fully democratic, or even reconciled to it. These include some elements within the Church, armed forces, police, bureaucracy, the judiciary, and elite groups. Many Spanish and Portuguese peasants and urban slum-dwellers have so far received few benefits from democracy and are not enamored of it, but these groups are declining in numbers in both countries. Note that we have used the term "pockets of resistance" and referred to "elements" within these groups: that is a far cry from the situation in the 1920s and 1930s, when half of society favored democracy and liberalism and the other half was adamantly opposed, leading to strife and civil war. The fact that three-quarters of the population now solidly and consistently favor democracy and only 15–20 percent are opposed represents a major step forward and a solid basis for Spanish and Portuguese democracy.

More worrisome are some Spanish and Portuguese political attitudes. It is one thing and relatively easy to change institutions to bring forth democracy; it is quite another to change basic, underlying attitudes or political culture. Spain and Portugal have now developed political parties, had numerous elections, written new constitutions, convened parliaments, and had several peaceful, democratically determined changeovers of government. These are the formal institutions of democracy. But if we use a broader conception of democracy that includes values, attitudes, and prevailing political culture, there are still worrisome features present in Spain and Portugal. These include a pervasive sense of hierarchy and inequality among persons, a haughty and condescending attitude on the part of elite groups, and a certain disdain for the lower classes. They also include a continuing desire to control, to regulate, to treat people like a herd of cattle rather than allow genuine freedom. Both politically and economically, the statist, mercantilist, top-down, authoritarian tradition seems still alive, although it is now transformed and less omnipresent. At the same time, there has been remarkably little growth in civil society in the years since Franco's death and the overthrow of Portuguese authoritarianism. Neither socially nor politically are Spain and Portugal yet fully egalitarian, pluralist, democratic societies.[3]

The message is, therefore, a mixed one. On the one hand, Spain and Portugal have made enormous strides in recent decades. On the other, there are important and not very democratic political and cultural currents from the past that are still very much alive. What may be equally interesting are Spain's and Portugal's efforts to try to combine and reconcile these older currents with its newer democratic ones or to pour new wine into the old bottles. For example, at the level of national political institutions, Spain and Portugal are clearly democratic, but in the way local governments and political groups deal with the state, corporatism is very much present. It is not the old-fashioned authoritarian corporatism of Franco and Salazar but neocorporatism: a system by which the state regulates interest groups and incorporates and coopts them into decisions making rather than allowing them genuine freedom and independence.[4] Similarly, in the political sphere, while elections and democracy are the formal coin of politics, behind the scenes, patronage, family connections, clan rivalries, and special access are critically important. And though Spain and Portugal have moved toward a system of individual human rights, in practice group rights and that ancient organic conception of the state and society may be predominant. In short, rather than definitively eliminating the past and substituting the new and the modern, including democracy, in its place, Spain and Portugal seem to have combined and fused past and present in new, interesting, but very Spanish and Portuguese ways. But is that really any different from what Japan, France, Germany, Great Britain, and other countries with long pasts have done?

We are now in a position to begin answering the questions posed earlier that have always been so difficult for Spain and Portugal and that serve as the main themes of this book. First, in terms of the conflict between traditional and modern, it is now clear that modernity has won, or else in a variety of areas the two have combined. It is no longer an even battle between traditional Spain and modern Spain or between traditional Portugal and modern Portugal. The "two Spains" and "two Portugals" concept has ended, terminated by the powerful currents of Europeanization and democratization and fueled by industrialization, prosperity, social change, rising literacy, the move from countryside to cities, and overall modernization and globalization. Modernity has won out. The older split in the Spanish/Portuguese "soul" and society has been overcome and is no longer capable of tearing these two countries apart. Or if not overcome, then it has been ameliorated, patched over, erased from memory (as with the Spanish civil war), or fused into modern forms. Spain and Portugal may still divide over other issues but the old ruptures that for two hundred years fragmented and fractured them are no longer threatening, let alone dangerous.

Second, there is the conflict between democracy and authoritarianism. At this stage, we can say that, while there are still many authoritarian and inegalitarian tendencies in Iberia, democracy has triumphed. Seventy-five percent or more of the population favors democracy; almost no one (publicly) favors authoritarianism anymore; and Marxism-Leninism has all but disappeared as an option. There are "pockets" and "elements" of authoritarianism in Spain and Portugal but no longer a societywide culture of authoritarianism, a whole way of life encompassing large sectors of the population. The strength of democracy is so great that even antidemocrats in the two countries now pay it at least lip service and feel they must operate within a democratic framework. Plus, Spain's and Portugal's membership in the EEC/EU/EMU now makes it unthinkable that anything besides democracy could triumph; indeed, there would be such extremely strong European economic and political sanctions if democracy were upset that no one can even contemplate that possibility. Democracy may come with fascinating Spanish and Portuguese twists to it (more organic, corporatist, patrimonialist), but it is democracy nonetheless.

A third question is whether Spain and Portugal are closer to the First World of modern, industrialized, capitalistic nations or to the Third World of poor, underdeveloped ones. It was not that long ago (twenty to forty years) that this would have been a difficult question to answer, and in the midst of the Revolution of 1974 Portugal proclaimed itself part of the Third World. But now the answer is unambiguous: Iberia is part of the modern, industrial, capitalist First World. Both countries are now classified as "industrial market economies"; both countries have "made it" into the World Bank's highest category of advanced nations—although along with Greece and Ireland still at the lower ranks within that category. Indeed, both economically and politically, Spain and Portugal are among the great success stories of the last third of the twentieth century and models for other nations.

Finally, there is the question of religion. Spain and Portugal began as theocracies; their social and political institutions were both shaped and locked in place by the sixteenth-century Counter-Reformation; their political theory or cosmology, fashioned by Thomas Aquinas and Francisco Suárez and based powerfully on medieval Catholic precepts, represented an alternative in Iberia and Latin America to the Lockean liberalism of the Anglo-American tradition. In the eyes of most outsiders, this cosmology helped hold Spain and Portugal back, but for a long time in the eyes of most of their own peoples, it was this belief system that gave them their essence, their place in the universe, their distinctiveness. Now both countries are more secular, less Catholic, and the strength of these beliefs has faded. Nevertheless, there are still powerful currents in both countries that reflect the earlier traditions: the presidency in Portugal and the monarchy in Spain are symbols and manifestations of the earlier concept of organic unity; corporatism and patrimonialism (although in new forms) are very much alive in both countries; there is still throughout both countries, beneath the surface secularism, a strong sense of the spiritual or the incandescent. It is not just Spain's and Portugal's democratization and economic accomplishments that are fascinating but also how they have blended old and new, traditional and modern, indigenous and imported in their own unique way.

The changes in both countries in recent decades have been enormous, including impressive economic development, vast social modernization, and democratization. In this conclusion we have so far concentrated on the parallels between the two Iberian nations in all these areas, but we should not neglect the considerable differences that still exist between them. Spain has a per capita income roughly one-third more than Portugal's and a gross national product five or six times as large. Literacy is higher in Spain and social modernization has proceeded farther. In addition, Spain's social, political, and economic foundations and institutions are considerably more developed.

Hence, it should not surprise us that Spanish democracy also seems firmer than the Portuguese, on a more solid base, better consolidated. Democracy in Spain, therefore, seems to be firmly in place, well institutionalized, with only small pockets of opposition. Portugal's democracy is also solid, particularly with the economic boom and greater stability that began in the mid-1980s; but its socioeconomic and institutional base is still weaker than Spain's. At this point, democracy seems strong in both countries, in no danger of being overthrown.

Both countries' accomplishments economically, socially, and politically in the last thirty years are little short of miraculous. They are all the more remarkable for having received so little worldwide attention. The fall of the Berlin Wall and the reunification of Germany, the collapse of the Soviet Union and the fall of communism, the end of the Warsaw Pact and the transformations in Eastern Europe have all made front-page headlines in recent years, but not the enormously impressive changes in Spain and Portugal. In fact, the transition from an underdeveloped to an advanced industrial economy, from social backwardness to modernity, and from authoritarianism to democracy is an enormously impressive, if little noted, accomplishment; and it deserves far greater attention and credit than so far have been given. The changes in Iberia rank right up there among the most significant events of the late twentieth century.

Although Spain and Portugal have indeed been transformed and in all areas of life, the continuities from the past must be borne in mind as well. Even with all the changes toward "European" values and a European-style political system, Iberia remains in many ways unique, distinctive. Pass five minutes, even blindfolded, in Spain or Portugal and you know immediately you are not in Germany, Great Britain, or Scandinavia. The Iberian nations now approximate the European economy and polity models, but they are not there yet; more than that, they retain—and are certain to continue to retain—particular Spanish and Portuguese features and ways of doing things that are uniquely their own, products of their own histories and sociocultural traditions. They are no longer "different" in the way Franco and Salazar emphasized for their own political purposes, but they retain their own culture, societal norms and institutions, and particular political forms and practices. Moreover, after twenty-five years of seeking to be European, there is now in Spain and Portugal a certain nostalgia for and renewed interest in the past, in their own history, in what made them different—including their Muslim past, which Spain and Portugal previously had preferred to forget. Iberia is rediscovering its roots to go along with its Europeanness, a healthy and long-overdue development in our view, which also reflects the often overlooked realities of their political systems—European, democratic, but also very Spanish, very Portuguese.

Spanish and Portuguese democracy, for instance, still seems closer to the organic, centralized, unified view of Aquinas, or perhaps in modern form of Rousseau, than to the individualistic, pluralist, decentralized, checks-and-balances form of Locke or Madison. And while Spain and Portugal have jettisoned the corporatist-authoritarian institutions and ideology of the past, they still practice corporatism in the way the central state and societal organizations (business, labor, the Church, etc.) interact. They are no longer corporatist in the old-fashioned, medieval sense but (and in contrast to U.S.–style competitive lobbying and pluralism) in the modern neocorporative sense in which organized labor, employers, and the state agree to a social pact to prevent disruptions and foment integral national development. There is room for further studies of how Spain and Portugal have gone not only from authoritarianism to democracy but from an older form of corporatism to a newer, more advanced, more open form, and how they have blended old and new in the process.

Intriguing also as a subject for further study is the notion advanced in chapter 8 of a contract state. The concept refers to the compacts ("fundamental" or "organic" laws) worked out between the state and the military, the state and organized labor, the state and local governments, (in Spain) the state and the autonomous regions, the state and virtually every organized group or entity in the country. What is so fascinating about these arrangements is that they have strong roots deep in the Iberian past and correspond closely to the historic Iberian understanding of democracy and representative rule. That is, when the state and its component social and corporate units are in harmony, are governed by mutually satisfactory compacts, and the rights and responsibilities of each are spelled out in law—this has historically been defined in Iberia as "democracy," a formulation that has now been combined with the electoral/institutional or modern Western definition of democracy.

Spain particularly and Portugal less explicitly have resurrected this ancient conception of Iberian "democracy" while at the same time creating all the institutions (parties, parliament, elections) of a Western and European form of democracy, and managing—often without explicitly thinking about or acknowledging it because to Spaniards and Portuguese that is the historic, almost "natural," way to operate the political system. In other words, Spain and Portugal have both an imported form of democracy that they have largely taken from Western Europe, and one with home-grown or indigenous roots, both of which seem to be working quite well. Again, some fascinating further studies could be carried out on these themes. But if it is accurate that Spain and Portugal have successfully blended both outside and home-grown forms of democracy, then that is not only a great accomplishment, it also has enormous implications for the field of comparative politics and for the future of other nations of the world. Many of these nations, especially in the Third World, also have the difficult task of taking what is best from the Western tradition (democracy) and fusing it with native, indigenous forms and ways of doing things. If Spain and Portugal can manage such a fusion successfully, then they will not only have provided a remarkable case study of impressive democratization and economic development but also a model that has global implications.

Spain and Portugal are now "regular," "normal," "ordinary" countries, democratic, with modern mixed economies, rather like their Western European neighbors. In both countries the great "systems" debate of the past (whether to be authoritarian, Marxist, or democratic) is largely over. Spain and Portugal are firmly in the democratic, European, free-economy camp. Ironically, now that they have made it to the front ranks and become thoroughly European, both countries are again rediscovering their roots, their origins, and what made them different. We find this healthy and invigorating, both the inspiring effort by Spain and Portugal to achieve first-rank status and recognition in Europe and the effort, now that these overriding national goals have been achieved, to also sort out and value what is distinctive and worth preserving from their past.

All countries need to find this healthy balance between global trends and their own indigenous experiences, and the Iberian nations are no exceptions. Meanwhile, Spain and Portugal must still solve some difficult equity problems, continue to modernize their economies and societies, and adapt to the newer currents of globalization which are certain to dominate in the twenty-first century.

NOTES

1. Howard J. Wiarda, *Corporatism and Development: The Portuguese Experience* (Amherst: University of Massachusetts Press, 1977).

2. Data in E. Ramón Arango, *Spain: Democracy Regained* (Boulder, Colo.: Westview Press, 1995), 311.

3. Peter McDonough, Samuel Barnes, and Antonio López Pina, *The Cultural Dynamics of Democratization in Spain* (Ithaca: Cornell University Press, 1998).

4. Howard J. Wiarda, *Corporatism and Comparative Politics: The Other Great "Ism"* (New York: M. E. Sharpe, 1996).

Selected Bibliography

Abel, Christopher, and Nissa Torrents, eds. *Spain: Conditional Democracy.* London: Croom Helm, 1984.

Aceves, Joseph. *Social Change in a Spanish Village.* Cambridge, Mass.: Schenkman, 1971.

Anderson, Charles W. *The Political Economy of Modern Spain: Policy-Making in an Authoritarian System.* Madison: University of Wisconsin Press, 1970.

Anderson, Jon Lee. "The Reign in Spain," *The New Yorker*, April 27, May 4, 1998, 110–19.

Aquinas, St. Thomas. *St. Thomas Aquinas on Politics and Ethics.* Translated and edited by Paul E. Sigmund. New York: Norton, 1988.

Arango, E. Ramón. *Spain: Democracy Regained.* Boulder, Colo.: Westview Press, 1995.

Arrighi, Giouahni, ed. *Semiperipheral Development: The Politics of Southern Europe in the Twentieth Century.* Beverly Hills, Calif.: Sage, 1985.

Baklanoff, Eric. *The Economic Transformation of Spain and Portugal.* New York: Praeger, 1978.

Bender, Gerald J. *Angola under the Portuguese: The Myth and the Reality.* Berkeley: University of California Press, 1978.

Bermeo, Nancy. *The Revolution within the Revolution: Workers' Control in Rural Portugal.* Princeton: Princeton University Press, 1986.

Bonine-Blanc, Andrea. *Spain's Transition to Democracy: The Politics of Constitution-Making.* Boulder, Colo.: Westview Press, 1987.

Brenan, Gerald. *The Face of Spain.* New York: Penguin, 1987.

______. *The Spanish Labyrinth: Account of the Social and Political Background of the Spanish Civil War.* Cambridge: Cambridge University Press, 1971.

Brettell, Caroline B. *Men Who Migrate, Women Who Wait: Population and History in a Portuguese Parish.* Princeton: Princeton University Press, 1986.

Bruneau, Thomas, ed. *Political Parties and Democracy in Portugal.* Boulder, Colo.: Westview Press, 1997.

Bruneau, Thomas, and Alex MacLeod. *Politics in Contemporary Portugal: Parties and the Consolidation of Democracy.* Boulder, Colo.: Lynne Rienner Publishers, 1986.

Bruneau, Thomas, Victor M. P. da Rosa, and Alex MacLeod, eds. *Portugal in Development: Emigration, Industrialization, the European Community.* Ottawa, Canada: University of Ottawa Press, 1984.

Carr, Raymond. *Spain, 1808–1939.* Oxford: Clarendon Press, 1966.

Carr, Raymond, and Juan Pablo Fusi. *Spain: From Dictatorship to Democracy.* London: Allen and Unwin, 1979.

Castro, Americo. *The Spaniards: An Introduction to Their History.* Translated by Willard F. King and Selma Margaretten. Berkeley: University of California Press, 1971.

Chislett, William. "Portugal" and "Spain" in *The Europe Review.* 11th ed. London: Walden Publishing, 1998.

Clark, Robert P. *The Basques.* Reno: University of Nevada Press, 1980.

Clark, Robert P., and Michael H. Haltzel, eds. *Spain in the 1980s: The Democratic Transition and a New International Role.* Cambridge, Mass.: Ballinger Publishing, 1987.

Collinson, Patrick, "The Late Medieval Church and its Reformation." In *The Oxford Illustrated History of Christianity.* Edited by John McManners. Oxford: Oxford University Press, 1990.

Cortada, James W., ed. *Spain in the Twentieth Century World.* Westport, Conn.: Greenwood, 1980.

Cottrell, Alvin J., and James D. Theberge, eds. *The Western Mediterranean: Its Politics, Economic and Strategic Importance.* New York: Praeger, 1974.

Crouch, Colin, and Anand Menon. "Organized Interests and the State." In *Developments in West European Politics.* Edited by Martin Rhodes, Paul Heywood, and Vincent Wright. New York: St. Martin's Press, 1997.

Crow, John A. *Spain: The Root and the Flower.* Berkeley: University of California Press, 1985.

Cutileiro, José. *A Portuguese Rural Society.* Oxford: Clarendon, 1971.

Eaton, Samuel D. *The Forces of Freedom in Spain, 1974–1979.* Stanford, Calif.: Hoover Institution Press, 1981.

Fletcher, Richard. *Moorish Spain.* Berkeley: University of California Press, 1992.

Gallagher, Thomas. *Portugal: A Twentieth-Century Interpretation.* Manchester, England: Manchester University Press, 1983.

Garcia, Soledad. "The Spanish Experience and Its Implications for a Citizen's Europe." In *The Anthropology of Europe.* Edited by Victora A. Goddard et al. London: Berg, 1996.

Gellner, Ernest, and John Waterbury, eds. *Patrons and Clients in Mediterranean Societies.* London: Duckworth, 1977.

Graham, Lawrence S., and Douglas L. Wheeler, eds. *In Search of Modern Portugal: The Revolution and Its Consequences.* Madison: University of Wisconsin Press, 1983.

Graham, Lawrence S., and Harry M. Makler, eds. *Contemporary Portugal: The Revolution and Its Antecedents.* Austin: University of Texas Press, 1979.

Gunther, Richard. *Politics and Culture in Spain.* Ann Arbor: Institute for Social Research, University of Michigan, 1988.

______, ed. *Politics, Society, and Democracy: The Case of Spain.* Boulder, Colo.: Westview Press, 1993.

______. *Public Policy in a No-Party State: Spanish Planning and Budgeting in the Twilight of the Franquist Era.* Berkeley: University of California Press, 1980.

Gunther, Richard, Giacomo Sani, and Goldie Shabad. *Spain after Franco: The Making of a Competitive Party System.* Berkeley: University of California Press, 1986.

Hamilton, Bernice. *Political Thought in Sixteenth-Century Spain.* Oxford: Oxford University Press, 1963.

Hayward, Jack, and Edward C. Page, eds. *Governing the New Europe.* Durham, N.C.: Duke University Press, 1995.

Herr, Richard. *An Historical Essay on Modern Spain.* Berkeley: University of California Press, 1971.

Heywood, Paul. *Politics and Policy in Democratic Spain.* London: Frank Cass, 1999.

Hooper, John. *The New Spaniards.* New York: Penguin, 1995.

Jackson, Gabriel. *The Spanish Republic and the Civil War, 1931–1939.* Princeton: Princeton University Press, 1965.

Ibn Khaldun. *The Muqaddimah: An Introduction to History.* Edited by N. J. Dawood. Translated by Franz Rosenthal. Princeton: Princeton University Press, 1967.

Kamen, Henry. *The Spanish Inquisition: A Historical Revision.* New Haven: Yale University Press, 1997.

Kay, Hugh. *Salazar and Modern Portugal.* London: Eyre and Spottiswoode, 1970.

Kohler, Beate. *Political Forces in Spain, Greece, and Portugal.* London: Butterworth, 1982.

Lancaster, Thomas D. *Political Stability and Democratic Change: Energy in Spain's Transition.* University Park: Pennsylvania State University Press, 1989.

Lancaster, Thomas D., and Gary Prevost, eds. *Politics and Change in Spain.* New York: Praeger, 1985.

Linz, Juan. "An Authoritarian Regime: Spain." Edited by E. Allardt and Stein Rokkan. In *Mass Politics.* New York: The Free Press, 1970.

______. "A Century of Politics and Interests in Spain." Edited by Suzanne Berger. In *Organizing Interests in Western Europe.* New York: Cambridge University Press, 1981.

Magone, José M. *European Portugal: The Difficult Road to Sustainable Democracy.* New York: St. Martin's Press, 1997.

Malefakis, Edward. *Agrarian Reform and Peasant Revolution in Spain: Origins of the Civil War.* New Haven: Yale University Press, 1970.

Maravall, José. *The Transition to Democracy in Spain.* London: Croom Helm, 1982; New York: St. Martin's Press, 1982.

Marias, Julián. *Understanding Spain.* Ann Arbor: University of Michigan Press, 1990.

Matthews, Herbert L. *The Yoke and the Arrows: A Report on Spain.* New York: Braziller, 1961.

Maxwell, Kenneth. *The Making of Portuguese Democracy.* New York: Cambridge University Press, 1995.

______. *Portugal in the 1980s.* New York: Greenwood Press, 1986.

McDonough, Peter, Samuel Barnes, and Antonio López Pina. *The Cultural Dynamics of Democratization in Spain.* Ithaca: Cornell University Press, 1998.

McKay, Angus. *Spain in the Middle Ages.* Madrid: Cátedra, 1977.

Medhurst, Kenneth N., ed. *Government in Spain.* Oxford: Pergamon Press, 1973.

Michener, James A. *Iberia: Spanish Travels and Reflections.* New York: Random House, 1968.

Mott, Margaret MacLeish. "The Rule of Faith over Reason: The Role of the Inquisition in Iberia and New Spain." *The Journal of Church and State* 40 (winter 1998): 57–81.

______. "Membership in the *Corpus Mysticum:* Metaphysical Politics in the Age of Saints." Ph.D. diss., University of Massachusetts, 2001.

Mujal-Leon, Eusebio. *Communism and Political Change in Spain.* Bloomington: Indiana University Press, 1981.

Muth, Annmarie, ed. *Statistical Abstract of the World.* 3rd ed. Detroit: Gale Publishing, 1997.

Opello, Walter C., Jr. *Portugal's Political Development: A Comparative Approach.* Boulder, Colo.: Westview Press, 1985.

Ortega y Gasset, José. *Invertebrate Spain.* New York: Norton, 1937.

______. *The Revolt of the Masses.* New York: Norton, 1932.

Orwell, George. *Homage to Catalonia.* New York: Harcourt, Brace, 1952.

Netanyahu, B. *The Origins of the Inquisition in Fifteenth-Century Spain.* New York: Random House, 1995.

Payne, Stanley. *Falange.* Stanford, Calif.: Stanford University Press, 1961.

______. *The Franco Regime, 1936–1975.* Madison: University of Wisconsin Press, 1987.

______. *A History of Fascism, 1914–1945.* Madison: University of Wisconsin Press, 1995.

______. *A History of Spain and Portugal.* 2 vols. Madison: University of Wisconsin Press, 1973.

______. *Politics and the Military in Modern Spain.* Stanford, Calif.: Stanford University Press, 1967.

______. *Spanish Catholicism: An Historical Overview.* Madison: University of Wisconsin Press, 1984.

______. *Spain's First Democracy: The Second Republic, 1931–1936.* Madison: University of Wisconsin Press, 1993.

Peces-Barba Martinez, Gregorio. *La Elaboracion de la Constitucíon de 1978.* Madrid: Centro de Estudios Constitucionales, 1988.

Pike, Frederick B. *Hispanismo, 1898–1936: Spanish Conservatives and Liberals and Their Relations with Spanish America.* Notre Dame, Ind.: Notre Dame University Press, 1971.

Pollack, Benny. *The Paradox of Spanish Foreign Policy.* New York: St. Martin's Press, 1987.

Porch, Douglas. *The Portuguese Armed Forces and the Revolution.* London: Croom Helm, 1977.

Pridham, Geoffrey, ed. *The New Mediterranean Democracies: Regime Transition in Spain, Greece, and Portugal.* London: Frank Cass, 1984.

Robinson, Richard. *Contemporary Portugal.* London: Allen and Unwin, 1979.

Sachar, Howard M. *Farewell España: The World of the Sephardim Remembered.* New York: Vintage, 1994.

Schmitter, Philippe. *Corporatism and Public Policy in Authoritarian Portugal.* Beverly Hills, Calif.: Sage, 1975.

Seward, Desmond. *The Monks of War: The Military Religious Orders.* New York: Penguin, 1995.

Solsten, Eric, ed. *Portugal: A Country Study.* Washington, D.C.: U.S. Government Printing Office, 1994.

______, ed. *Spain: A Country Study.* Washington, D.C.: U.S. Government Printing Office, 1990.

Stuart, Douglas T., ed. *Politics and Security in the Southern Region of the Atlantic Alliance.* Baltimore: Johns Hopkins University Press, 1988.

Thody, Philip. *An Historical Introduction to the European Union.* New York: Routledge, 1997.

Trythall, J.W.D. *Franco: A Biography.* London: Rupert Hart-Davis, 1970.

Vicens Vives, Jaime. *Approaches to the History of Spain.* Berkeley: University of California Press, 1970.

Walsh, Michael. *Opus Dei: An Investigation into the Secret Society Struggling for Power within the Roman Catholic Church.* San Francisco: Harper Collins, 1992.

Welles, Benjamin. *Spain: The Gentle Anarchy.* New York: Praeger, 1965.

Wheeler, Douglas L. *Republican Portugal: A Political History, 1920–1926.* Madison: University of Wisconsin Press, 1978.

Wiarda, Howard J. *Corporatism and Development: The Portuguese Experience.* Amherst: University of Massachusetts Press, 1977.

______. *From Corporatism to Neo-Syndicatism: The State, Organized Labor, and the Changing Industrial Relations Systems of Southern Europe.* Cambridge: Harvard University, Center for European Studies, Monograph no. 4, 1981.

______. *Iberia and Latin America: New Democracies, New Policies, New Models.* Lanham, Md.: Rowman and Littlefield, 1996.

______. *Politics in Iberia: The Political Systems of Spain and Portugal.* New York: Harper & Row, 1990.

______. *Transcending Corporatism? The Portuguese Corporative System and the Revolution of 1974.* Columbia: University of South Carolina, Institute of International Studies, 1976.

______, ed. *The Iberian-Latin American Connection: Implications for U.S. Policy.* Boulder, Colo.: Westview Press, 1986.

Wiarda, Howard J. and Iêda S. Wiarda. *The Transition to Democracy in Spain and Portugal.* Washington, D.C.: University Press of America, 1989.

Williams, Allan, ed. *Southern Europe Transformed: Political and Economic Change in Greece, Italy, Portugal, and Spain.* London: Harper & Row, 1984.

Index

Abbasid Dynasty, 15
Abortion, 102, 112, 154
Absolutism, 28, 127
Accão Nacional Popular (ANP), 50, 130
Afonso Henriques, 20
Afrancesados, 30, 100
Africa, 59, 62, 183–85
AIDS, 118, 180. *See also* Health
Alcalá Zamora, Niceto, 34
Alfonso VI, 19
Alfonso X (the Wise), 20
Alfonso XIII, 34, 70
Aliança Democrática (AD), 66, 135
Alianza Popular (AP), 72, 75, 114, 136
Anarchism, 33, 35, 127
Ancien regime, 107
Angola, 62
Antidemocratic elements, 195
Arías Navarro, Carlos, 70, 71
Aristotle, 12, 42, 85–86
Armed Forces Movement (MFA), 64, 65, 153
Army, 50, 107–9, 127. *See also* Military; *Pronunciamiento*
Asia, 187
Assembly of the Republic, 155, 156
Asturias, 12, 115
Augustine, Saint, 14
Autarky, 55, 164. *See also* Mercantilism
Authoritarianism, 48–49, 92–93, 128–130
Autonomous communities, 118
Autonomy, 137
Azaña, Manuel, 34
Aznar, José María, 98; economic policies of, 136, 169; election of, 75–76, 158; relationship with EU, 147
Azores, 187–88

Balkans, 179
Balsemão, Francisco Pinto, 66
Banks, 52, 114, 150
Basque regional parties, 138, 154

Basques, 75, 108
Belgium, 121
Berbers, 15, 18. *See also* Moors
Birthrates, 149
Bourbon Monarchy, 27–28, 100, 126
Brenan, Gerald, 96
Bullfight, 13–14, 98, 119, 154
Bureaucracy, 120, 146, 151
Bureaucratic state, 43, 44, 51
Business, as interest group, 120; popular opinion of, 102; regulation of, 114; under Franco, 47, 52; under Salazar, 44; under Suárez, 72. *See also Confederación Espanola de Organizaciones Empresariales* (CEOE)

Caciques, 107
Caetano, Marcello, 58–59
Calvo-Sotelo, Leopoldo, 73
Carillo, Santiago, 72, 132
Carlist Wars, 31
Carlos, Don, 31
Carmona, Óscar Fragoso, 33
Carrero Blanco, Luis, 58, 70
Carthaginians, 11
Castro, Fidel, 75
Catalonian parties, 138
Catholic Monarchs, 23–24. *See also* Hapsburg Monarchy
Catholic social teachings, 40–41, 42–44
Catholicism, 28–29, 97–100. *See also* Roman Catholic Church
Caudillos, 18, 93
Cavaco Silva, Aníbal, 67, 135, 156
Cave dwellers, 10
Celts, 11
Censorship, 95
Centro Democrático y Social (CDS), 135
Ceuta, 180
Charles I (V), 24–25
Charles II, 27
Christian-Democrats, 52, 65
CIA, 65, 182
Cities, 98, 102
Civil service, 120
Civil society, 102, 105, 106, 119, 150
Civil War of 1936–1939, 35–36, 95, 113
Class structure, 138
Coimbra, University of, 34, 40, 41, 84
Columbus, Christopher, 22
Communist countries, 53
Communist parties, 65–66, 72, 116, 127, 130–32. *See also* Portuguese Communist Party
Communists, 35, 53, 54, 110. *See also* Communist parties
Confederación Española de Organizaciones Empresariales (CEOE), 114, 115
Congress of Deputies, 157, 158
Constituent Assembly, 152, 153
Constitution of 1812 (Spain), 30, 127
Constitution of 1933 (Portugal), 44
Constitution of 1976 (Portugal), 122, 152–153
Constitution of 1977 (Spain), 72, 122, 153–155
Contract state, 121
Conversos, 22
Convivencia, 6
Corporate groups, 12, 43, 91, 119, 121
Corporatism, Catholic roots, 87–88; defined, 94–95; under Franco, 46; under Salazar, 41–46; varieties of, 193. *See also* Neocorporatism
Cortes, history of, 19, 25, 30; institution of 153, 157; under Franco, 47; under Suárez, 72
Council of Bishops, 112
Council of Ministers, 156, 158
Council of State, 153, 159
Council of the Revolution, 153
Council of Trent, 84
Counter Reformation, 25, 102

Cuba, 75, 182

Democracy, 3, 151, 195
Democratic Alliance. *See Aliança Democratica*
Democratic deficiency, 122
Demographics, 146, 148
Development models, 2
Devolution, 146, 157, 159–61
Diaz del Castillo, Bernal, 25, 88
Divine law, 88–89
Divorce, 102, 110, 112
Domestic policy, 164–65. *See also* Economic policy, Education, Health, Welfare

Eanes, Ramalho, 66, 155
Economic development, 77, 112, 150, 169–70, 170–74
Economic elites, 56
Economic growth, 54, 55, 147
Economic policy, under Franco, 147, 167; under Salazar, 44–45, 55, 172
Education, 55, 110, 122, 127, 149
El Cid, 18, 92
Elections, 72, 75, 129–130, 141, 143. *See also* Voting
Emigration, 53, 101, 114, 147
Enlightenment, 29, 126, 127
Esquivá de Balaquer, Josemaría, 111, 112
Ethnic groups, 117–18
Euro, 148
Eurocommunism, 132
European Economic Community (EEC), 67, 69, 134, 169. *See also* European Union
European Union (EU), 6; catalyst of change,114, 122, 147; foreign policy with, 176–78, 185–86; hostility toward, 97, 118; relationship with regions, 160
Euskadi Ta Askatasuna (ETA), 118
Exiled, 131

Factions, 53
Falange Movement, 36, 46, 50, 52, 127. *See also* Movement, The
Fascism, 39, 45
Fátima, 99
Ferdinand VII, 30
Foreign policy, 176–83, 183–89
Fraga, Manuel, 72, 75, 136
France, 29, 178, 186
Franco, Francisco, decline, 58; relationship with banks, 114; relationship with political parties, 125; rise to power, 36, 39–40, 41–42; use of force, 93, 115
French occupations, 29–31
French Revolution, 29
Fueros (foros), 17, 25, 117, 160

Galicia, 11
Geertz, Clifford, 81, 82
Germanic tribes, 14
Germany, 147, 178, 186
Globalization, 122
Godoy, Manuel de, 29
González, Felipe, 71, 74–75, 102, 108, 134, 168
Goya, Francisco, 97
Great Britain, 26, 29, 186
Greeks, 11
Gross national product, 51
Grupos, 150–51
Grupos Anti-Terroristas de Liberación (GAL), 108
Guardia Civil, 1, 51
Guinea-Bissau, 62
Gulf War, 109
Guterres, António, 67, 134, 148, 156

Hapsburg Monarchy, 23–26
Hapsburgian model, 23–26
Health 122, 148–49
Hermangildas, 16
Herri Batasuna (HB), 118, 138
Hispanismo, 182

Hitler, Adolf, 128
Holy Warrior, 15, 16

Ibn Khaldun, 15, 92–93
Iglesias, José, 142
Income, 147
Individualism, 122
Industrialization, 55, 166
Industry, 54
Inquisition, 3, 17, 89, 113
Institutional Law of the State, 108
Integralist, 52, 128
Intellectuals, 54, 130
Intereses, 107, 145
Interest groups, 105, 120
International Monetary Fund (IMF), 173
Intersindical, 116
Isidore, Saint, 98
Islamic influence, 15–18
Italy, 121
Izquierda Republicana (IR), 34

James, Saint, 18, 88, 98
Jesuits, 27–28, 101
Jews, 17, 20–23, 180
John Paul II, Pope, 102, 111
Juan Carlos, King, 93, 98, 103, 113; and coup attempt, 1; and democracy, 71–72, 96; and military, 108
Juan, Don, 70–71, 113
Judiciary, 118

Labor, 115–17, 120; under Franco, 47; under Salazar, 44; under Suárez, 72
Labor statue, 44
Latin America, 181–82, 187
Ley Orgánica del Derecho de la Educación (LODE), 111
Liberalism, 31, 49, 95, 127, 193
Liberals, 35, 52
Limpieza de sangre, 113
Linz, Juan, 48–49
Literacy, 55, 149
Local saints, 98
Locke, John, 26, 31, 83
Lusitania, 12

Maastricht Treaty, 117, 147–48, 152
Manuel (King of Portugal), 23
María Christina, 31
Mariana, Juan de, 24, 27
Marxism, 65, 74, 94, 193
Melilla, 180
Mercantilism, 91, 114, 164–66
Merchant class, 113–14
Middle class, 56, 119
Middle East, 179, 188
Military, 30–31, 155. *See also* Army
Military orders, 16, 107
Militias, 107
Ministry of Syndicates, 47
Modernization, 100
Molina, Luis de, 84
Monarchists, 96, 106, 128
Monarchy, 96–97, 157
Moncloa Pact, 72
Monteíro, Manuel, 137
Moors, 15
Moran, Fernando, 74
Morocco, 180, 188
Movement, The, 71, 128, 130. *See also* Falange
Mozambique, 62
Mozarabs, 17
Mudejars, 17
Mussolini, Benito, 40–41, 128

Napoleon, 29
National identity, 9, 129, 146
National Popular Action. *See Accão Nacional Popular*
Natural law, 4, 12, 83, 88–90
Navarre, 117, 121
Neocorporatism, 78, 120, 140, 196
Netherlands, The, 26, 65
Newspapers, 58
Nobility, 113–15

North Africa, 14–15, 42
North American Trade Organization (NATO), 6, 74, 109, 118, 134

Oil prices, 62
Oligarchy, 151
Olive oil production, 97
Opposition groups, 52–54
Opus Dei, 50, 55, 111–12
Organicism, 94
Organization for Economic Cooperation and Development (OECD), 189
Ortega y Gasset, José, 106

Parliament, 141. *See also* Assembly of the Republic
Partido Comunista Español (PCE), 72, 132–33
Partido Nacionalista Vasco (PNV), 138
Partido Popular (PP), 75, 114, 134
Partido Socialista Obrero Español (PSOE), 34, 71–75, 132, 134, 139, 154, 168
Patrimonialism, 90–92
Patronage, 86, 129, 140, 151
Patronato Real, 14, 112
Paul, Saint, 86–87, 94
Peasants, 119, 127, 138
People's Party (PP). *See Partido Popular*
Perón, Juan, 5
Personalismo, 139
Philip II, 25
Phoenicians, 11
Pilgrimage, 99, 100
Pluralism, 71, 105–6, 119, 121
Political culture, 77, 81–82
Political parties, 50, 53, 76, 78, 102, 129, 142–43. *See also individual party names*
Political Reform Act of 1976, 72
Pombal, Marquis de, 28, 100, 126
Popular Party (PP), in Portugal, 137, 138
Popular Party (PP), in Spain. *See Partido Popular*
Portuguese Communist Party (PCP), 133
Portuguese First Republic, 32, 127
Presidential powers, 153, 155
Preto, Rolão, 52, 128
Prime Minister's powers, 155–56, 157
Primo de Rivera, José Antonio, 36
Primo de Rivera, Miguel, 33–34
Privatization, 152
Pronunciamiento, 30, 33, 95, 107, 109, 127
Protestant Reformation, 3, 25–26
Protestant values, 82, 91

Quadragesimo Anno, 94
Quran, 15

Reconquest, 17–20, 88
Reforma, 68, 150
Regionalism, 73, 137, 145–46, 160
Religious orders, 111
Representation, 72
Repression, 47, 48, 92–93
Republicans, 106
Rerum Novarum, 94
Revolution of 1974 (Portugal), 1–2, 62, 64
Rights, corporate, 18–20
Roman Catholic Church, constitutional protections, 154–55; cultural influence, 43, 100, 101, 109–13, 121; history of, 14; role in politics, 51, 109–13; social programs, 166. *See also* Catholicism
Roman Empire, 12–14
Rotativismo, 32, 95
Ruptura, 68, 150
Rural life, 98

Sá Carneíro, Francisco, 66, 135, 156

Salazar, Antonio de Oliveira, decline, 58; political parties, 125; rise to power, 34, 39–40; use of force, 93
Sampaio, Jorge, 98, 103, 155
Santiago de Compostela, 98, 99. *See also* James, Saint
Secret police, 51
Senate, 72
Seneca, 86
Seville, 75
Siesta, 114–15
Siete Partidas, 20
Siglo de Oro, 25
Sindicatos, 45, 47, 130
Slavery, 13, 17
Soares, Mario, 66, 133, 155, 156
Social and Democratic Center. *See Centro Democrático y Social* (CDS)
Social change, 56, 57, 100–101
Social Democratic Center Party (CDS), in Portugal, 137, 138
Social Democratic Party (PSD), 66, 67, 135–36, 138
Social democrats, 52, 65, 130
Social programs, 55, 150, 166
Socialist International (SI), 74
Socialist parties, 127, 130, 131, 133. *See also* Socialist Party (PS)
Socialist Party (PS), in Portugal, 133, 139, 156
Socialist Revolutionary Party (PSR), 132
Socialist Workers' Party. *See Partido Socialista Obrero Española*
Socialists, 35, 54; in Portugal, 66, 108; in Spain, 108
Sofía (Queen of Spain), 113
Soto, Domingo de, 84
Soviet Union, 62, 128, 145, 181
Spanish Communist Party (PCE). *See Partido Comunista Español*
Spanish Republic, 127
Spanish Socialist Workers' Party (PSOE). *See Partido Socialista Obrero Español*
Spanish-American War of 1898, 33–34
Spínola, Antonio de, 63
State–society relations, 90, 117, 149–50
Statism, 121
Strait of Gibraltar, 180
Strikes, 115, 116–17, 130
Students, 54, 119, 120, 130
Suárez, Adolfo, 71, 139, 154
Suárez, Francisco, 27, 84

Taxes, 110
Territorial integrity, 108–9
Thomas Aquinas, Saint, 42, 83–84
Tocqueville, Alexis de, 105, 106
Topography, 11
Totalitarianism, 48, 49
Tourism, 57, 69, 100, 101
Towns, 98
Trade unions, 94, 102, 116–17
Transitions to democracy, 61–62; Portuguese, 62–68; Spanish, 68–76, 78, 168
Two Portugals, 192
Two Spains, 192

Umayyad Dynasty, 15
Unemployment, 146, 148
União Nacional, 50, 128, 130. *See also Accão Nacional Popular* (ANP)
Unión del Centro Democrático (UCD), 72, 73, 134, 135, 139, 154
Union of the Democratic Center (UCD). *See Unión del Centro Democrático*
United States, 65, 74, 145, 182–83, 187–88

Vatican II, 100. *See also* Catholicism; Roman Catholic Church

Virgin of Fátima, 99
Vitoria, Francisco de, 84
Voting, 76–77, 102, 138, 143

Weber, Max, 81
Welfare, 117, 121
Wildavsky, Aaron, 81
Women, 13, 17, 118–19
Workers' Statute of 1980, 116
World War II, 45, 54, 175

Yugoslavia, 109, 181

Zamora, Niceto Alcalá, 34

About the Authors

HOWARD J. WIARDA is Professor of Political Science and the Leonard J. Horwitz Professor of Iberian and Latin American Studies at the University of Massachusetts/Amherst. He also is Senior Associate of the Center for Strategic and International Studies in Washington, D.C. A prolific scholar, he is the author of numerous studies, including *American Foreign Policy, Introduction to Comparative Politics, Latin American Politics and Development, Transitions to Democracy in Spain and Portugal,* and *Politics in Iberia.*

MARGARET MACLEISH MOTT is Professor of Political Science and Writing at Marlboro College. She has published in the *Journal of Church and State* and has twice walked across Spain on the Road of St. James.